THE
MODERN AMERICAN
URBAN NOVEL

THE MODERN AMERICAN URBAN NOVEL

NATURE AS "INTERIOR STRUCTURE"

ARNOLD L. GOLDSMITH

 Wayne State University Press   Detroit

Library of Congress Cataloging-in-Publication Data

Goldsmith, Arnold L.
　　The modern American urban novel : nature as "interior structure" /
Arnold L. Goldsmith.
　　　p.　　cm.
　　Includes bibliographical references and index.
　　ISBN 0-8143-1994-7 (alk. paper)
　　1. American fiction — 20th century — History and criticism.　2. City
and town life in literature.　3. Cities and towns in literature.
4. Nature in literature.　I. Title.
PS374.C5G65　　　1990
813'.509321732 — dc20　　　　　　　　　　　　　　　　90-37925
　　　　　　　　　　　　　　　　　　　　　　　　　　　　　　　CIP

This book was designed by Joanne Elkin Kinney

An earlier version of chapter five was published as "Nature in Bernard Malamud's *The
　　Assistant*" in *Renascence* 4 (summer 1977): 211–23.
Quotations from *Manhattan Transfer* and "The beginnings of the Contemporary Chron-
　　icles" used with the permission of Mrs. John Dos Passos.
Quotations from *Studs Lonigan: A Trilogy* by James T. Farrell. Copyright © 1932,
　　1933, 1934 by Vanguard Press, Inc. Used by permission of Vanguard Press, a Divi-
　　sion of Random House, Inc.
Quotations from *Call It Sleep* by Henry Roth, copyright © 1934 and 1962 by Henry
　　Roth, used by permission of Roslyn Targ Literary Agency, Inc., New York.
Quotations from *The Dollmaker* by Harriette Arnow, copyright © 1954 by Harriette
　　Arnow Simpson, used with permission of Macmillan Publishing Company.
Quotations from *The Assistant* by Bernard Malamud. Copyright © 1957 by Bernard
　　Malamud. Used by permission of Farrar, Strauss, and Giroux.
Quotations from *The Pawnbroker* by Edward Lewis Wallant, copyright © 1961 by Ed-
　　ward Lewis Wallant, used by permission of Harcourt Brace Jovanovich, Inc.
Quotations from *Mr. Sammler's Planet* by Saul Bellow. Copyright © 1969, 1970 by
　　Saul Bellow. Used by permission of Viking Penguin.
Quotations from "The Waste Land" and "The Love Song of J. Alfred Prufrock" in *Col-
　　lected Poems 1909-1962* by T. S. Eliot, copyright © 1936 by Harcourt Brace
　　Jovanovich, Inc., copyright © 1963, 1964 by T. S. Eliot, used by permission of the
　　publisher.
Quotations from *The Writing on the Wall and Other Literary Essays*, copyright © 1970
　　by Mary McCarthy, used by permission of Harcourt Brace Jovanovich, Inc.
Quotations from *Gardner's Art Through the Ages*, sixth edition, revised by Horst de la
　　Croix and Richard G. Tansey, copyright © 1975 by Harcourt Brace Jovanovich, Inc.,
　　used by permission of the publisher.

*To
Alana,
Andrew,
Shira,
and Samuel,
the next generation
of readers*

CONTENTS

Introduction

I do call the city to be laid out by the name of
Philadelphia. Let every house be placed in the middle
of its plot, so there may be ground on each side for
gardens or orchards or fields, that it may be a green
country town, which will never be burnt, and always
be wholesome.

        William Penn, Charter to Philadelphia

J oyce Carol Oates once asked, "If the City is a text, how do we read
it?"[1] The seven essays in this book take Oates's question one step
farther and provide a viable way of reading seven modern American
novels that deal with the urban experience. I do not claim that this study
of nature in scenes, imagery, and symbolism is the only way to read
Manhattan Transfer (1925), *Studs Lonigan* (1932, 1934, 1935), *Call It
Sleep* (1934), *The Dollmaker* (1954), *The Assistant* (1957), *The Pawnbroker* (1961), and *Mr. Sammler's Planet* (1970), but I do feel that the
close textual analyses that follow provide a fresh perspective from which
to study the city novel.

    Nature in these essays is used in the simple way that Emerson defined
it, as "essences unchanged by man; space, the air, the river, the leaf."[2] Since
nature and the city are often thought of as polarities, the search for nature
as the dialectical pole of the urban world central to these novels might,
at first, seem fruitless, but such is not the case. Mary McCarthy is only
partially right when she laments the disappearance in modern fiction of
the great outdoors setting so common in nineteenth-century fiction, influenced, to a considerable extent, by the great Romantic poets. Nature,
McCarthy remembers, used to be one of the cast of characters, "sometimes
as a chorus, jeering or sympathetic, sometimes as one of the principal ac-
tors, even the prime antagonist, the role it inevitably plays in stories of
the sea."[3] With all the literary discussion of the absence of plot, even
character, from modern fiction, she is surprised that

> nobody has called attention to the disappearance of another element, as though
> nobody missed it. We have almost forgotten that descriptions of sunsets,
> storms, rivers, lakes, mountains, valleys, used to be one of the staple ingre-

dients of fiction, not merely a painted back-drop for the action but a component evidently held to be necessary to the art.[4]

James T. Farrell, while seemingly in agreement with McCarthy about this change, does not share her sense of loss. Arguing that "an author does not pick his images out of a grab bag," he explains that "they grow out of his own background and changing experiences. . . . [I]t is apparent that romantic literary conventions have already passed their efflorescence and that they reflect an ideology of dualism completely dead and antiquated for many of us."[5] Contemporary American novelists, says Farrell, because they are "the products of urban life," reject romantic symbolism as no longer meaningful.

> In their immediate sensory experiences they have been most affected by the sights, sounds, odors, and objects of an industrial city. In their first stages of reading particularly, they have absorbed much of the romantic poets, and in their early writing there has been some imitation of the romantics. Generally speaking, the charms and attractions of nature have been peripheral if not non-existent in their lives. Hence they often have sensed a dichotomy between the objects and sensations they have sought to describe and the language and symbolism they have inherited.[6]

Despite Farrell's disclaimer, a close reading of his *Studs Lonigan* trilogy reveals that the novelist's interest in nature is not "peripheral" and that the "dichotomy" of which he speaks has been effectively turned into a creative tension central to the characterization of the protagonist. And contrary to McCarthy's lament, nature in *Manhattan Transfer, Studs Lonigan, Call It Sleep, The Dollmaker, The Assistant, The Pawnbroker,* and *Mr. Sammler's Planet* has definitely not disappeared. In these novels it is neither principal character nor mere backdrop, but an integral part of the setting, language, symbolism, and even characterization. The scale may be greatly reduced, the appearance less spectacular, but the results are aesthetically impressive and thematically effective.

Nature continues to be one of the richest sources for the creative imagination, and the modern urban novelist is no exception. Perhaps the explanation lies in our collective unconsciousness, as Jung argued, or perhaps the influence of the English Romantics is too deep to be erased by new sources of imagery and symbolism found in an environment of concrete, glass, and steel. Whatever the explanation, Blanche Gelfant, who has written one of the first important studies of the modern American urban novel, should not go unchallenged when she theorizes that "a language that draws heavily upon metaphors and symbols taken from nature seems incongruous and outmoded" because these novelists "deal with . . . a mechanized world of man-made structures,"[7] and that it is "the city itself" which "has provided a vocabulary for the urban novel." That the urban environment has developed its own vocabulary (what Irving Howe has sarcastically called "the flavorless language of sawdust, we associate with naturalism")[8] is indisputable, but Gelfant is mistaken in her disparaging comment on the incongruity of nature imagery and symbolism in the city novel, as the seven essays in this book will show.

Contrary to Gelfant, American urban novelists from Dos Passos to Bellow *have* drawn "heavily upon metaphors and symbols from nature," and the resulting contrast serves multiple purposes and strategies that greatly enhance their works. As might be expected, nature imagery is used to express mood and feelings and to reinforce theme. But it is also an important part of character delineation and social criticism, and it can be a delightful source of humor. It can serve as a bridge between the harsh world of urban reality and the surrealistic world of dreams and fantasies. It can serve as an ironic counterpoint and foreshadowing, and it can supply a mythic substructure to universalize a contemporary story. In short, whether it is used consciously or unconsciously, nature imagery is an important part of a novel's "interior structure," to borrow an apt phrase from Henry Roth.

When Roth speaks of "interior structure" in regard to *Call It Sleep*, he has in mind, I think, what he calls the "lyric . . . or poetic quality" of his novel. A synonym for "interior structure" could be *texture*, that interweaving of physical description and symbolism, metaphor and characterization, theme and imagery. Scenes set in and images taken from nature thus provide a rhythmical, incremental pattern which helps to unify the disparate elements of the novel and contribute to its form.

In the essays that follow, three primary areas of focus emerge. The first encompasses those scenes set in parks, on rivers and lakes, or on green belts separating the city from its suburbs. Since such settings are less common in these works than paved streets, streetcar tracks, apartment houses, restaurants, and office buildings, a second focus is the wordscape of metaphor, simile, and analogy. All seven authors draw on a cornucopia of natural images taken from the world of animals, insects, birds, flowers, plants, trees, and water. (The change of seasons also contributes important symbolism to this kind of imagery.) The third area of focus depicts the cityscape as reflected in sunlight and moonlight, stars and clouds, rain and snow. (The outstanding example of this treatment of the city is Dos Passos' impressionistic portrait of Manhattan.)

Four of the seven novelists in this study—Roth, Malamud, Wallant, and Bellow—though endowing their major characters with a love of nature, reject the Arcadian myth. According to Leo Marx, who has written one of the best books on the subject, this myth has always been an important part of the negative view of the city in literature. In nineteenth-century America,

> In its simplest, archetypal form, the myth affirms that Europeans experience a regeneration in the New World. They become new, better, happier men — they are reborn. In most versions the regenerative power is located in the natural terrain: access to undefiled, bountiful, sublime Nature is what accounts for the virtue and special good fortune of Americans. It enables them to design a community in the image of a garden, an ideal fusion of nature with art. The landscape thus becomes the symbolic repository of value of all kinds — economic, political, aesthetic, religious.[9]

Ironically, none of the four European emigrant protagonists — Albert Schearl, Morris Bober, Sol Nazerman, and Artur Sammler — experienced regeneration upon coming to the New World, nor did they become "new, better, happier men" in their roles as milkman, grocer, pawnbroker, and retired journalist. Nevertheless, the first three characters have warm memories of having enjoyed nature in their youth in Europe: Schearl herding bulls in Austrian pastures, Bober as a boy running through the Russian fields, and Nazerman on his family picnics in the Polish countryside. To Arthur Sammler, "leafy reverie" may also be "a thing of the past," but he is still capable of enjoying his natural surroundings ("The sun feels good pouring through his gaps as if he were a Henry Moore sculpture").

Another kind of myth concerning nature that appears in all seven of these novels is what John Ruskin demeaningly called the "pathetic fallacy," that is, the use of nature sympathetically to reflect or reinforce the mood of a particular character or scene. In these modern urban novels this sentimental kind of imagery usually reinforces the character's feelings of frustration or victimization in the city. For example, when Dos Passos describes the death wish of the unhappily married Ellen Oglethorpe as she stands by the open hotel window, "the rain lashed in her face spitefully stinging her flesh, wetting her nightdress." When Farrell describes the depression of Studs Lonigan, now thirty, returning to Chicago from the funeral of one of his old pals, "the sky seemed to be heavier, to be pressing down close to the earth as if from the force of tremendous tons of lead." And in Malamud's *The Assistant*, Morris Bober, the struggling grocer, as he walks through the streets of New York, feels that "Winter still spits in [his] face," while his unhappy daughter, Helen, standing forlornly at the winter seashore, listens "to the winddriven, sobbing surf." Each of these passages, seen from the perspective of one of the characters, not the author's, shows the lingering influence of the Romantic writers into the twentieth century.

Typical of the ambivalence that is one of the hallmarks of the American urban novel is the reverse image of the pathetic fallacy — the naturalistic belief that nature is totally indifferent to man. One example can simply counterpoint the other in the same work, as when the depressed Studs Lonigan, late in *Judgment Day*, the third volume of Farrell's trilogy, appears at the beach with his fiancée Catherine. Like the persona in Steven Crane's brief poem who challenges nature with the announcement of his presence ("A man said to the universe: / 'Sir, I exist!'"), Studs is met with complete indifference. It is not the hostility of nature that brings on his heart attack. Hundreds of people are frolicking on the sand and in the refreshing waters of Lake Michigan on this beautiful summer day. Another example is found in Wallant's *The Pawnbroker* the day of Sol Nazerman's fifteenth anniversary of his family's horrible murder in the Nazi death camp: the air in New York City is clear and shiny "with a quality of richness." When Sol painfully remembers the scene in which his friend Rubin is trapped by the Nazis' dogs against the barbed wire fence, the pigeons around the barracks roofs fly over "the monotonous horizon of the camp." The mundane routine of the birds makes the terror below more obscene and implies a condemnation of a divine being who allows such things to happen.

All seven authors in this study have used scenes and images from nature to reinforce themes in their novels. A few examples will suffice here. The early discovery of a ram's skull and horns in *Manhattan Transfer* ties in metaphorically with the Biblical allusions to Sodom and Gomorrah, Nineveh and Babylon, and introduces the themes of corruption, ultimate judgment, and destruction implicit in the urban environment. Dos Passos' impressionistic cityscape of Manhattan brilliantly underscores his theme of the failure of the American city to fulfill the American Dream. Bellow expands this theme of urban degeneration and adds a cosmic dimension with the new option of lunar exploration and colonization. Nature imagery plays a major role in Bellow's dialectical approach to the Adamic theme in *Mr. Sammler's Planet*, just as it contributes significantly to the themes of survival and the intrusion of the machine in the garden in Arnow's *The Dollmaker*. In *The Pawnbroker*, especially, and in some of the other novels, nature imagery underscores the difference between appearance and reality, and the crucial need of the survivor to know the difference.

The use of nature scenes, imagery, and symbolism as part of character delineation and development turns out to be one of its most important functions in these novels. For example, flower images are identified with Ellen Oglethorpe and Nellie McNiel in *Manhattan Transfer*, but the addition of worms, thorns, and faded blossoms supplies an effective note of ominous foreshadowing in their lives. The blue flowers in the cornfields of Austria serve as an important part of the characterization of the loving and passionate Genya Schearl, in contrast to the bull's horns so symbolic of Albert's brutal strength and the Oedipal conflict that develops in Roth's *Call It Sleep*. Gertie Nevels's close identification with the rich Cumberland soil in Kentucky is essential to Arnow's portrayal of her as an Earth Mother figure struggling to adapt to a wartime housing development and to keep her family together in Detroit. Seasonal symbolism, as Jonathan Baumbach has observed, is part of the "metaphysical climate" of Malamud's *The Assistant*: "The seasons mirror the inner conditions of the central characters"[10] in this novel about the Fall, Death, and Redemption of Man. In Wallant's *The Pawnbroker*, Marilyn Birchfield's name identifies her as another fertility figure, joining the ranks of Hilma Tree (*The Octopus*), Lena Grove (*Light in August*), and Rose of Sharon (*The Grapes of Wrath*). Animal images proliferate in *Mr. Sammler's Planet*, as Bellow depicts the "creatureliness" of man in constant conflict with his higher aspirations ("make Nature your God, elevate creatureliness, and you can count on gross results"). The black pickpocket identified with a puma is but one example. Perhaps the outstanding example in these seven novels is James T. Farrell's use of nature scenes and imagery to reinforce the duality of Studs Lonigan: his poetic, romantic, soft feelings versus his tough guy exterior as he tries to impress his gang. In the words of Edgar Branch, "Urban images are constantly used to suggest the limitations and lifelessness in Studs' character," whereas nature imagery is used "to reveal the inner Studs. . . ."[11]

In all seven novels, nature scenes and imagery provide a bridge between the harshness of urban reality and the world of spirituality, dreams, and fantasies. Jimmy Herf, as a boy in *Manhattan Transfer*, reads R. S. Ballantyne's *The Coral Island* and fantasizes heroic adventures, seeking escape from the city and the debilitating illness of his mother. Years later he remembers a pastoral interlude with his pregnant wife, Ellen, but such reveries are ironic, as the beautiful but unfeeling actress is in reality as cold as porcelain and incapable of giving herself in a loving relationship. Studs Lonigan has a mystical experience in an oak tree in Washington Park with his girlfriend, Lucy Scanlan. As he views the beautiful lagoon and the people boating below, he feels that his inner self separates from the dirty demands of his body and that he is for the moment in transcendental harmony with the idyllic scene around him. This rhapsodic mood is broken when a bird on the branch above suddenly defecates on him. When David Schearl, in *Call It Sleep*, slips into a mystical trance on the pier, staring at the brilliance of the sun glinting off the water, the voice of a captain of a passing tugboat saves him from falling into the river and drowning. Gertie Nevels and Cassie, in *The Dollmaker*, dream of the Tipton Place, the farm they will never possess, as they and the rest of their family move to Detroit to be reunited with Clovis, who dreams not of stars, but of trucks and jigsaws. Morris Bober, in *The Assistant*, has reveries of his boyhood in the snow-filled forests of Russia, but dies of pneumonia shoveling the snow for the comfort of the infrequent customers walking in front of his store. Even Sol Nazerman, the stone-hearted pawnbroker in Wallant's novel, has the pain of daily existence eased temporarily by a reverie of his family's picnicking in Europe before the horrors of the Nazi Holocaust, and later imagines himself on a barge flowing toward eternity on the Harlem River.

And finally, in each of the works studied here, nature is also used in a scene, image, or incident that, seemingly insignificant at first, can later be viewed as an objective epitome of the whole novel, or at least the protagonist's condition. Such a scene is the one in *Manhattan Transfer* were Jimmy Herf catches a fly in his hands and then crushes it with his fingers. Shakespeare used a similar image long before the American naturalists, but to the latter it suggests not so much cruel deities as the impersonal forces in a deterministic environment that torture human individuals. The "golden decay" of autumn in Washington Park in *Young Lonigan* aptly expresses the human potential of Studs and his friends going to waste as they make the wrong decisions in the streets of Chicago. In *Call It Sleep*, another fly image appears, this time in a humorous yet chilling parable when David's friends feed a live but wounded fly to their favorite spider. As the boys shout encouragement to the combatants, Roth portrays a Darwinian world in which the strong prey on the weak, adding to the fears of a sensitive child. In *The Dollmaker* there is the parable of the potato bugs (that is, the Nevels and their neighbors), some of which, though scorched and maimed, manage to survive the destructive force of the burning coal oil which, in Enoch's analogy, represents the atomic bomb dropped on Hiroshima and Nagasaki. In *The Assistant*, it is the Chaplinesque scene in which Frank Alpine falls into the open grave of Morris Bober, as he strains too hard to watch the rose Helen threw on her father's casket. In *The Pawnbroker*, it is the image of Sol as a "Mammoth . . . preserved in ice." And in *Mr. Sammler's Planet*, it is the exposed genitals of the puma-like black pickpocket who tries unsuccessfully to intimidate a tough old man.

Thus it is evident that nature, whether in landscape, wordscape, or symbolism, plays an important part in the "interior structure" of the American twentieth-century urban novel. Nature takes its place along with other image patterns clustered around imprisonment, sex, and religion, in the total texture of each work as the seven authors weave together the strands of their stories. The kinds of patterns of images are limited only by the imagination and artistry of the writer. The only limitations are those of the reader, and the objective of these essays is to help this reader discover from a different perspective some of the richness, beauty, and complexity of modern American fiction at its best.

CHAPTER 1

The Naturalistic Impressionism of
Manhattan Transfer

From the beginning of his career, John Dos Passos was fascinated by the contrasts he found in Manhattan. Reminiscing years later in "What Makes a Novelist," he explained, "New York was the first thing that struck me. It was marvelous. It was hideous. It had to be described. . . . Fragmentation. Contrast. Montage. The result was *Manhattan Transfer*."[1] In this same reminiscence, he spoke of the readiness of so many of the aspiring artists of his generation "to attempt great things. . . . It was up to us to try to describe in colors that would not fade, our America that we loved and hated. . . ."[2]

Through the technique of rapidly changing vignettes involving a large cast of characters, many of whose lives intersect in Manhattan, Dos Passos succeeded in capturing the restiveness and despair of a whole generation. "Direct snapshots of life," he called this technique years later in "What Makes a Novelist."

> Reportage was a great slogan. The artist must record the fleeting world the way the motion picture film recorded it. By contrast, juxtaposition, montage he could build drama into his narration. Somewhere along the way I had been impressed by Eisenstein's motion pictures, by his version of old D. W. Griffith's techniques. Montage was his key word.[3]

"From such sharp and kaleidoscopic sensuous impressions of urban scenes," says Blanche Gelfant, "the city is registered immediately in its color, odor, din, and gaudy brilliance. And as it comes to life, it is its own indictment."[4] In an early appreciation of Dos Passos' artistic achievement, Joseph Warren Beach pointed out that where the reader may first see mainly discontinuity and lack of development in *Manhattan Transfer*, he eventually realizes that the opposite is true: "there is composition in the arrangement of incidents from the private lives of Gotham. The thing has its own form in its modernistic manner; by suggestion, by implication, by contrast and irony. The more one examines it, the more one finds of studied implication."[5]

Beach's praise of the aesthetic form of *Manhattan Transfer* with its striking juxtaposition of incidents and characters is commonly accepted today, but less evident, perhaps, is the "studied implication" of the many scenes, images, and symbols drawn from the world of nature. Sometimes they are in contrast to and sometimes they complement the thousands of urban images. Together they reinforce Dos Passos' love-hate relationship with the American metropolis and the ambivalence that was to become the hallmark of the American twentieth-century urban novel.

Although skyscrapers, office buildings, apartments, boarding houses, restaurants, bars, and city streets are the most frequent settings in *Manhattan Transfer*, there is also an extensive pattern of images taken from nature. Repeated references to snow, rain, animals, insects, birds, flowers, and trees become an important part of the novel's texture, and contribute significantly to its interior structure. Many scenes are set at dawn or dusk, and sunlight and moonlight bathe the novel in various shades of yellow, pink, orange, and red. Gelfant perceptively observes that in Dos Passos' mood, "The beauty of the city lies in its color formations, sometimes brilliant and gaudy, sometimes muted and subdued,"[6] but she goes too far when she claims that "all other sensory details, those of sound, weather, and odor, are oppressively ugly."[7] The occasional glimpse of beauty in the reflections of the falling snow colored by streetlights or in the shine put on the paint of vehicles by the fresh rain reveals the tantalizing beauty the writer can find even in a metropolis that frustrates and dehumanizes its inhabitants.

Much has already been written about the European cultural influences that helped mold the technique and style of the young Dos Passos. Linda Wagner, using the University of Virginia collection of Dos Passos' manuscripts, quotes the author as saying that he was influenced by the New York Armory Show in 1913 while he was a college student, and by the Imagist poets.

> Everything looked different in the light of what was happening in Europe. After the armistice, while still in the army, I had managed to get myself inducted into what was known as the Sorbonne detachment. An early form of the G. I. bill of rights. . . . This was the Paris of socalled [sic] modern painting which was really modern in those days: Modigliani, Juan Gris, Picasso. This was the Paris of futurism, expressionism in literature, of new schools of music: Poulenc, Milhaud, Stravinsky, Diagheleff's Russian Ballet.[8]

In the definitive essay on the subject, "Dos Passos and Painting," George Knox points out that Dos Passos was both a student of modern art and, for a while, a painter himself. Over the course of his career, according to Knox, Dos Passos moved in his fiction "from simple realism in color composition to Monet-like impressionism, to explosions of force, cacophony, and finally a handling of cubistic techniques suitable to depicting the confused planes and psychic dimensions of metroplex life."[9] Knox concludes, however, that "Dos Passos certainly contributed as much as he derived from the climate of Impressionism and Cubism, and I have implied no lack of originality by entertaining the possibilities of 'influence.'"[10]

Impressionism is the key to understanding Dos Passos' artistic achievement in *Manhattan Transfer*. In correspondence with Knox, Dos Passos revealed that Flaubert's realism and Impressionism were early influences on his writing. According to Gelfant, in *Manhattan Transfer* Dos Passos used "a technique of abstraction which proceeds through an impressionistic method."[11] The objective of this method "is to give an impression of reality, rather than to give, like Dreiser, a total catalogue of actual details."[12] His "cityscapes," says Gelfant, "are only fleeting sensuous impressions of scene. His people are only representatives of a human state of mind intrinsic to the city—they are not fully realized flesh and blood people, but abstract states of being."[13] To Gelfant, "the rapid transition from one impression to another accelerates the novel's pace to suggest the incessant restless movement within the city itself." Throughout the novel, "static scenes become dynamic relationships of color and of light and shadow."[14]

Comments of R. W. Stallman and Richard Chase about Stephen Crane, an important late-nineteenth-century forebear of Dos Passos, provide a fresh perspective from which to view Dos Passos' impressionistic naturalism. Stallman points out that the impressionist writers of the late 1880s all aimed to create, in Henry James's phrase, "a direct impression of life."[15] Joseph Conrad supplied their manifesto when he announced their objective as follows: "by the power of the written word, to make you hear, to make you feel — it is, before all, to make you *see*."[16] Stallman views Crane as anticipating French post-Impressionism with his pointillistic prose style. His seemingly disconnected images coalesce and form a meaningful pattern, and the intensity of his story is the result of "this patterned coalescence of disconnected things, everything at once fluid and precise."[17] Richard Chase goes beyond Stallman and attempts to connect Impressionism with late-nineteenth-century Naturalism. This connection should not be surprising, says Chase,

if we reflect that, despite its peculiar effectiveness and beauty, impressionism, like naturalism, has implications that are pessimistic, irrational, and amoral since its technique is to break down into a shimmering flow of experience the three dimensions that symbolize rationality and religious and social order in traditional art.[18]

The connection between Naturalism and Impressionism becomes even clearer with the comments of Helen Gardner, in her well-known study *Art through the Ages*. According to Gardner, in the last half of the nineteenth century,

> when the Realists are discarding romantic subject matter in order to represent what they see around them, Manet (in his later work) and the Impressionists seem to raise the question whether *what* we see is not a matter of *how* we see it. What is more real for a painter who seeks the "real"—a world of solid objects moving in space or simply his optical sensations of light and color in fleeting patterns? In a sense, naturalistic Impressionism continues the Romantic preoccupation with the *self* of the artist, except that now he consults not so much his feelings and imagination as his purely visual sensations.[19]

Thus the Impressionist studies "light as the source of our experience of color," and this approach reveals "the important truth that local color—the actual color of an object—is usually modified by the quality of the light in which it is seen, by reflections from other objects, and by the effects produced by juxtaposed colors."[20]

Manhattan Transfer is a casebook study of Impressionism. Dos Passos evidently agrees with Phil Sandbourne, the architect in his novel, who shares the dream of his former employer to use colored tile, "bands of scarlet round the entablatures of skyscrapers."[21] Sandbourne tells George Baldwin, "we could evolve new designs, new colors, new forms. If there was a little color in the town all this hardshell inhibited life'd break down. . . . There'd be more love and less divorce. . . ." Sandbourne is an incurable romantic who, because he is distracted by the sight of a beautiful woman (Ellen) passing in a cab, is hit by a car as he crosses the street. Dos Passos, himself, is the artist evolving "new designs, new colors, new forms" on every page of his novel. Dawn and dusk, as mentioned above, are his favorite times of day, and the Impressionist author is fascinated by the effect of the rising and setting sun on the local color of Manhattan. A few examples will show this technique at work.

In the opening section, the radical Marco, Emile, and Congo Jake are drinking and talking on the steps of a restaurant:

> Outside the lemoncolored dawn was drenching the empty streets, dripping from cornices, from the rails of fire escapes, from the rims of ashcans, shattering the blocks of shadow between buildings. The street-lights were out. At a corner they looked up Broadway that was narrow and scorched as if a fire had gutted it. (39)

The Joycean device of combining words (for example, "lemoncolored") has the effect of wide, long brushstrokes on canvas. The patches of light soften the ugly fire escapes and the lids of garbage cans, as shadows are obliterated. Beauty is in the eye of the beholder. Each dawn gives Marco new hope; Congo, however, is going back to sea, fed up with New York. The image of "fire-scorched" streets suggests that Congo's vision is the more realistic, though ironically, he is one of the few characters who succeed in making a fortune (illegally) in the metropolis.

Toward the end of the long middle section of the novel, the drunken Stan Emery looks at Manhattan from a ferryboat. "Across the zinc water the tall walls, the birchlike cluster of downtown buildings shimmered up the rosy morning like a sound of horns through a chocolatebrown haze. As the boat drew near[,] the buildings densened to a granite mountain split with knifecut canyons" (251). There is something beautiful about the approaching city, as buildings look like birch trees and steep walls of granite canyons. Stan watches the gulls above his head: "three gulls wheeled complaining. A gull soared in a spiral, white wings caught the sun, the gull skimmed motionless in whitegold light. The rim of the sun had risen above the plumcolored band of clouds behind East New York. A million windows flashed with light." But such beauty is illusory. The drunken Stan, who is soon to die senselessly in a tenement fire, drops his eyes from "the whitening light tinfoil gulls"[22] to the broken boxes and floating garbage as the ferryboat docks. This repetition of the epigraph to section 1, with slight variations, is a grim reminder of the broken hopes and aborted dreams of the crushed masses.

Dos Passos' impressionistic depiction of Manhattan at dawn can also be seen in the first section as Gus McNiel delivers milk from his wagon: the "sky behind cornices, tanks, roof peaks, chimneys becomes rosy and yellow. Hoarfrost glistens on doorsteps and curbs" (45). Preoccupied with his "visual sensations," the Impressionist finds considerable beauty as the light alters his view of the city. Chapter 3 of the second section finds poetry in the dawn breaking over Manhattan: "Over Chatham Square the sky was brightening redviolet through the latticework of elevated tracks" (181). Section 2 begins with an epigraph describing the city waking up: "*Daylight rattles through the windows, shaking the old brick houses, splatters the girders of the L structure with bright confetti*" (129). The paragraph immediately following shifts the focus from the impressionistic to the naturalistic: "The cats are leaving the garbage cans, the chinches are going back into the walls, leaving sweaty limbs, leaving the grimetender necks of little children asleep." Scavengers, garbage, and bedbugs are as much a part of Manhattan as the delicate confetti-like patterns of sunlight through the girders of the elevated railway.

Sunlight plays an important part in the characterization of Ellen (Elaine) Thatcher Oglethorpe.[23] At the beginning of section 2 there is a Renoir-like description of Ellen: "Sunlight dripped in her face through the little hole in the brim of her straw hat. . . . through the thin china silk the sunlight tingled like a hand stroking her back" (136). The morning she runs away from her husband, the homosexual actor John Oglethorpe, nature reflects her mood of intense happiness. In the taxi, she takes "deep breaths of the riversmelling morning air" (167). As the cab "turned down into the very empty sunlight of Broadway a feeling of happiness began to sizzle and soar like rockets inside her. The air beat fresh, thrilling her face." In the early morning, "Fifth Avenue was white and empty and swept by a sparkling wind. The trees in Madison Square were unexpectedly bright green like ferns in a dun room" (168). After she undresses in her new room, admiring her naked body in the mirror, she puts on a yellow nightgown and gets into bed. Dos Passos' choice of color in this sensual scene identifies Ellen with the sun she loves, but again the pessimistic Naturalism intrudes: "She felt hungry and alone. The bed was a raft on which she was marooned alone, always alone on a growling ocean. A shudder went down her spine. She drew her knees up closer to her chin" (168). This is the cocoon-like position Ellen favored even as a child. She needs protection from a hostile environment, a world in which she will never find lasting happiness as she drifts from man to man. In another morning scene later in the same section, Ellen is awakened by the sunlight, "Red buzzing in her eyelids," but momentarily she "sinks back into purpling cottonwood corridors of sleep" before awakening again, pulling "her knees up to her chin to pull the drowsysweet cocoon tighter about her" (240).

A favorite device of Dos Passos is to interject into such tranquil moments a jarring street sound (often a fire engine)[24] to foreshadow distress ahead. With a slight variation in this case, "A truck jangles shatteringly along the street, the sun lays hot stripes on her back" (240). The sense of intrusion is reinforced by a second noise from the city, followed by a very effective organic image rich in ominous undertones: "From far away through streets and house-walls the long moan of a steamboat whistle penetrates to her like a blunt sprout of crabgrass nudging through gravel." A final example of sun imagery associated with Ellen appears on the next page as she walks down Fifth Avenue worried about the missing Stan, the only man she has ever loved. "The sun is heavy like his arm across her back, strokes her bare forearm the way his fingers stroke her, it's his breath against her cheek" (241). In this case, the hot sun becomes a conventional metaphor for love and passion.

Impressionism is also evident in many of Dos Passos' descriptions of sunset. Some, such as the following, are mainly ornamental and depend simply on a large blob of color with little dabs reflecting the glow: "Rosy twilight was gushing out of the brilliant west, glittered in brass and nickel, on buttons, in people's eyes. All the windows on the east side of the avenue were aflame" (395). Earlier, in this same section, the sky was described as "glittering with motherofpearl flashes of sunset" (358). In what is one of the most effective examples of Impressionism in *Manhattan Transfer*, Dos Passos combines the colors of sunset with the Fourth of July fireworks observed by a child, Jimmy Herf. The result is a firewheel of spinning colors, allowing Dos Passos to use his whole palette to express the kaleidoscopic beauty and excitement so characteristic of the big city:

> Blue chunks of dusk melting into the squarecut uptown streets. Rockets spurting bright in the blue dusk, colored balls falling. Bengal fire, Uncle Jeff tacking pinwheels on the tree outside the apartmenthouse door, lighting them with his cigar. Roman candles you have to hold. . . . Hot thud and splutter in your hands, egg-shaped balls soaring, yellow, green, smell of powder and singed paper. (71)

The beauty of this sensuous description is immediately followed by the intrusion of a fire engine, reminding the reader that a consequence of this dazzling display of color is danger, destruction, and even death. "Down the fizzing, glowing street a bell clangs near, clangs faster. Hoofs of lashed horses striking sparks, a fire engine roars by, round the corner red and smoking and brassy."

While many spectators are thrilled by the visual effects and exploding sounds of the fireworks, defeated individuals like Bud Korpenning are in too much pain to enjoy the sunset or America's birthday celebration. Cheated by the woman who hired him to move a pile of coal into her house, he fights off cramps, not wanting to vomit because he needs the nourishment of the food inside his stomach. As he lies on "the rubbish slide beside the wharf,"

> The light of the sunset flamed in the portholes of tugs, lay in swaths of curling yellow and orange over the swift, brown green water, glowed on the curved sails of a schooner that was slowly bucking the tide up into Hell's Gate. Inside him the pain was less. Something flamed and glowed like the sunset seeping through his body. He sat up. Thank God I aint agoin to lose it. (66)

The naturalistic Impressionism of this scene is repeated at dawn, the day of Bud's eventual suicide leap from Brooklyn Bridge. Having come to New York after killing his brutal father, Bud repeatedly informs acquaintances that he is searching in the city for the elusive "center of things" (24). Tired of running, Bud watches the darkness lighten: "An edge of the blue night had started to glow behind him the way iron starts to glow in a

forge. . . . All the darkness was growing pearly, warming" (124). Ominously, "The river was smooth, sleek as a bluesteel gunbarrel" (125). Bud is
desperate. "Dont matter where I go; can't go nowhere now. The shadows
between the wharves and the buildings were powderly like washingblue.
Masts fringed the river; smoke, purple chocolatecolor fleshpink climbed
into light. Cant go nowhere now." Dreaming of the wedding he will never
have, of the alderman he will never become, he sits "on the rail of the
bridge. The sun has risen behind Brooklyn," but the beauty surrounding
him is totally indifferent to his needs. "The windows of Manhattan have
caught fire. He jerks himself forward, slips, dangles by a hand with the
sun in his eyes. The yell strangles in his throat as he drops."

In the description of Bud Korpenning's leap from Brooklyn Bridge,
Dos Passos perfectly fits Helen Gardner's description of the Impressionist
artist attempting to reproduce "purely visual sensations." The novelist is
more concerned with the pink and white glow dissipating the blue darkness,
the mast-fringed river below, and the fiery sun in Bud's eyes than he is
with the terror of the moment. *Manhattan Transfer* is filled with examples
of Dos Passos' conscious effort to make the reader *see* the reality of the
urban scene through the interplay of light and shadows and the intermixture and juxtaposition of various colors. The implications that result are,
as Chase claims, frequently "pessimistic, irrational, and amoral."

The brilliant sunrise as the setting for Bud's suicide is but one example. Another is the epigraph to chapter 5, "Steamroller," the conclusion
to section 1:

> *Dusk gently smooths* [sic] *crispangled streets. Dark presses tight the steaming*
> *asphalt city, crushes the fretwork of windows and lettered signs and chimneys*
> *and watertanks and ventilators and fireescapes . . . into blue chunks, into black*
> *enormous blocks. Under the rolling heavier heavier pressure windows blurt*
> *light. Night crushes bright milk out of arclights, squeezes the sullen blocks*
> *until they drip red, yellow, green into streets resounding with feet. All the asphalt*
> *oozes light. Light spurts from lettering on roofs, mills dizzily among wheels,*
> *stains rolling tons of sky.* (112)

In the scene that follows, to be analyzed later in this chapter, young Jimmy
Herf is walking away from the cemetery where his mother has just been
buried. Traditional religious hope and Christian prayers offer him no consolation. The darkness of night in the epigraph is equated with death; verbs
like "press," "crush," "Squeeze," and "ooze" are heavy with pessimistic implications.[25] The steamroller analogy is just one more vivid example of the
overwhelming cosmic forces that burden the lives of Dos Passos' characters.

Nature imagery, an important part of Dos Passos' naturalistic Impressionism, does not always have heavy pessimistic undertones in *Manhattan Transfer*. There are a few relatively minor scenes set in parks which

supply a contrast to the urban environment and give the author an opportunity to record his visual impressions of another side of the metropolis.
In one such scene, Ellen is walking through the park on a Sunday to meet
George Baldwin. "All the shady benches were full of people . . ." (136),
seeking relief from the hot sun. Sailors look at her lustfully, and a man
in a car tries to pick her up. "Two pigeons with metalgreen necks and feet
of coral waddled out of her way. An old man was coaxing a squirrel to
fish for peanuts in a paper bag." The scene could be a canvas by Claude
Monet. "Sunshades, summer dresses, straw hats were bright in the sun that
glinted in squares on the upper windows of houses, lay in bright slivers
on the paint of limousines and taxicabs" (137). With his typical mixture
of the urban, natural, and human, Dos Passos conveys Ellen's impression
of the odors surrounding her in the park: "It smelled of gasoline and asphalt, of spearmint and talcumpowder and perfume. . . ." Sometimes,
however, Dos Passos loses control and the resulting impressionistic description is overwritten. An example is the description of Ellen walking with
Harry Goldweiser up the Mall in Central Park

> in her wide hat in her pale loose dress that the wind now and then presses
> against her legs and arms silkily, swishily walking in the middle of great rosy
> and purple and pistachiogreen bubbles of twilight that swell out of the grass
> and trees and ponds, bulge against the tall houses sharp gray as dead teeth
> round the southern end of the park, melt into the indigo zenith. (202)

More effective is the unstrained impressionistic description of Cassie eating ice cream and walking in the park with her boyfriend, Morris Mc-
Avoy, after a date at the movies: "The path between round splashes of
arclights ducked into darkness. Through slant lights and nudging shadows
came a smell of dusty leaves and trampled grass and occasionally a rift
of cool frangrance from damp earth under shrubberies" (161). Dos Passos
effectively counterpoints the romantic setting with the following realistic
contrast: "'Oh I love it in the Park,' chanted Cassie. She stifled a belch.
'D'you know Morris I oughtnt to have eaten that icecream. It always gives
me gas.'"

Though the Impressionism of John Dos Passos is most in evidence in
scenes set at sunrise and sunset, the two times of day when the change
of light and its effect on local color would be most noticeable, other examples involving moonlight, snow, and rain can also be cited. In chapter
5 of the second section, Dos Passos describes a "night . . . marbled with
clouds and moonlight. The toads in the ditches sounded like sleighbells,"
as Jimmy, a newspaperman, takes Ellen to the scene of a recent murder.
Dos Passos supplies only a few details of the crime, but mentions that
there are a locust tree behind the house and a policeman on guard in

front. "A mildewed scrap of moon came out from behind the clouds for a minute, made tinfoil of a broken glass in a gaping window, picked out the little rounded leaves of the locust and rolled like a lost dime into a crack in the clouds" (230). The alliteration of the soft *m*'s, *n*'s, and *l*'s contrasted with the hard *g*'s and *c*'s, the touch of assonance, and the rhythm of the prose counterpoint the antiromantic imagery ("mildewed scrap of moon," broken window, and policeman on guard after a murder), giving the sentence a lyrical bent, the purpose of which, however, is simply aesthetic embellishment.

Snow and rain in *Manhattan Transfer* give Dos Passos the opportunity to present a scene under even different lighting conditions. In the example that follows, he tries to capture Jimmy Herf's mood rather than the specificity of the streets through which he and Ellen are walking to dinner at a speakeasy: "Big snowflakes spun and spiraled about them mottling the glare of the streets with blue and pink and yellow, blotting perspective" (298). These last two words are the key to his artistic intentions. Here is a perfect example of what Gardner meant when she explained that the Impressionist is more interested in *how* an object is viewed than *what* he is viewing. It is a question of altered perspective. Jimmy hates the city ("Why did we come back [from France] to this rotten town anyway?" [301]), and the mixed colors of the snow in the reflection of the street lights temporarily take his mind off his precarious change of jobs, the economic insecurity of the young couple who are now parents, and the cold, untouchable beauty of Ellen, who is slipping away from him ("He felt paralyzed like in a nightmare; she was a porcelaine figure under a bellglass" [300]). During dinner, "A current of fresh snowrinsed air from somewhere eddied all of a sudden through the blurred packed jangling glare of the restaurant, cut the reek of food and drink and tobacco." The romantic Jimmy fantasizes about the nightingales he heard in France when Ellen and he were traveling by train "among the silverdripping poplars" (301). As the couple spend their meager funds on yet another cocktail, Jimmy cries out, " . . . Ellie for heaven's sake what's the matter with us?" Then they spend their last dollar on a taxi to take them home: "The street was a confusion of driving absintheblurred snow" (302). The words "Blotting perspective," "blurred . . . glare," "confusion," and "absintheblurred snow" all emphasize Jimmy's visual and emotional reaction to his immediate surroundings as he tries to find his way in a world that offers so much beauty, bewilderment, and pain.[26]

Rain is described more often than snow in *Manhattan Transfer*. Sometimes the effect is gratuitous Impressionism, as in chapter 4 of section 2, when Joe O'Keefe is leaving George Baldwin's law office and thinks enviously of the beautiful secretary he has just met. In the street, a summer storm has begun, as people run to cover. "Two girls had made hoods of news-papers over their summer bonnets. He snatched blue of their eyes, a glint of lips and teeth as he passed" (207). The eroticism of O'Keefe's thoughts car-ries over into a striking sensual image in the next impressionistic sentence: "The rain advanced down the street in a solid sheet glimmering, swishing, beating newspapers flat, prancing in sliver nipples along the asphalt, striping windows, putting shine on the paint of streetcars and taxicabs" (207).

When the unhappily married Ellen is on her honeymoon with John Oglethorpe, it rains steadily for days. Running through her head are the lyrics of a song:

> Oh it rained forty days
> And it rained forty nights
> And it didn't stop till Christmas
> And the only man that survived the flood
> Was longlegged Jack of the Isthmus. (118)

Ellen fights depression as "Rain lashed down the glaring boardwalk and crashed in gusts against the window like water thrown out of a bucket. Beyond the rain she could hear the intermittent rumble of the surf along the beach between the illuminated piers" (116). John is asleep in the bed beside her, but she cannot stand the touch of his body. Even though she is "icy cold," she opens the window. "The rain lashed in her face spitefully stinging her flesh, wetting her nightdress." She wants to die and vomits in the bathroom before getting back into bed. "Through a crack in the cold stiffness the little tune trickled warm as blood. . . . And it rained forty nights." The drunken Stan later sings snatches of the same song not long before he dies. He is not one of the survivors of the flood. Lacking the redeeming qualities of Noah, he is not saved by an ark. Thus, avoiding any sermonizing, Dos Passos can imply through the symbolism of the rain, through fragments of popular song, and biblical echoes, the need for redemption in the wasteland of twentieth-century Manhattan. The rain fails to cleanse Ellen, who, carrying the child of the now dead Stan in her womb, throws open the window of her stifling apartment "and breathes deep of the wet air full of the cold rot of autumn" (260).

Only Jimmy Herf will be purged; it is he who will become the "long-legged Jack of the Isthmus." It is he who likes the cleansing effect of the rain after the "biting taste of whiskey and cigarettes" (235). As he walks alone in the rain feeling sorry for Tom Hunter, a homosexual who plans to commit suicide, Jimmy

> rammed his hat down on his head and yanked his coatcollar up. He wanted to run along yelling sonsobitches at the top of his lungs. Lightning flickered

up along the staring rows of dead windows. The rain seethed along the pavements, against storewindows, on brownstone steps. His knees were wet, a slow trickle started down his back, there were chilly cascades off his sleeves onto his wrists, his whole body itched and tingled.

As Jimmy walks through the streets of Brooklyn, his thoughts are not of himself, but of all the miserable solitary souls in their tiny rooms, the beginnings of World War I, and the recent murder of a daughter by her father. "As far as he could see the street stretched empty in the rain between ranks of dead windows studded here and there with violet knobs of arclights. Desperately he walked on" (236).

The desperation, confusion, and misery of so many of the characters in *Manhattan Transfer* are typical of the mood of the major characters in naturalistic fiction. Murray Baumgarten sees this pessimism as part of the dialectical polarity of the city. "If the city is freedom, dignity, activity, possibility," writes Baumgarten, "it is also limiting, and personal experiences will surely add potentially imprisoning and degrading to the list of its characteristics."[27] To reinforce his pessimistic view, Dos Passos uses many animal images[28] to suggest the degrading effect of the city on its inhabitants. The title of chapter 5, section 2, "Went to the Animals' Fair," pretty well sums up Dos Passos' picture of Manhattan as a farm or zoo. This theme is introduced much earlier in the novel's second chapter, "Metropolis," when in a fancy restaurant scene, a "moonfaced man" tries to address a group of noisy revelers: "'Silence in the pigsty . . .' piped up a voice. 'The big sow wants to talk,' said [another] . . ." (30). Then, when Fifi Waters, a vivacious, uninhibited actress arrives and is greeted lavishly with champagne, a young man following her sings to the crowd:

"O we went to the animals' fair
And the birds and the beasts were there
And the big baboon
By the light of the moon
Was combing his auburn hair." (33)[29]

Fifi kicks off a man's top hat, and in the process bloodies his eye. This is the same song heard over two hundred pages later as the drunken Stan enters a dancehall. It is in this scene that Stan insults the Pope and is consequently beaten and thrown out. When he wakes up on a ferryboat and thinks he is having the D.T.'s, he asks the sobering questions, "Who am I? Where am I?" and answers mechanically, "City of New York, State of New York . . . . Stanwood Emery age twenty-two — occupation student" (250–51). In another restaurant scene, George Baldwin supplies the animal image that best describes the trapped situation of himself and so many of Dos Passos' characters. Bored with his wife and his success as an attorney, George craves fun and tells Ellen, "The terrible thing about having New York go stale on you is that there's nowhere else. It's the top of the world. All we can do is go round and round in a squirrel's cage" (220).[30]

The catalog of animal images to describe different characters trapped in the cage of Manhattan is extensive. In an expensive restaurant, the waiter Emile observes "a weazlish man with gold teeth . . . a voice like a crow's and . . . a diamond the size of a nickel in his shirtfront" (27). Congo Jake has "a deep gorilla chest" and "very hairy hands" (223). A bouncer is "a small broadshouldered man with deepset tired monkey eyes" (370). Ellen gives balloons to "three monkeyfaced girls in red tams" in Central Park (203). Harry Goldweiser shakes "his calf's head" (211), and Jimmy laughs at a woman who has "a face exactly like a llama" (132). Madame Soubrine, Ellen's dressmaker, has a "catlike smile" (396), and she circles Ellen "like a cat that wants its back rubbed." In one of the novel's most stereotyped animal images, the destitute Joe Harland looks at a picture of The Stag at Bay. His desperate lament is, "I got to do something. I got to do something" (157).

Various animal images are especially associated with Jimmy Herf. As a child he wonders "what it'd be like to be a seal, a little harbor seal" (81). "Very chilly I should think," his mother replies, but Jimmy explains that the animal wouldn't feel the cold. "Seals are protected by a layer of blubber so that they're always warm even sitting on an iceberg. But it would be such fun to swim around in the sea whenever you wanted to. They travel thousands of miles without stopping." His mother reminds him that *they* have traveled thousands of miles without stopping; and when the novel ends, Jimmy, with no protective insulation, will be on the road again, still restless, still seeking his utopia, knowing only that Manhattan is not for him. Earlier, in a bar, dancing with Ellen, Jimmy "was suddenly full of blood steaming with sweat like a runaway horse" (228). When he quits his newspaper job, he is elated: "His thoughts ran wild like a pasture full of yearling colts crazy with sundown" (352). After having some amusing fantasies on a bench in Washington Square, he notices "A little yellow dog . . . curled up asleep under the bench. The little yellow dog looked very happy" (352), mirroring his own momentary contentment. Earlier in the novel, Jimmy takes a cold shower, jumps out, and stands "shaking himself like a dog, the water streaming into his eyes and ears" (172). Such animal images are relatively minor and lack the atavistic import of those found in Crane and Norris, but one ominous image involving two cats is used when Jimmy's marriage to Ellen is in trouble. At her selfish suggestion, he rents a separate room where he can work (and sometimes sleep) uninterrupted. One cold night as he walks back to see Ellen, he notices two black cats chasing each other on West Twelfth. "Everywhere was full of the crazy yowling. He felt that something would snap in his head . . ." (345). When he awakens Ellen and asks if she loves him, she admits that she cannot love anyone unless he is dead (that is, Stan).

One additional animal image that is especially significant appears in Chapter 2. Coming so early in the novel it introduces an important theme and helps put the coming incidents into perspective. An anonymous realtor is trying to sell a lot to a customer who is told that with the growth of New York City it will make a good investment. "Poking amid the dry grass and the burdock leaves Mr. Perry [the client] had moved something with his stick. He stooped and picked up a triangular skull with a pair of spiralfluted horns. 'By gad!' he said. 'That must have been a fine ram'" (15). It is as though a paleontologist has uncovered the bones of an extinct creature. One effect of this seemingly minor incident, never mentioned again, is to arouse the reader's curiosity about the new civilization that has replaced the old. Will it survive? What will bring about *its* destruction? The fact that the paleontological find is a ram's head and horns is particularly significant since the ram's horn is a venerated religious object still used by people who have survived a history of almost six millennia. In Jewish ritual, the ram's horn is blown to signal the beginning and the end of the holiest time of year, the annual period of atonement for one's sins and the judgment of God, who will decree who shall live and who shall die in the year to come. Since Dos Passos later refers explicitly to Sodom and Gomorrah, Babel and Babylon, Nineveh and Noah's Flood, and introduces an Old Testament prophet figure who predicts the imminent destruction of New York City,[31] it would seem that the ram's skull and horns are used to reinforce these biblical references and introduce the theme of urban corruption, ultimate judgment, and destruction that permeate the novel.

The pessimistic Naturalism of *Manhattan Transfer* is also evident in Dos Passos' use of insect imagery, particularly flies. There is more truth than he realizes when the drunken Martin Schiff, who calls Jimmy and his lost companions "a peewee generation," continues, "You are all bored, bored flies buzzing on the window-pane" (361). Ellen is awakened one morning by "a fly blundering about her face. The fly vanishes in the sunlight, but somewhere in her there lingers a droning pang, unaccountable, something left over from last night's bitter thoughts" (240). Earlier, when the theatrical producer Harry Goldweiser proposes to Ellen in Central Park, "She feels very helpless, caught like a fly in his sticky trickling sentences" (203). Later, in a taxi, as he offers her a role in *The Zinnia Girl*, his "broad short knees pressed against hers; his eyes were full of furtive spiderlike industry weaving a warm sweet choking net about her face and neck" (244).

The fly image does not appear explicitly here, but it is implied. Like Dreiser's Carrie Meeber, also a lovely, aspiring actress, Ellen is passive, more acted upon than acting, frequently caught in a web of circumstances over which she has little control.[32]

Two fly images involve Jimmy Herf. In one he is compared to a fly after he has quit his job and is unemployed: "Life was upside down, he was a fly walking on the ceiling of a topsy-turvy city" (351). The other fly image involving Jimmy is much more important. Jimmy has locked himself in his room at his aunt and uncle's apartment after his mother's stroke, and suddenly he observes a fly on the window ledge

> scrubbing his wings with his hind legs. He cleaned himself all over, twisting and untwisting his forelegs like a person soaping his hands, stroking the top of his lobed head carefully brushing his hair. Jimmy's hand hovered over the fly and slapped down. The fly buzzed tinglingly in his palm. He groped for it with two fingers, held it slowly squeezing it into mashed gray jelly between finger and thumb. (96)

Here is another of the novel's objective epitomes to illustrate implicitly the effect of the vast metropolis on its inhabitants, who are crushed by implacable forces over which they have no control.

One other important insect image merits inclusion here. Again in the naturalistic tradition, it emphasizes the smallness of man and his inability to satisfy his cravings. This time, however, the unobtainable object is Ellen, who is surrounded by men in evening dress and women in gowns. Harry Goldweiser praises her for her latest theatrical success, but Ellen sits in an armchair, aloof, cold, unemotional. Her physical beauty attracts all the men drawn into her orbit. She just sits there

> drowsily listening, coolness of powder on her face and arms, fatness of rouge on her lips, her body just bathed fresh as a violet under the silk dress, under the silk underclothes; she sits dreamily listening. A sudden twinge of men's voices knotting about her. She sits up cold white out of reach like a lighthouse. Men's hands crawl like bugs on the unbreakable glass. Men's looks blunder and flutter against it helpless as moths. But in deep pitblackness inside something clangs like a fire engine. (182)

Another image suggesting futility and helplessness is the figure of a caged bird. It is a further extension of Dos Passos' naturalistic philosophy. Early in the novel the birdcage image is introduced humorously, as the stout widow, Madame Rigaud, sings to entertain her suitor Emile in her delicatessen shop:

Just a birrd in a geelded cage
A beautiful sight to see

You's tink se vas 'appee
And free from all care
Se's not zo se seems to be. . . . (60)

The second stanza reinforces the sad story of a wasted, unhappy life as "Beautee was sooooled / For an old man's gooold." Immediately following the song is a tragic vignette in which Bud Korpenning observes a man in a carriage with a woman wearing "a gray feather boa round her neck and gray ostrich plumes in her hat" (60). As the carriage passes, the man puts a pistol to his head and kills himself. While the man vomits blood on the curbstone, his female companion explains to the police that his wife was taking him to Europe, and the lovers were parting forever. "The woman stood tall and white beside him twisting her feather boa in her hands, the gray plumes in her hat nodding in the striped sunlight under the elevated" (61). The shadowy lines of the elevated suggest another cage in which someone is imprisoned, just as the feather boa and gray ostrich plumes relate the woman to the bird in the song. Later in the novel, Cassie, one of the aspiring actresses who lives in the boardinghouse with Ellen, is explicitly identified with the caged bird. Cassie tells her boyfriend, Morris, that the stage manager of a second road company is going to try to pull strings for her and get her out of the show which she finds "vulgar and howid." "I want to do such beautiful things," she tells Morris. "I feel I've got it in me, something without a name fluttering inside, a bird of beautiful plumage in a howid iron cage" (162). Cassie's lisp and romantic sentimentality as she tries to keep in check the lusty ardor of her boyfriend make of her a comic figure, but her pregnancy later in the novel adds just one more victim to the list of trapped characters.[33]

Many bird images appear throughout the novel, mainly for descriptive purposes,[34] but they are much less important than those found in Henry Roth's *Call It Sleep*, analyzed in chapter 3. In *Manhattan Transfer*, for example, a taxi driver is described as having a "red hawk face" (261), and Goldweiser's "pigeonbreasted" sister has "a little voice like a parakeet's" (242) and "little birdeyes" (244). The affected John Oglethorpe recites poetry to his bride Ellen and exclaims, "Behold thou art fair my love, thou art fair, thou hast dove's eyes within thy locks" (116). A favorite cliché of Dos Passos is to describe the sky as "robin's egg blue" (112, 351). More important than any of these bird images is the scene mentioned earlier that takes place while Jimmy is walking on a suburban road away from the cemetery where his mother has just been buried. Significantly, the chapter is entitled "Steamroller," and outside the gate of the cemetery, workers are tarring the road. The epigraph to this chapter, it is to be remembered, describes night coming over the city like a gigantic steamroller, obliterating everything it touches. Jimmy removes his black mourner's tie as he tries to free himself from the oppressive gloom of the setting. Echoing in his head are the mourners' prayers he has just heard to comfort the living: "There is one glory of the sun and another glory of the stars: for one star differeth from another star in glory. So also is the resurrection of the dead . . ." (112–13). Jimmy wants to block out the meaningless words, get the feeling of black crêpe off his fingers, to forget the smell of lilies" (113). As he moves farther into the countryside, suddenly

> From a fencepost came the moist whistling of a songsparrow. The minute rusty bird flew ahead, perched on a telegraph wire and sang, and flew ahead to the rim of an abandoned boiler and sang, and flew ahead and sang. The sky was getting a darker blue, filling with flaked motherofpearl clouds. (113)

The singing bird, as it flits from one spot to the next, suggests through its natural beauty and movement the elusive happiness of this world. The connotations of "rusty" and the "abandoned boiler" are reminders of the decay of modern urban civilization. Thus, through his subtle imagery, Dos Passos effectively reinforces his theme of the corruption of the natural by the advances of urban technology. The polar opposites of the dialectic are neatly fused.

Eventual departure from the city is Jimmy's only hope, but it will be years before Jimmy realizes this. Meanwhile, he seeks escape from the city through his fantasies and reading. Nature is involved in most of these instances. For example, when Jimmy goes out to play because his mother is having one of her terrible headaches, he imagines that "The dungeon gates opened. Outside was an Arab stallion and two trusty retainers waiting to speed him across the border to freedom" (86). When he is sent away to school after his mother's stroke, he enjoys escapist books to remove himself from the taunts of the boys who try to make him fight. Interestingly, the one book Dos Passos alludes to in some detail is R. S. Ballantyne's *The Coral Island*, the same popular romantic adventure mentioned so prominently a quarter of a century later in William Golding's *Lord of the Flies*. Jimmy's wish to escape to nature is seen throughout his reverie and dream about this book:

> The surf thundered loud on the barrier reef. He didn't need to read Jack was swimming fast through the calm blue waters of the lagoon, stood in the sun on the yellow beach shaking the briny drops off him, opened his nostrils wide to the smell of the breadfruit roasting beside his solitary campfire. Birds of plumage shrieked and tittered from the tall ferny tops of the coconut palms. The room was drowsy and hot. Jimmy fell asleep. There was a strawberry lemon smell, a smell of pineapples on the deck and mother was there in a

white suit and a dark man in a yachting cap, and the sunlight rippled in the milkytall sails. (97–98)

But even this idyll is invaded by an ominous intruder: "A fly the size of a ferryboat walks towards them across the water, reaching out jagged crabclaws." A man urges a reluctant Jimmy to jump and beats him before he snaps back to reality.

Much later in the novel, when Jimmy is a struggling reporter working on an article on the violence of bootlegging, he remembers a pastoral interlude with Ellen:

> The time on the hill when she had suddenly wilted in his arms and been sick and he had left her among the munching, calmly staring cows on the grassy slope and gone to a shepherd's hut and brought back milk in a wooden ladle, and slowly as the mountains hunched up with evening the color had come back into her cheeks and she had looked at him that way and said with a dry little laugh: It's the little Herf inside me. (322)

The Ellen of Jimmy's bucolic reverie and the real Ellen who aborts the dead Stan's baby after telling Jimmy she would never do so, are very different. Ellen is no Madonna figure, and the pastoral imagery in Jimmy's recollection is heavily ironic.[35]

Two other pastoral fantasies involve Gus McNiel and Bud Korpenning. In the first, Gus, then a milkman, dreams of owning a farm out West. While driving his milkwagon early one morning, he fantasizes about telling his wife Nellie that he has applied "for free farmin land in the state of North Dakota, black soil land where a man can make a pile of money in wheat; some fellers git rich in foive good crops" (47). Feeling sorry for the policeman on the beat in the cold city, he sentimentally thinks it would be better as "a wheatfarmer an have a big farmhouse an barns an pigs an horses an cows an chickens. . . . Pretty curlyheaded Nellie feedin the chickens at the kitchen door . . . ." Urban reality intrudes as George's horse wanders onto the railroad tracks while his master dozes and causes the accident that puts George into the hospital.

The other pastoral fantasy is revealed in a Bowery flophouse where Bud tells another sleepless drifter how for twelve years he has dreamt of returning to the countryside: "Every spring I says to myself I'll hit the road again, go out an plant myself among the weeds an the grass an the cows comin home milkin time, but I don't; I juss kinder hangs on" (121–22). The romantic sentimentality of Bud's dream is undercut by the tragic truth he then reveals — patricide. Bud's cruel father beat the thirteen-year-old boy with a chain. "We was grubbin the sumach outa the old pasture to plant pertoters there . . . ." when Bud "mashed his head in with the grubbinhoe, mashed it in like when you kick a rotten punkin. . . . A bit of scrub along the fence hid him from the road. Then I buried him an went up to the house an made me a pot of coffee" (123).

These pastoral fantasies, reveries, dreams, and reminiscences on the parts of Jimmy, Ellen, Gus, and Bud are all part of Dos Passos' antiromanticism and constitute an important ingredient of his Naturalism. Life and people are often not what they appear to be. The romance goes out of Jimmy and Ellen's marriage, Ellen is not an innocent shepherdess, enterprising and noble youth do not always conquer their challenging environment, and the countryside can breed child abuse and murder, as the best laid plans of young and old go astray.

One of the most effective patterns of nature imagery in *Manhattan Transfer* involves flowers. Early in the novel George Baldwin, desiring an affair with Nellie McNiel, brings her flowers to further his seductive advances. "Out of a pot of narcissus still wrapped in tissue paper starshaped flowers gleamed with dim phosphorescence, giving off a damp earthsmell enmeshed in indolent prickly perfume" (55). Narcissus is an appropriate choice of flower for the self-centered, unscrupulous lawyer; in Greek myth Naricissus falls in love with his own image and then is punished for scorning the love of a maiden. Much later, when George tells Ellen about his old affair with Nellie, he says that the milkman's wife "was like a wild rose, . . . fresh and pink and full of the Irish," but adds, "and now she's a rather stumpy businesslike looking little woman" (220). When love-smitten George loses control of himself and threatens the unresponsive Ellen with a gun in a restaurant, Dos Passos describes Nellie's compassion for her former lover with a beautiful flower image, although one strangely inconsistent with her characterization: "Remembering the insupportable sweetness of Chinese lilies, she felt her eyes filling with tears" (231). Such compassion is wasted on George, whose active love life produces as much pain as pleasure. Trapped in a miserable marriage and nervous about his risky affair with his mistress Nevada, George asks the question many of Dos Passos' characters eventually contemplate: "Good God how am I going to get my existence straightened out?" (279). The novelist uses a striking garden image as a contrast to the lawyer's messy life. Stopping to look in a florist's window at a "miniature Japanese garden with brokenback bridges and ponds . . . and goldfish [looking] as big as whales," he finds a lesson for himself: "Proportion, that's it. To lay out your life like a prudent gardener, plowing and sowing." Such resolve is quickly abandoned as he sends a bouquet of yellow, coppery roses to Nevada and two dozen Gold of Ophir roses to Ellen.

Flower imagery is also used to characterize Ellen.[36] Flowers reflect both her stunning beauty and her desire to avoid the ugliness of reality. They also foreshadow her destiny. In chapter 3 of the second section, the imagery is present in the print of a chintz curtain which she uses to "hide with its blotchy pattern of red and purple flowers the vista of desert back-yards and brick flanks of downtown houses" (186). She is wearing "a daf-fodilcolored kimono." The sharp contrast between the beauty of the flowers (this time real) and the ugliness of the city is revealed again late in the third section when Ellen gets off a bus and buys a bunch of arbutus "and pressed her nose in it. May woods melted like sugar against her palate" (395). However, as the boy selling the flowers brushes against her, she shrinks from the contact.

> Through the smell of the arbutus she caught for a second the unwashed smell of his body, the smell of immigrants, of Ellis Island, of crowded tenements. Under all the nickelplated goldplated streets enameled with May, uneasily she could feel the huddling smell, spreading in dark slow crouching masses like corruption oozing from broken sewers, like a mob. (395)

Dos Passos' choice of language here is, of course, a parody of Emma Lazarus's sonnet inscribed on the pedestal of the Statue of Liberty, welcoming the new immigrants to New York: "Give me your tired, your poor, / Your huddled masses yearning to breathe free, / The wretched refuse of your teeming shore." Ellen, however, shuns physical contact with the sweating world of the flower vendor and becomes more like a porcelain figurine than a flesh and blood woman.[37]

Three earlier flower images associated with Ellen are especially significant with their foreboding implications. In the first, Ellen has brought her father roses and announces her forthcoming divorce from John Oglethorpe. In the awkward silence that follows, Ellen "leaned over to breathe deep of the roses. She watched a little green measuring worm cross a bronzed leaf" (198). Equally ominous is the statement moments later that her eyes focus on "the faded roses of the carpet" (199). The third flower image also involves roses, and again casts a shadow on her future happiness. In this scene, Ellen arrives in a restaurant where her divorce lawyer George Baldwin introduces her to the McNiels. "Laying her gloves away on the edge of the table her hand brushed against the vase of rusty red and yellow roses. A shower of faded petals fluttered onto her hand, her gloves, the table. She shook them off her hands" (219). Asking George to have the flowers re-moved, she says, " . . . I hate faded flowers." This shower of faded petals is another of the novel's objective epitomes. Each of Ellen's relationships with men is doomed to failure, any love and feeling quickly fading.[38]

Flower and plant imagery is also used in the characterization of Jimmy Herf. After his mother's stroke, he has to live with his Aunt Emily and her family. His cousin Maisie asks him if he knows the game of jacks, but all he can think of are the Jack roses his mother loves. Maisie, the spoiled rich girl, likes only American Beauties. Jimmy's sensitivity to the suffering of others is seen in Dos Passos' choice of imagery to describe his thoughts as he walks in the rain and thinks "of all the beds in all the pigeonhole bedrooms, tangled sleepers twisted and strangled like the roots of potbound plants" (235).[39] The most important flower images involving Jimmy appear symbolically in the novel's conclusion. They effectively counterbalance Ellen's repulsion at the smell of the immigrant flower vendor already described. As Jimmy boards the ferry to leave New York, destitute but inwardly very happy with his decision, he observes a horse and wagon coming aboard,

> a brokendown springwagon loaded with flowers, driven by a little brown man with high cheekbones. Jimmy Herf walks round it; behind the drooping horse with haunches like a hatrack the little warped wagon is unexpectedly merry, stacked with pots of scarlet and pink geraniums, carnations, alyssum, forced roses, blue lobelia. A rich smell of maytime earth comes from it, of wet flowerpots and greenhouses. The driver sits hunched with his hat over his eyes. Jimmy has an impulse to ask him where he is going with all those flowers, but he stifles it and walks to the front of the ferry. (403)

When he exits, Jimmy walks along the dump heaps with their burning rubbish[40] and then spends his last quarter on breakfast at the Lightning Bug lunchwagon. As *Manhattan Transfer* ends, Jimmy hitches a ride with a friendly trucker and responds to his question, "How fur ya going?" with the vague but determined, "I dunno. . . . Pretty far" (404).

Jimmy Herf's departure from Manhattan to transfer to places unknown is his refusal to become part of the "grayfaced" masses described in the epigraph to chapter 3 ("Revolving Doors") of the third section: *Like sap at the first frost at five o'clock men and women begin to drain gradually out of the tall buildings downtown, grayfaced throngs flood subways and tubes, vanish underground"* (305). Jimmy does not want to become like them or like his cousin, whose name he shares, and again Dos Passos ironically chooses an organic tree image to express the negative. Jimmy tells Stan early in the novel, "You ought to see my cousin James Merivale. Has done everything he was told all his life and flourished like a green bay tree . . . " (176). The images of the sap and the green bay tree must be seen in conjunction with the epigraph to chapter 1 of the third section, in which Dos Passos describes hospital ships secretly unloading wounded soldiers at night and excoriates the obscene war profits of American entrepreneurs. The sarcasm is evident as he intersperses glimpses of the American flag, brass bands, snatches of patriotic war songs, and subway graffiti announcing APOCALYPSE with the following lyrics from a popular song: "O the oak and the ash and the weeping willow tree / And green grows the grass in God's

country" (271). On the next page, Captain James Merivale, D.S.C., returning war hero, reappears.

When the novel ends, Jimmy is painfully aware of the modern debase-
ment of the original words and spirit of the Declaration of Independence.
Vanderwerken sees him as "a contemporary Lot, . . . the only man allowed
to flee the City of Destruction. . . . to remain in the city is to risk the loss
of one's humanity, to risk metamorphosing, like Ellen Thatcher Herf, into
a porcelain doll—hollow, rigid, artificial, and cold."[41] Carrying his perceptive analogy one step farther, Vanderwerken sees Ellen as Lot's wife looking back at the city and, "figuratively speaking," turned "into modern glass
instead of Biblical salt. . . ."[42] In Jimmy's final nightmarish fantasy, sky-
scraper windows collapse all around him as he walks around buildings
desperately seeking an entrance. Follies girls with Ziegfeld smiles beckon
from windows, one of them Ellie in a golden dress, but her world is no
longer his. "If only I still had faith in words" (365) is his lament, as he
prepares to flee Manhattan.

This failure of the American city to fulfill the American Dream becomes
the overriding theme of Dos Passos' novel, and the author's extensive use
of nature imagery and symbolism both serves as an important touchstone
against which to measure this failure and enriches the novel's interior structure. Walcutt sees *Manhattan Transfer* as "a picture of Chaos, a blind,
formless struggling frantic world. . . ."[43] To Walcutt, "the fragmented
presentation suggests that life is not integrated by purpose or order, that
it is a flow of sensation, that man is controlled by his basic physical response."[44] Such a reading supports Walcutt's view of Dos Passos as "a
tremendously significant figure in the development of naturalism. . . ."
With this it is difficult to argue, but Jimmy's response to the horse and
flower wagon gives the reader hope, and, in the words of Vanderwerken,
"suggests that Herf is returning to a pastoral world where he may create
new values to replace those rejected."[45] Herf, in other words, "is reborn
and redeemed by the spirit of the great words of the patriarchs." His flight
and redemption in no way diminish the novel's Naturalism, but they make
a "morally affirmative" statement, "And therein," says Vanderwerk, "lies
Dos Passos' hope for the nation."

CHAPTER 2

"Golden Decay":
The World of Nature in *Studs Lonigan*

W riting on the use of setting in the violent fiction of Dostoevski and Dreiser, Frederick Hoffman concludes that "one of the major contributions of nineteenth-century realism and naturalism has been the growing importance of *scene* as a literary focus of what an artist wishes us to accept as a *state of mind*."[1] To Hoffman, "the value of scene in this case comes primarily from its function in defining and describing the moral and psychological condition of the protagonist." Although Hoffman is writing about Dreiser's Clyde Griffiths and not Farrell's Studs Lonigan, the latter serves as a fascinating example of this thesis. Many of the scenes of Farrell's trilogy reflect the moral and psychological state of Studs Lonigan, and what is most surprising is the fact that so many of them take place in verdant rather than asphalt settings.

In Farrell's trilogy, according to Edgar Branch, "Urban images are constantly used to suggest the limitations and lifelessness in Stud's character."[2] These urban images become the "metaphors of his mind and culture." Nature imagery, on the other hand, is used to reveal a different Studs— soft, spiritual, poetic—craving beauty and love. Donald Pizer agrees with Branch and observes that "Characters, activities, and setting are . . . all part of the iconographic texture of *Studs Lonigan*."[3] One might also say that they are part of the trilogy's interior structure. Studs's search for his inner self, as Pizer points out, often takes place "in a natural setting or while Studs is engaged in a 'natural' activity, like swimming." To Pizer, " . . . Farrell is remarkably successful in finding in the heavily populated and overbuilt urban world of *Studs Lonigan* symbolic equivalents of the traditional opposition between man confined in thought and feeling by a restrictive society and man alone and free in nature."

Farrell's use of nature imagery to reflect Studs's mood and to develop the tension between his inner sensitivity and the external pressures to conform is even more complex than Branch and Pizer have indicated. Despite Farrell's belief (as quoted in the Introduction to this book) that "the charms and attractions of nature have been peripheral if not non-existent" in the lives of modern American urban novelists, the pervasiveness in his trilogy of such scenes and images proves otherwise. Farrell has used nature in various ways; characterization is the most important, but there are others. He has used nature imagery for comic effect, for social and religious satire, and for irony. Following the lead of Dos Passos in the twenties, he has used the lyrics of popular songs to counterpoint events in the novel, with nature imagery playing an important part. Furthermore, nature scenes and images are used to express metaphysical ideas. Sometimes they even foreshadow and advance the plot. And finally, nature provides a rhythmical and incremental pattern that contributes to the novel's form and helps unify the episodic structure of the three volumes.

A clue that nature has been used for comic purposes, to add a light touch to an otherwise dark story, can be seen in the epigraph Farrell supplies for the middle volume, *The Young Manhood of Studs Lonigan*. It is the speech from *Moby-Dick* in which Fleece, the victim of a prank of the Pequod's second mate, is asked to preach a quieting sermon to the noisy sharks feasting on a dead whale. Farrell quotes just part of it:

> *Your woraciousness, fellow critters, I don't blame ye so much for; dat is natur, and can't be helped . . . . No use goin' on; de willians will keep a scrougin' and slappin' each oder, Massa Stubb; dey don't hear one word; no use a-preaching to such dam g'uttons as you call 'em, till dere bellies is full, and dere bellies is bottomless; and when dey do get 'em full, dey won't hear den; for den dey sink in de sea, go fast to sleep on de coral, and can't hear not'ing at all, no more, for eber and eber.*[4]

The relevance of this epigraph to the events of the novel can be seen in chapter 21, when Father Shannon, the popular missionary, returns to Chicago to conduct the first mission in St. Patrick's, the magnificent new church in the badly deteriorating South Side of Chicago. He begins by telling the young people in his audience that he cannot blame them for wanting good times, but they must ever be on the alert to avoid the temptations of the devil — "jazz, atheism, free-love, companionate marriage, birth-control" (*YMSL*, 351). He lambasts the free-thinking universities; modern writers like Sinclair Lewis, H. G. Wells, and H. L. Mencken; Russian radicalism and the theory of evolution. The only hope for America in these paganistic, immoral times is "the Catholic young men, the Catholic girls of this nation. They must be the leaders" who will supply the "Self-

Control!" (*YMSL*, 355) that is so sorely needed in the eternal fight to resist the sins of adultery and drinking. Unlike the sharks in Melville's passage, Studs and his friends listen attentively to and admire Father Shannon's sermon, but ironically, "*dey don't hear one word.*" That Sunday morning they all go to mass, but that evening "They got drunk and raised hell around the corner. They hung around until Slug talked them into going to a new can house, a small place. They went and had the girlies, and gypped them out of their pay. It was a big night" (*YMSL*, 368). Their voraciousness and sensuality temporarily appeased, Father Shannon's words forgotten, their energy spent, Studs and his friends sink a little lower into the gutter.

A kind of humor different from that which results from the juxtaposition of the epigraph above with the irony of situation in chapter 21 can be seen in the graduation speech of Father Gilhooley in *Young Lonigan*. Here Farrell piles cliché upon cliché, one stale image drawn from nature after another, to emphasize the ineffectuality of the Catholic Church to reach the real problems beneath the pompous platitudes. Father Gilhooley tells the good Catholic parents in his audience that their financial sacrifice to provide their children a religious education is now being rewarded as their "fears and worries must be scattering like the fog dissipating before the warming rays of Gawd's golden morning sunlight. Your little ones have been safely steered beyond all the early rocks and shoals and sands . . . ," and their diplomas symbolize the arrival of the children at "the first safe haven on their journey across the stormy and wave-tossed sea of life" (*YL*, 28). After two more pages of such deadly commencement oratory, Farrell interrupts his expert mimicry with the delightful observation that Father Gilhooley's "verbal thickets grew thicker and thicker with fat polysyllables. They wallowed off his tongue like luxurious jungle growths as he repeated everything he had said" (*YL*, 30–31). The only effective image in his entire speech is his comparison of the relentless passage of time to "some lonely bird that comes to the banquet hall of this earth where man is feasting: it comes from a black unknown, flies through while man eats, and is gone in the black of night. . . ." (*YL*, 32), but even this figure of speech is unoriginal, having been borrowed from the Venerable Bede's *Ecclesiastical History of the English People*, written in the eighth century. As Richard Mitchell has perceptively concluded, the clichés of Studs, his peers, and his family reveal that "they have been provided with no other terms in which to think. They have, in fact, been sheltered from all need for thought."[5] The Catholic Church and capitalism have been dependable sources of "ready-made solutions" to all problems of daily living. In short, "The whole education of Studs is designed to teach him not to think."[6]

A mildly amusing (and sometimes annoying) example of trite verbal patterns is the repeated use of animal images by most of the characters.

Popular similes and metaphors from the animal world inundate the trilogy. Paddy Lonigan remembers how in his youth he used to be "a young buck" (*YL*, 13); when he was courting Mary at picnics, she "could run like a deer" (*YL*, 14). Weary Reilley calls Sister Bertha "the old cow" (*YL*, 39) and says that she is "blind as a bat" (*YL*, 40). After beating up Weary, Studs is "now the cock of the walk" (*YL*, 86). Jewboy Schwartz, running with the football, is "graceful as an antelope" (*YMSL*, 124). Even Studs's nickname falls into this category. Eager for his sexual initiation with Iris, Studs tells Kenny that he can hardly wait to be led to her. Kenny replies, "Well, at that you're talkin' horse sense," and Studs jokes, "Horsey sense" (*YL*, 142).

Although a few of the examples just mentioned are meant to be complimentary, most of the comparisons with animals are made in a derogatory sense, as was the case in *Manhattan Transfer*, and many of Farrell's demean the sex act. For example, after having made love to Catherine for the first time, Studs feels guilt-stricken and humble. He is afraid that he was messy and crude and that Catherine will hate him for what he did "and only remember him on her like a goddamn, wheezing bull" (*JD*, 262). And later, when Mrs. Lonigan cruelly tricks Catherine into a confession of her pregnancy as Studs lies dying, she puts all of the blame on her son's fiancée and tells her that a girl "should have more pride and self-respect and a sense of decency than to act like a mongrel dog or an alley cat" (*JD*, 417). Like Dos Passos, Farrell incorporates some of the popular songs of the twenties and thirties, their lyrics and catchy tunes, providing the mindless formulas and "ready-made solutions" to everyday problems that induce euphoria in the listener. The most significant of these involving nature is "Singin' in the Rain," which Farrell humorously juxtaposes with the argument that Studs and Catherine are having in the restaurant just before she breaks their engagement. As the couple fight, Farrell underscores the difference between the dream world and reality by counterpointing the dialogue with such lyrics as *"Singin' in the rain, just singin' in the rain, / What a glorious feelin', I'm happy again"* (*JD*, 199), and *"Little brooklets breaking free, Work their way down to the sea"* (*JD*, 200).[7] As this chapter ends with Studs having difficulty falling asleep, worried about Catherine, his poor health, and the falling stock market, he succumbs to the easy optimism of the song: "He and Catherine would patch it up, prosperity might now really be around the corner, it would all turn out hotsy-totsy, and Studs Lonigan would be singing in the bathtub, and singing in the rain, and singing" (*JD*, 210). The devastating irony of such shallow optimism is revealed at the climax of the trilogy (to be discussed later) when Studs overtaxes his weakened body by job hunting in the rain and has his fatal heart attack.

Rarely in *Studs Lonigan* does Farrell use nature simply to reflect the ugliness of the event taking place, as in his description at the end of *The Young Manhood* of the slow coming of "The dirty gray dawn of the New Year" (*YMSL*, 411), while a drunken and beaten Studs lies in his own vomit and blood in the gutter. Much more common is Farrell's use of nature to reflect Studs's mood. For example, at the end of section 2 of *Young Lonigan*, having just licked Red Kelly and won the admiration of the gang from Fifty-eighth and Prairie, "Studs felt pretty good again. He felt powerful. Life was still opening for him, as he'd expected it to, and it was going to be a great summer. And it was a better day than he imagined. A sun was busting the sky open, like Studs Lonigan busted guys in the puss. It was a good day" (*YL*, 131). The opposite of this mood can be seen at the beginning of *Judgment Day* when Studs, now thirty, and his friends are on the train to Chicago after the funeral of Shrimp Haggerty in Terre Haute. The dismal Indiana landscape "in the early drizzling twilight" (*JD*, 3) reinforces Studs's depressed mood as he envisions the train speeding him to death. He looks at the "flat farmlands, dreary and patched with dirty snow at the end of February, houses, barns, silos, telephone posts, steel towers connecting lines of strung wire, with a row of wintry trees in the distance, bare like death, and appearing to speed as swiftly as the train travelled" (*JD*, 4). Night falling over the fields becomes in Studs's imagination "like a coat of gloom being buttoned on, and it was like a coat of even heavier gloom being spread over, buttoned tightly down on, his own thoughts. And the sky seemed to be heavier, to be pressing down close to the earth as if from the force of tremendous tons of lead" (*JD*, 6). As Studs identifies compassionately with the lonely, inarticulate farm people, even the clearing weather and the half moon that looks "almost like a fire of whiteness and silver" cannot lighten his mood. To Studs, "the growing early darkness seemed itself to be sorrowing, to be carrying through it an unseen and awful sadness, and it made all the world seem . . . like a graveyard" (*JD*, 16).

In some of the passages just cited, especially the last one, Studs, not Farrell, is obviously indulging in the pathetic fallacy. In his attributing to nature human characteristics to reflect his own feelings, the imagery is stale, the thought commonplace. However, as part of the characterization of Studs and the foreshadowing of his early death, these passages are surprisingly effective. On rare occasions Studs can be more original in his choice of figures of speech, the result beging more naturalistic than romantic. In *Judgment Day*, worried about his failing health, Studs watches "A cloud . . . floating just over the apartment hotel, white, puffy, its edges like strand or even like the hockings of a man with the con" (*JD*, 207). As he worries about the possibility of his having consumption, "He rolled over to look at the shadowy wall, trying to shutter out of his mind the image of that cloud, which seemed to grow into an enormous lump of consumptive spittle."

Undoubtedly the most important way that nature is used throughout the trilogy is to present the duality of Studs Lonigan. Studs's favorite poses are the tough gangster in the movies, the virile athlete, the caveman conqueror of women. The antithesis of these is the effeminate poet. In *The Young Manhood*, when Davey tells Studs that the radical waiter Christy, who is translating Whitman into Greek, is "a nice fellow. . . . a poet" (*YMSL*, 337), Studs sneers, "For Christ's sake! I suppose he writes about the birdies and the stars, and my heart in love." Ironically, Studs himself has a warm feeling for the beauties of nature and wishes that he could communicate the love in his heart for Lucy, but he is too self-conscious, too afraid of being made fun of. In *Judgment Day*, right after the silly fight in the restaurant, Studs and Catherine are walking moodily along the street: "It was clear and pleasant out, and he glanced absently up at the skies, seeing star galaxies as if he were discovering them. It was nice. But he'd get a stiff neck and look like a sap walking along with his hands in his pockets and his eyes raised this way. Ahead he saw the sidewalk, the red lanterns hanging from the railroad gates . . ." (*JD*, 201). The red lanterns serve almost as a symbolic warning to Studs to beware of this emasculating softness. But Studs's innate sensibility continually rises to the surface as when he observes the rain from his apartment window three days after the quarrel with Catherine:

> He returned to the window and forgot his worried thoughts by watching the rain hit the street, turn silver, almost bounce. The drops hung like crystals to the leaves of the small tree in front of the apartment hotel, slid off. An automobile passed with a clatter, and the rain splattered on its tarpaulin top. The sky, dull, heavy black clouds ranked above the tall apartment hotel. (*JD*, 243)

Toward the end of *Judgment Day*, in a vignette of seeming insignificance, Farrell deftly counterpoints Studs's romantic view of the rain as silver crystals. Wet, tired, angry, and depressed, unable to find a job in the pouring rain, Studs overhears the following conversation between a man and a woman:

> "Look at the rain, just like a silver stream from the heavens, Martha," a sallow fellow with a ruined panama hat said to the girl.
> Studs glanced at them, sneered. But she was nice.
> "It just looks wet to me," she said.
> "But you don't see it with the poet's lyric eye." (*JD*, 381)

Studs's bitter reaction to this scene: "That pansy poet. Silver rain. B.S. A cold rain-drop spattered on his cheek."

These are the thoughts of an embittered, dying young man. Studs has not always felt this way about nature. Throughout the trilogy Farrell uses scenes and images from nature to suggest Studs's longing for a better life — for purity, quietness, a sense of identity, fulfillment, serenity. For example, in *The Young Manhood*, after enjoying an exciting movie about love in Alaska, Studs thinks about the many "things in life he's been missing."

> He was doing a lot of the things he dreamed of doing when he had been a kid. He wanted more and felt that somewhere there was something else for him in life, and it was the ticket that would satisfy the feeling he always got from the movies, from seeing a nice jane on the street, sometimes from walking in the park in summer and maybe looking at the sky, sometimes when walking home from work in the sunset. (*YMSL*, 147)

It is the considerable attention Farrell gives to the soft side of Studs that makes his character more interesting, complex, and, above all, sympathetic.[8]

Although most of the novel's scenes take place in the city's alleys, streets, poolrooms, bars, restaurants, places of entertainment, and tenements, a surprising number take place in three of Chicago's parks — Grant, Jackson, and Washington. This fact does not mean that the parks always represent an idyllic interlude, a contrast to the perversions and ugliness of the city. On the contrary, in the parks there are attempted robberies, homosexual solicitations, beatings, and sordid sex; in one encounter Studs contracts syphilis. According to Edgar Branch, who discusses the thematic significance of the many park scenes, Studs goes to Washington Park for various reasons, depending on his mood. "The park answers to many needs and moods, shaping itself to the conformations of his spirit. Whatever the dominant impulse, the park is where he can go to be Studs Lonigan. There he can dream and act, or release the bottled up feelings and face up to his real condition."[9] To Branch, "The imagery of the park best typifies Studs's complete self, the actual and the potential. Symbolically it is the area of indeterminism in his character and destiny, yet like Farrell's other symbols it remains a solid part of empirical reality."

The earliest and one of the most important park scenes takes place in *Young Lonigan* and is repeated throughout the trilogy like a poetic refrain. The summer before entering high school, Studs goes to Washington Park with Lucy Scanlan, the girl he most wants to impress. "Everything was sun-colored, and people walked around as if they had nothing to do. It was nice out, all right, with the sky all so blue and the clouds all puffed and white and floating as if they were icebergs in a sea that didn't have any waves" (*YL*, 108). As Studs and Lucy walk around the playground, watching the rhythmic movement of the children on the swings, "their feet sank in the asphalt drive that was gooey on account of the heat, and they moved onto grass that was like velvet and bright with many colors from the sun." Hand in hand they walk over to the wooded island "until they came to a full-leaved large oak that stood near the bank. It looked nice and they decided to climb it, and sit on one of the large branches." It is at this moment that Studs has a vision that will haunt him for the rest of his life. As he helps Lucy up the tree, he sees "her clean wash bloomers. He was tempted, and wondered if he ought to try feeling her up" (*YL*, 109–10), but he controls himself and just sits there enjoying the cool breeze. What happens next is crucial in the development of Studs's character. Against his better judgment he reveals to Lucy his poetic thoughts, telling her that "the wind was like the hand of a pretty girl, and when it touched the leaves it was like that pretty girl" (*YL*, 111). This is the only time in the trilogy that the inarticulate Studs tries to express to a confidante his deepest feelings, and he is ridiculed. "She laughed, and said that it was very funny and a very silly thought for a person like Studs to have. It made him ashamed of himself, and very silent. . . ."

However, even Lucy (the "light" of Studs's life as her name implies)[10] cannot destroy his mood as he gazes at the beautiful lagoon and the people boating. Listening to the many sounds in the park, he has the first of several mystical, transcendental experiences:

> it seemed as if they were all, somehow, part of himself, and he was part of them, and them and himself were free from the drag of his body that had aches and dirty thoughts, and got sick, and could only be in one place at one time. He listened. He heard the wind. Far away, kids were playing, and it was nice to hear the echoes of their shouts, like music was sometimes nice to hear, and birds whistled, and caroled, and chirped, and hummed. It was all new-strange and he liked it. (*YL*, 112)

The sylvan interlude builds to a climax when Studs kisses the willing Lucy, who sits in the tree, swinging her legs, singing "The Blue Ridge Mountains of Virginia." To Studs this ecstatic moment is the turning point of his life, better even than his victorious fight with Weary Reilley. But the pattern of Studs's life is expectation, experience, and disillusionment, and nature has a little surprise for the youth as part of his education. "A bird cooed above them. He usually thought it was sissified to listen or pay attention to such things as birds singing; it was crazy, like being a guy who studied music, or read too many books, or wrote poems and painted pictures. But now he listened; it was nice; he told himself how nice it was" (*YL*, 113). At this rhapsodic moment, as he gazes up at the bird, "Some white stuff dropped on him, and somehow, seeing the bird that sang like this one doing that, well, it kind of hurt him, and told him how all living things were, well, they weren't perfect. . . ."

This is the lesson Studs will have to learn about his dream girl Lucy, but it will take him years to find out how imperfect she really is — and even then the dream persists.[11] As the visit to the park is coming to an end, Studs

> wanted to let her know about all the dissolving, tingling feelings he was having, and how he felt he might be the lagoon, and the feelings she made inside of him were like the dancing feelings and the little waves the sun and wind made on it; but those were things he didn't know how to tell her, and he was afraid to, because maybe he would spoil them if he did. (*YL*, 114)

Many of the novel's themes radiate from this important scene. One of them is the relentless passage of time and, concomitantly, the imminence of death. Again Farrell uses natural images, here of wind and sunset, to express metaphysical concepts of passing time and the finality of death: "And Time passed through their afternoon like a gentle, tender wind, and like death that was silent and cruel. . . . They sat, and about them their beautiful afternoon evaporated, split up and died like the sun that was dying a red death in the calm sky" (*YL*, 114). The afternoon, of course, is not all that evaporates. The "red death" of the sun foreshadows both Studs's failure to consummate his love for Lucy and his early death at the age of thirty.[12]

Washington Park is the setting again in a short but particularly effective passage that ends the last section of chapter 4. Studs has returned alone a few days later and is walking in the park when he sees Danny O'Neill's beautiful Airedale snapping at the heels of the park sheep until a policeman chases it away. Studs watches the dog take its daily swim in the lagoon and then race around. At the same time that he admires the animal's alertness and agility, he thinks "of getting even with Danny [for his having made fun of Studs's liking Lucy] by doing something to the dog, but when he watched it run, its movements so graceful, its body so alert, its ears cocked the way he liked to see a dog's ears cocked, he couldn't think of hurting it" (*YL*, 121). The scene ends with Studs playing with the dog and wishing he owned one like it, but his father refuses to buy one because he considers dogs dirty, and Studs's ignorant, superstitious mother says they bring bad luck "because sometimes dogs were the souls of people, who had put a curse on you, come back to life" (*YL*, 122–23).

Farrell has Studs, Weary, and Paulie return to Washington Park in the next-to-last scene of *Young Lonigan*. At first the seasonal symbolism and description of the park reflect the barrenness, degeneration, and ugliness of the lives of these youths who just five months ago looked forward to a future bathed, according to Father Gilhooley, in "the warming rays of Gawd's golden morning sunlight." Now it is November. "The park was bare. The wind rattled through the leaves that were colored with golden decay. The three kids strolled around, crunching leaves as they walked. Almost nobody was in the park, and their echoes traveled far" (*YL*, 195). On the wooded island the trees are "gaunt and ugly."

> They stood gazing at the chilled-looking lagoon that was tremulous with low waves. Leaves drifted, feebly and willy-nilly, on its wrinkled surface, and there was no sun. They wandered on along the shore line, and Weary broke off a branch from the shrubbery. He whittled a point on it and stopped to poke some ooze out of a dead fish. (*YL*, 195)

In this appropriate setting the discussion turns to death, but the therapeutic power of nature, even in her gray state, lightens their mood and gives the day a special cast. "[T]he day seemed so different from other days. Nothing happened, and it wasn't dull. The three kids felt something in common, a communion of spirit, given to them by the swooning, cloudy, Indian summer day that was rich and good and belonged to them" (*YL*, 196). As they stop on the bridge and watch the current of the water sweep along the leaves and branches, they can even make light of Paulie's syphilis and forget their troubles. "It's swell here," says Weary, in a statement of surprising softness for him. But with dusk, the mood changes. Although the following passage begins with an echo of the Romantic poet Longfellow, it quickly changes to one of fear and guilt, with ominous implications for the future:

> Darkness came, feather-soft. The park grew lonely, and the wind beat more steadily, until its wail sounded upon Studs' ears like that of many souls forever damned. It ripped through the empty branches. It curved through the dead leaves on the ground, whipped bunches of them, rolled them across bare stretches of earth, until they resembled droves of frightened, scurrying animals. Studs wanted to get out of the park now. (*YL*, 199–200)

Young Lonigan ends with Studs's father wistfully promising Mrs. Lonigan an excursion next summer to Riverview Park, a trip much talked about throughout the trilogy but never taken, while Studs, like the persona in Frost's "Tree by My Window," sits "listening to night sounds, to the wind in the empty tree outside. He told himself that he felt like he was a sad song. He sat there, and hummed over and over to himself . . . *The Blue Ridge Mountains of Virginia*" (*YL*, 201).

Washington Park is the setting of several scenes in *The Young Manhood*, but with a significant difference. Four of these scenes involve ugly incidents in which the bucolic purity and quiet are invaded by corruption and violence. The first of these occurs early in chapter 3, when Studs, who is supposed to be looking for a job, falls asleep under a shady tree, dreaming of girls. Once again the wind and sun are identified with Lucy and some vague desires Studs cannot articulate. The mood is romantic, as nature soothes and comforts him. But then a stranger tries to engage him in a homosexual relationship before Studs can send him on his way. This incident makes Studs feel ashamed of his body and thoughts. "He heard birds chirping and the winds above him in the tree leaves, pure like Lucy, and he looked up at the waving bushes, first one group of bushes flaunting, then another, then all of them whipping back and forth, and through them he could see patches of sky. He felt as if somebody had rubbed him all over with horse manure" (*YMSL*, 52). This time no bird excrement drops on him, but the pattern of events is similar — blissful expectation followed quickly by disenchantment.

The second scene in Washington Park occurs after Studs's father has slapped and cursed him. In violent reaction, Studs takes his empty gun, runs to the park, and pretends he is Lonewolf Lonigan, acting out gangster roles he has seen in the movies. Embarrassed when he realizes how closely he resembles his younger brother Martin playing cops and robbers, he leaves the park and nervously attempts a holdup, only to be foiled when his victim laughs in his face.

The third park scene takes place one month after the Chicago race riots. As Studs walks with Paulie and his wife enjoying the cool air, Studs is preoccupied with side glances at Eileen and thoughts of sex. His frustrated desires erupt in violence as he transfers his guilt feelings to a man who has ogled Eileen and joins Paulie in beating him up. Shortly thereafter, Studs picks up a fourteen-year-old tramp and takes her to the wooded island. "They found a spot right near the tree where he and Lucy had been. She didn't offer him any resistance" (*YMSL*, 81). At first Studs enjoys having intercourse under the stars, but the incessant demands of the girl wear him out, and he is horsewhipped by her father as he walks her home. To add to his disillusionment, this encounter in the park leaves him with syphilis.

The fourth major scene in Washington Park is one of the best pieces of writing in the book — Farrell's description of the football game that ends in a violent free-for-all after the crippling of the Monitor star, Jewboy Schwartz, by Studs and his vicious teammates. Here is a prime example of what Branch meant when he said that the park fulfills many of Studs's needs, that "Whatever the dominant impulse, the park is where he can go to be Studs Lonigan." Here Studs can act out his frustrations, engage in violent competition for the approval of his peers, and act the sports star he cannot be in real life. But even here Studs must suffer disappointment. Because of the dirty play and riot, he knows that the Cardinals will lose their permit to play in Washington Park, no team will play them on the road, and his football career will be over. He wishes he had stayed at high school and been properly coached. His only consolation is the admiration of his friends.

The Young Manhood contains two more scenes of some significance set in Washington Park. Section 3 begins with "dreary February weather" (*YMSL*, 205) and Studs longing for a new and better life as he leaves a drunken companion at the poolroom. Farrell expresses Studs's hope for regeneration through his deep love of nature and the faint signs of renewal in the park.

> He could see the lagoon, steely, dark, glittering here and there with the moon and stars. The world, the night, the park, spring that was going to come, it was all new. He felt as if he were discovering them for the first time in his life, as if the sense of budding things, of leaves coming out on the branches, the gradual warming and laziness in the air, the grass bursting green through the cold, hard, wintry earth, as if all these were inside of him. He wished that it were spring already. He determined that it was going to be a different spring and summer for him. (*YMSL*, 209)

Studs's love of nature in this scene is in the transcendental tradition. Despite the triteness of the imagery, which, of course, is appropriate for him, in the following passage Studs undergoes a genuine religious experience as he questions the meaning of life, subconsciously feels some correspondence between the distant stars and man's conduct below, and intuitively feels a reverent awe for the creator of such beauty. Standing by the lagoon,

> He glanced up at the sky and was quickened with surprise and elation because it was so clear, with such clean clouds, and a moon which seemed like frothy ice or frozen snow. And he had never realized there were so many stars in the sky, some of them blue like signal lights far, far off. They were all over the sky like jewels flung on a dark carpet and they made him wonder about life, and what it was and why people had such curious feelings. But he guessed that God had made life and the stars just as they were so that people would wonder like that, and marvel at His handiwork.
>
> He had a feeling of freshness and cleanness, even if he, too, had often been drunk like a pig. (*YMSL*, 210)

Even though such romantic passages as the above are undercut by the events of the novel and Studs's weakness of character, his feelings about nature are sincere and make him more likable. It is his genuine love of nature's beauty and purity in contrast with the continual foulness of his own life that creates one of the major tensions of the trilogy.

Inspired by the epiphany he has just experienced Studs eagerly anticipates getting to know the attractive girl who had sat next to him in church. He envisions her becoming the "center of his new life" (*YMSL*, 210), and is confident that "some day he'd see her, meet her, speak to her, tell her how he had been in the park this very night, and of the things he'd thought, and how she had been in them so much, as if she were the trees and flowers of the new spring growing inside of him. He suddenly remembered Lucy. Hell with her!" For the second time in the trilogy Studs identifies a woman he idolizes with lovely objects in nature and feels that he now has the willpower he has always lacked in the past. As he walks through the park he is "again aware of the wind sweeping through the shrubbery. It was a sad song, and it seemed to sing through him. It made him sad, but it was a pleasant sadness, because he knew he was different from all the mopes at the poolroom, he was going to do different things and be more than they" (*YMSL*, 212). However, Studs's relationship with this new girl proves even less fruitful than the one with Lucy. The wavelike pattern of expectation ending in disappointment continues. The motif of the wind as a suggestion of something sad, intangible, and distant—previously equated with fear, guilt, or death—here has a bittersweet quality as Studs tries to convince himself that the future will be better.

Washington Park is the setting for one last series of scenes in *The Young Manhood*. In chapter 19 Studs and his gang walk over to the Bug Club and listen for a while to the soapbox orators debate such things as Einstein's theory of relativity, the existence of God, Chicago's race problems, and Senator La Follette, but the freedom of discussion and intellectual level of ideas are more than they can tolerate or understand, and their reaction is best summed up by the vulgarity of Studs's gesture in goosing one of the fanatical speakers. The scene ends with Studs and his gang becoming drunk and brutally tormenting innocent Negroes.

The equivalent of Washington Park in *Judgment Day* is Grant Park, and paralleling the scene with Lucy in *Young Lonigan* is a walk Studs takes with Catherine the night he has matter-of-factly proposed to her. As the couple cross a bridge to the park, Farrell faintly echoes an incident that occurred fifteen years ago in the tree with Lucy. While they are discussing the growth of Chicago and the coming World's Fair, a train suddenly passes below them and "a flurry of hot cinders struck Studs' face causing him to grumble" (*JD*, 42). Although the couple are not yet in the park, and cinders are not quite from the world of nature as was the bird's excrement in the first volume, the effect is similar. Romance is spoiled by the intrusion of the ugly world of reality, and the difference between the dream world and actuality is seen in Catherine's remark, "Yes, isn't it a shame to have smoke in such a beautiful city."

Once the couple are in the park, Studs's mood is reflected by his surroundings, and just as he had previously identified Lucy with light, he does the same with Catherine:

> He looked ahead feeling soft, and the dazzling rays of the fountain seemed, somehow, to be part of his mood. And his feelings about Catherine and the spray were like so many diamonds lifting and falling, and to him, Catherine was like a diamond, and his feelings were like the fountain, so many diamonds rising and falling that way in the light, and the light was Catherine. (*JD*, 44)

Not having changed much in the last fifteen years, Studs feels like a "chump" to have such thoughts. As he smells the lake breezes and hears "the dry-sounding clatter of a train" behind them, Studs senses the contrast between the loveliness of nature and the sterility of the city as a wasteland. He longs once again for the elusive happiness that has always escaped him, and Farrell expresses this longing through the imagery of a parched person's unquenchable thirst for the fruit of life. Lucy, the girl in the church, and now Catherine — all of whom have repeatedly been identified with the loveliness of nature — represent to Studs "a happiness he hadn't known but only wished for. It had always seemed ahead of him, and now he was on the verge of catching up with it. It had been, he guessed, a feeling like always being so thirsty that he could never get enough to drink, or like eating a fruit that he could never suck all the juices from, and now, he would" (*JD*, 45).

As Studs and Catherine walk near the lake, the wind ominously "rubbed their faces like a brush with sharp fibrous hairs" (*JD*, 46). Hope for the future and regret over lost opportunities in the past are mixed with Studs's fear for his deteriorating health. He feels the strength and permanence of nature in contrast to the puniness of man as he and Catherine stand

> on the jagged breakwater rocks, his left arm encircling her waist. Foaming with noisy whitecaps, the waters came in with a rush, pounded, dragged outward to the visible wall of darkness and mist. A path of moonlight, like a gleaming aisle, slanted over the water, away from them. Listening to the waves, and perceiving their merciless and resilient strength as they smashed into the breakwater and lifted, he felt how weak he himself was, how weak, perhaps, anybody must feel standing here. He felt that for years, and forever onward until the Day of Judgment, these waves would be pounding and smashing, day and night. (*JD*, 47)

The third Chicago park that Farrell uses as a setting in *Studs Lonigan* is seen less often, but it, too, plays a part in Studs's characterization. Studs and Catherine visit Jackson Park in March after Sunday morning church services. Once again it is the season of new life and regeneration, and Studs, observing the golfers, thinks that it might be good exercise for him to drive golf balls. The reader is constantly reminded of Studs's failing health, but as he admires the "shoots of fresh green bursting amidst dead wintry grass" (*JD*, 164), there seems to be hope for the future.

Shortly thereafter Studs pays a second visit to Jackson Park alone, hoping that he will meet some attractive girl, even though he is engaged to Catherine. The beauty of the area momentarily drives away his worries about his stock market losses, but his problems are too great. "He stopped to stare at an oak, its limbs rattling a trifle in the wind, hoping that by concentrating on it he would drive the worry away" (*JD,* 180). However, like the Studs of old, he is embarrassed by these poetic reveries and thinks, "Christ, he was getting goofy as a loon!" The previously established pattern of romantic idyll interrupted by some ugly intrusion, some threat or danger, is hinted at with the golfers yelling "Fore" and the ball landing near Studs. Even more ominous is Studs looking up and seeing "a bank of clouds smothering the sun and draping shadows over the park." A less subtle indication of what is in store for Studs follows when he is invited by some young men to join them in a pickup baseball game. Studs plays right field but does poorly. At bat he is no better. His arm hurts and he tires easily, so he quits the game and sits on a bench in the sun.

Here Studs has another religious experience similar to the one in *The Young Manhood.*

> He leaned back and with shaded eyes looked up at a sky whose shimmering and pervasive brightness brought water to his eyes. He blinked at a squirrel moving swiftly across the walk and into the bushes. He was humble and soft, and felt that there was something behind all this that he saw, sun, and sky, and new grass, and trees, and birds, and the bushes, and the squirrel, and the lagoon, and people moving by him, and street cars and automobiles, and it was God. God made all this, moved it, made it live, himself, that Red he'd met who was against Him, the fellows playing ball. And God was the spirit behind it all and behind everything. Gee, if Catherine was only here now! He shook his head, as if to drive all these thoughts away because if he told them to anybody, it would just sound goofy. He wasn't a poet. (*JD,* 189)

Momentarily at peace with the world, Studs falls asleep on a park bench.

Studs is right when he fears that even Catherine will make fun of him for his soft side. Some time later while walking with Catherine he suggests that they walk to the park. Her sarcastic reply is: "You want to go to Jackson Park and enjoy nature" (*JD,* 281). When he asks her what they should do instead, she says, "I know what we shan't do. . . . Go to the park and catch cold on the damp grass finding out that nature is grand. . . . Go on, you're making me blush." But by the beginning of the next chapter, Farrell informs the reader that the blushing Catherine has made love with Studs in Jackson Park and is now pregnant.

From this point on, *Judgment Day* moves quickly to the fateful day at the beach when Studs has his heart attack. Before analyzing Farrell's use of nature in this crucial scene, however, it is necessary to go back and look briefly at some of the other swimming scenes in the trilogy. That water imagery has played an important part throughout the novel has already been evident from the many references to Lake Michigan as well as to the lagoons and fountains in the various parks. According to Branch, "Farrell uses water imagery to reveal the inner Studs: not the 'iron man,' but the unique, unknown individual in need of love. Fluidity is constantly associated with Studs's deepest feelings and desires, with his ideal moments and dreams, and with important maturing experiences."[13] Water in *Studs Lonigan*, as Branch points out, "often suggests health, freedom, self-mastery, as when Studs swims in the 'Y' pool and feels 'removed from the world, clean.'" Paradoxically, as David Owen has observed in his unpublished dissertation, "A Pattern of Pseudo-Naturalism: Lynd, Mead, and Farrell,"[14] water imagery in the trilogy also suggests death, but Branch effectively dissolves the paradox with the argument that "if he gave in to his feelings death indeed would be the fate of Studs Lonigan the tough guy; but to Studs the man of feeling, death subconsciously appeals as a release from his hell on earth."[15]

The first of the three swimming scenes occurs in *Young Lonigan* when Studs and Kenny Killarney go to the Fifty-first Street beach after Kenny steals a bathing suit. The two boys dive, swim, float, and splash around with "animal glee" (*YL*, 143), exhilarated by the hot sun and cold water. Studs experiences complete freedom — release from the confinement of the city and from all the sensual thoughts and guilt feelings that have been bothering him. Like a poet he identifies himself with an aimless cloud drifting in the sky and is no longer ashamed of his body and its urges. As he floats he pretends that "he was the most powerful whale in all the seas and oceans, floating along, minding its business, because all the sharks were leery of attacking it" (*YL*, 145). But Studs's reverie is suddenly shattered by the fear of cramps "and drowning and dying, so he turned over and swam."

In this scene Farrell again uses nature to present the two sides of his protagonist. The tension between the tough exterior and the tender inner being is relaxed until the intrusion of the perpetual fear of death that haunts Studs throughout the trilogy. Young Studs makes light of this fear, dives deep and pretends to be drowning to attract attention, but he is happy to be alone. "He felt far away from all the world now, and he didn't care" (*YL*, 145). Finally Studs and Kenny sprawl on the sand, "the sun fine and warm on their backs, evaporating all the wet." In the serene quiet, "Studs forgot everything, and felt almost as good as when he had been by himself way out in the deep water. He just lay there and pretended that he wasn't Studs or anybody else at all, and he let his thoughts take care of themselves."

As in *The Young Manhood* and *Judgment Day*, such idyllic interludes are quickly shattered. Studs cannot isolate himself from the real world. He is "snapped out" of his reverie "by Kenny cursing the goddamn flies and the kids who ran scuffling sand over everybody" (*YL*, 146). The only release from these intrusions is death, and Studs's death wish is expressed through water imagery, as he looks "out over the lake where the water and sky seemed to meet and become just nothing. He thought of swimming out into the nothingness, and just floating, floating with nothing there, and no noises, no fights, no old man, no girls, no thinking of Lucy, no nothing but floating, floating" (*YL*, 146). Once again, the intrusion of Kenny's voice breaks his thoughts.

The second swimming scene takes place in *The Young Manhood*, but since it occurs indoors at the YMCA, it does not qualify as an example of Farrell's use of nature. However, it is carefully related to the beach scenes as Studs, trying to reform and regain his former good health, enjoys swimming in the nude in the Y pool, "Feeling . . . complete bodily freedom. . . . removed from the world, clean. It was like losing all the gripes that had been piling up within him" (*YMSL*, 235).

Balancing the swimming scenes in the two earlier volumes is the third one in *Judgment Day*. Both Studs's and Catherine's families are unhappy over the sudden announcement of their forthcoming marriage. Catherine is depressed as the couple go to the beach for an excursion. Nature is not in sympathy and does not reflect their mood. On the contrary, "Her mood and his own both seemed to press down the more forcibly because of the sunny appearance of the Sunday street, the people dressed up, strolling along . . . " (*JD*, 325).

At the beach Studs ogles the other girls, feeling sorry for himself and disappointed in the "chunky" Catherine. Nature makes him aware again of his own insignificance. Pausing by the pebbles at the edge of the water, "Studs suddenly felt himself small and puny, and he stood, with the incoming waters curling over his feet, sticking his shoulders back and throwing out his chest" (*JD*, 327). This defiant gesture is more to impress Catherine than the universe. Studs dives and shows off in front of Catherine and begins to feel "a part of this scene, of many people all having a good time" (*JD*, 328), but as a result of all this exertion he begins to feel chest pains. Catherine's pregnancy makes him feel "trapped like a rat in a cage" (*JD* 320). Studs looks "around the beach, as if looking through the bars of a cage, and he saw all these people in swimming suits, so many girls, so many fellows, and he wondered how many of them were trapped as he was, or would be trapped in the same way?" (*JD*, 330)

Nature, the vast lake blending with the sky, symbolizes at this point the enigma of life. Man, Farrell suggests, can at best only swim toward a distant goal against difficult odds, until, tired of the struggle, he sinks.

Studs, overwhelmed by his problems, sees death as an inviting release. He looks

> wistfully over the lake at the horizon, where the merging of sky and water was like some mystery. He was struck with the desire to swim out to it and reach the center of where the sky fell into the water, and he knew there was no such place, and if he swam out, he would finally just sink, and this wish was like so many others that he had had all along. He was like a swimmer going out and out, and the farther he swam the more tired he got and the harder he had to swim. (*JD*, 331)

Unlike Clyde Griffiths, who finds himself in a somewhat similar predicament with his girlfriend in *An American Tragedy*, Studs never thinks of using the lake to hurt Catherine.

As Studs lies on his back and looks up at the sky, he realizes "what a big place the world was after all, and he was sort of lost in it. He felt that he had always been like this. Ever since he had been a kid, he had wished and waited, and there had been no change except for the worst" (*JD*, 335). Wishing that he were a handsome six-footer, built like a fullback, attracting the attention of the crowd of bathers," Studs plunges into the water to end the second part of chapter 15. Part 3 begins with Studs at the center of attention, lying on the sand, having been pulled from the water after a heart attack.

Nature's indifference toward Studs is in keeping with one part of naturalistic tradition. The lake does not drown Studs. The temperature of the water cannot be blamed for his heart attack. When Studs challenges nature with the announcement of his existence, the universe feels no need to reply. Where the Romantic poet might indulge in the pathetic fallacy and have nature weep for the fallen victim, undeserving of such a fate, the naturalist is less sentimental. Perhaps the basic difference between the Romantic and naturalistic attitude toward nature can best be seen at the climax of *Judgment Day*, when Studs hunts for a job in the rain. As Studs wanders the streets of Chicago, miserably wet, Farrell's presentation of nature is somewhere between Crane's view of its indifference to man in "The Open Boat" and Norris's portrayal of its hostility in the death of McTeague in the desert.

Studs does not have to look for a job this particular day. He has never been portrayed as being especially ambitious or industrious, though it is true Catherine's pregnancy and his forthcoming marriage have given him new responsibilities. The most probable explanation of his driving himself so hard under such adverse conditions is his subconscious death wish. Death will provide him with the permanent release from his disappointment and worries. "He wished to all holy hell that he didn't have to go through with all this, and he stood watching the splattering rain. He felt sorry for himself" (*JD*, 362). He becomes short of breath as he gets soaked, walking through puddles. "Rain beat off his hat and back, and a drop oozed inside his collar, slid coldly down his back." Actually, Studs is role playing again, even though the movies are not mentioned. "He saw himself walking in the rain, wet and tired, with things crashing down on his head, being screwed at every turn, forced to do something" (*JD*, 380).

In a miserable mood Studs tries unsuccessfully to cheer himself up at a burlesque show, after which he takes the train home. Impulsively, despite a high fever and nausea, he then runs the last hundred yards down the street. Finally, "He stopped and like a drunken man watched an automobile splash by. Suddenly, a cold chill iced his body, and the rain slapped against his cheeks, dripped from his hat" (*JD*, 387). Dizzy, his body racked with stabbing pains, Studs staggers around. "With the sleeve of his raincoat, he wiped his dripping nose, streaking his upper lip. The rain beat on him." At last he manages to stumble into his parents' apartment, where he collapses.

The closest Farrell comes in this crucial scene to portraying nature as hostile is his writing that the rain "slapped" Studs and "beat on him," but nature's hostility exists only in Studs's mind. It is part of his role playing, his self-pity. Studs is, in reality, punishing himself and, as he has been throughout his life, he is his own worst enemy.

Some readers have been tempted to see Studs as a helpless victim of his environment in the naturalistic tradition, but Farrell is angered by such a misinterpretation of his intentions. In the interview with Flynn and Salzman, he insists that "The environment alone doesn't kill Studs."[16] Studs, Farrell argues, makes many decisions, some of them bad, in his struggle to survive. His choices do not always work out, but other people have made similar choices and survived. No one knows why. "You can't even say that [any particular reason] causes his disintegration. You don't know. I mean, there's a simple enigma about Studs. You see, he's a human being. And there's a mystery about every human being. And there's a mystery about Studs,"[17] but, to Farrell's disappointment, the critics fail to see it. Farrell claims that his objective presentation of Studs's thoughts and actions has purposely excluded any "signposts for the reader" who is "on his own. . . . There is no clue what to think. You've got to think for yourself about it." That he has succeeded admirably in his goal of making the reader think and care about Studs Lonigan is undeniable, but he is not to be believed when he claims that there are no clues. The clues are there and some can be found in his nature scenes, images, and symbols. In his court testimony defending his trilogy against charges of obscenity, Farrell argued that his goal was "to present life as it is, in so far as I can see it, to present it in terms of patterns of thought and consciousness, which I can grasp and open, or which I imagine with the conviction that this is the way it is."[18] It was Farrell's creative imagination that led him to use nature in setting, image, and symbol to express the moral and psychological conditions, the anguished state of mind, of his defeated protagonist.

CHAPTER 3

Nature as "Interior Structure":
Henry Roth's *Call It Sleep*

I n an interview with Bonnie Lyons in 1972, Henry Roth explained that in the three and one-half years he was writing *Call It Sleep*, "especially towards the end, the whole novel was in my consciousness at once. I thought of it musically — that's how I really felt about it. My attitude toward it was what a musician must feel about his composition."[1] When Lyons asked if the mythological motif was "consciously developed," he replied, "I think the motifs were conscious — I think I felt the need of them. When you speak about . . . how to achieve form in the course of a long work like that — this is one of the few things that I recognized that I needed. Really it gives added interior structure."[2] Since Lyons and others[3] have already written perceptively about the intricate patterns of imagery, symbols, and motifs in Roth's novel, this study will focus on only one such pattern — nature imagery — and show how it is a crucial part of the novel's conscious "interior structure."

As suggested in the Introduction, "interior structure," as conceived by Roth, is synonymous with texture, and texture contributes to form. Roth's analogy to music in the Lyons interview indicates that he was probably thinking in terms of the interrelationship of such things as melody, rhythm, harmony, dynamics, and instrumentation. This interweaving of melodies, with its exposition and recapitulation, is similar to the fiction writer's blending motifs and images, symbols and metaphors, physical description and characterization, to give internal form to the external narrative.

Nature imagery in *Call It Sleep* serves this function. The repeated references to animals, flowers, birds, snow and rain, water and sunlight, do more than just embellish a given scene; they contribute significantly to what Roth called in an interview with John S. Friedman, "the summary impact . . . the apocalyptic impact of"[4] the novel. Nature imagery also reinforces themes, like the struggle for survival in a hostile universe, the acceptance of death, the Oedipal conflict, and the inextricable mixture of good and evil. It contributes to the characterization of David Schearl, Roth's child-protagonist, and his father, mother, and Aunt Bertha. Certain nature images become identified with a particular character, for example, flowers with Genya, bulls and horns with Albert, and Austrian peaks with Aunt Bertha. Some nature images poetically soften the harshness of urban reality, contribute humor, or suggest the dreamlike quality of the events and psychological state being depicted. And finally, nature imagery becomes an important ingredient in presenting the mindscape of the protagonist, offering clues to the quality and extent of David's transformation at the climax and denouement.

Call It Sleep spans approximately three years in the life of an immigrant child consumed with fear and guilt as he tries to adjust to a new urban environment, first in Brownsville and then the east side of New York. David Schearl's fears range from dark cellars and closets, rats, and a lame temptress with an iron brace on her leg, to fights with neighborhood children, getting lost on strange streets, enrollment in a dark cheder (Hebrew School) with a volatile rabbi, violations of the Sabbath, and a whip-wielding father with an incendiary temper. Not the least of David's fears is his fear of death, of spending eternal years in a narrow box. David's one sanctuary is his mother, Genya, but she has problems of her own, trying to adjust to a foreign city in a new land, to placate a violent, temperamental husband, and to discourage a lusty boarder named Luter. Genya's love for her son is undeniable, but she does not fully understand what he is going through. On one occasion she tells him: "I really believe . . . that you think of nothing. Now honest, isn't it so? Aren't you just a pair of eyes and ears! You see, you hear, you remember, but when will you know?"[5] Genya is wrong. Even in the final section of the novel, she understands him no better. In chapter 11 of "The Rail," she tells him: "The skein the cat's played with is easier to unravel than my son" (331). She compares him to "those large bright flies in Austria that can fly backwards and forwards or hover in the air as though pinned there. And what will you do after you're fed — stay here till the Messiah comes?" (332). On the contrary, David is not just flitting around but always thinking, always questioning the world around him. By the novel's denouement, he is beginning to *know*.

One of the nature images that Roth uses occasionally to describe David is that of a hunted animal, the prey of his fears. An early example occurs when David goes downstairs on his way to school and stumbles in fear before the cellar door, "but the next moment shot to his feet again, and sped like a hunted thing to the pale light of the doorway" (58). The next evening, when Yussie, a neighbor, hits David in the knee with a clothes-hanger hatchet, David kicks him in the face and bloodies his nose. Yussie's screams draw the attention of Albert Schearl, who looms over his terrified son as judge and executioner. "Like a cornered thing, he [David] shrank within himself . . . and waited" (83), as Albert strikes him in the face, knocks him down, and then beats him on the shoulders with the hanger, ironically calling him "Wild beast!" (84). In the street the following day, the terrified David bares his teeth when attacked, runs away after knock-ing his attacker unconscious, and finds himself lost in another neighbor-hood. "He ran faster, sensing beside him the soft pad of easy-loping fear. The next corner would be haven or bay, and as he neared it, he burst into the anquished spring of a flagging quarry—" (96). Another example ap-pears when David's mother brings him home from the police station. Near an empty lot he finally recognizes his neighborhood. "There was a wind that prowled over that area of rock and dead grass, that would spring at them when they passed it. And the wind did" (109–10).

Much later in the novel, in chapter 15 of "The Rail," Roth uses a very effective nature image related to the motif of the pursued and the pursuer, in a scene that crystallizes the theme of the struggle for existence and sur-vival in a hostile universe. It is reminiscent of an episode in Dreiser's *The Financier*, where young Frank Cowperwood observes the daily combat be-tween a lobster and a squid in an aquarium window of a fish store. In Roth's novel the boys are smoking a straw-reed outside of Rabbi Pankower's cheder. Izzy lets Strooly take a puff for the cost of one of the gray horse-flies he has caught around the tenement garbage cans and bottled. "The horse-fly, wing-stripped, crawled impotently about on Izzy's hand" (363), while Izzy decides which spider he is going to feed it to. As the boys go down the cellar steps outside the cheder to find Choloimis, their favorite spider, David's fears are reawakended; he realizes that his cousin Polly must have told her mother by now about David's serving as pimp during Leo and Esther's sexual play in Aunt Bertha's cellar. Under the humor of the dialect and the excitement of the boys, Roth presents a parable. David's guilt is crying out for punishment, and he feels as impotent as the wingless fly being fed to the fat spider.

> "Dere! Look! Look! T'row it now! Easy don' bust id! Look o' him! He's walkin' roun'. Whee! Dere he comes! Dere he comes! Lyow! He glyabth 'im! Fight! Fight! Gib'm, haws-fly! In de kishkis—nudder one! C'mon Choloimis! Yowee! Tie 'im op! He's god 'im. Wid de legs! Waddye big wungl! Pullin' him! Pullin' him! Hully Muzzis! Look! In de hole! Bye! Bye! Buzzicoo! Yea! Yea!" Excited

voices fused into a treble dirge. "Bye! Bye! Buzzicoo! Yea Spider! Yea!"
(364)

The boys' dirge parallels David's fear of his own destruction at the hands
of his father. Thus the wounded insect deftly echoes Genya's comparison
of her son with "the bright flies in Austria" and the scene with the hungry
spider becomes a semi-humorous objective epitome of David's innermost
thoughts.

The hunter/hunted, victimizer/victim relationship is reinforced by
means of two predatory bird images. One suggests that David is a small
creature or animal caught by a bird of prey. After a tense dinner in honor
of Bertha's introducing her beau, Nathan Sternowitz, to the family, David
feels the threatening silence as the couple go for a walk: "silence only made
his father more ominous. But the silence continued, and David feeling
himself caught as if in talons of stress, dared not move — at least not until
his father spoke and eased the strain . . . "(188). The bird-of-prey image
is echoed at the novel's climax when David almost electrocutes himself
by plunging the milk ladle into the streetcar tracks: "*The hawk of radiance
rak[ed] him with talons of fire, battering his skull with a beak of fire, braying
his body with pinions of intolerable light . . .*" (419).[6]

An effective extension of the hunter/hunted, victimizer/victim motif
appears when David learns a Passover folk song in Hebrew school, at the
same time he hears about Isaiah and the coal, and the two become linked
in his mind. According to Lyons, who discusses this song in a very brief
chapter on motifs in *Call It Sleep*, "Since David is searching throughout
the novel for the meaning of the universe, a sense of God's order and justice,
it is fitting that he should catch upon this nursery rhyme as a possible
clue."[7] In the words of the folk song "*Chad Godya*," a father buys a kid
for two zuzim, but in the pecking order of this predatory world, the baby
goat is eaten by a cat, which is bitten by a dog, and so on in a long chain
of events. The song ends blessing God, who "killed the angel of death,
who killed the butcher, who killed the ox, who drank the water, that
quenched the fire, that burned the stick, that beat the dog, that bit the
cat, that ate the kid, that my father bought for two zuzim. One kid, one
only kid" (233). As David fearfully accepts Rabbi Pankower's challenge
to translate the Aramaic folk song into Yiddish, he has the feeling that
the other boys "were crouching to pounce upon him should be miss one
rung in the long ladder of guilt and requital. Carefully, he climbed past
the cow and the butcher and the angel of death." To Mary Edrich Redding,
in her study of myth in Roth's novel, the depiction in the song of the need
"for a divine champion against the shadows of death," combined with the
parental inadequacies of Albert Schearl, serves "as a moving comment on

the insecurities of a small boy who has been rejected by his own father."[8] Both Redding and Lyons, who relates the "*Chad Godya*" motif to the theme of deliverance in the Passover celebration and then traces the echoes of the song later in *Call It Sleep*, are much closer to the mark than Gary Epstein, who concludes that "David, looking for the God who purified Isaiah, finds instead the all-powerful destroyer, who answers guilt with requital. The 'kid' has been sacrificed to demonstrate God's utter power and lack of compassion."[9] On the contrary, the Passover song, sung at the conclusion of the seder, celebrates the compassion of God whose mercy saves the Jews and overwhelms the forces of death in a Messianic future. Thus Roth's explicit identification of Albert with the angel of death in chapter 8 of "The Picture," when Albert furiously warns Genya that her sister Bertha is pushing him too far—"if she thinks she can make light with me because she has a man with her, she'd better be careful. She's jesting with the angel of death!" (189)—subtly foreshadows the father's defeat at the climax of the novel, to be discussed later.

Redding exaggerates when she claims that "The set of symbols most important to *Call It Sleep* derives from the corn-spirit and related agricultural myths,"[10] but she does highlight the importance of Genya's and Albert's rural origins in Austria. Just as Albert is identified with bulls on his father's farm, so Genya is identified with flowers. David, entranced by the lyrics of the song of the girls playing in the street,

"Waltuh, Waltuh, Wiuhlflowuh,
Growin' up so high;
So we are all young ladies,
An' we are ready to die" (23)

recalls his mother's telling him that Walter Wildflower was a little boy who lived in the country where David had been born. In his imagination, David "had seen him standing on a hill, far away. Filled with a warm, nostalgic mournfulness, he shut his eyes. Fragments of forgotten rivers floated under the lids, dusty roads, fathomless curve of trees, a branch in a window under a flawless light. A world somewhere, somewhere else." What David does not know at first is that his mother was once like the romantic young ladies in the song, in love with a man who made love to her among the blue cornflowers. The last time Genya saw her faithless Christian lover, who married an older woman for her money, Genya was standing among the blue cornflowers, comforted by their beauty. This memory led to her purchase in New York of the picture of a cornfield, "at the foot of which tiny blue flowers grew" (172). Genya tells David, "That's how it grows. It grows out of the earth you know, the sweet corn in the summer—it isn't made by pushcart pedlars." Then she adds, "In July those flowers come out.

They're pretty, aren't they? You've seen them, only you've forgotten, you were so young."

Roth, in addition to using flowers symbolically to relate Genya to her past, also uses them metaphorically to describe Genya through David's adoring eyes. Thrilled to hear that his mother has a secret past, even though he does not understand Genya's revelations to Aunt Bertha, David is aware that his mother is blushing. "Looking up, he saw a deep rose in his mother's throat and fainter petals dappling the waxen sheen of her flat cheek" (164). A little later, he sees Genya on the street. "Catching sight of her accidentally this way always gave him an intense pleasure. It was as though the street's shifting intricacy had flowered into the simple steadiness of her presence" (164). In this manner Roth weaves both the pictured and the imagined flowers into the texture of Genya's portrait, thus contributing to what he calls the novel's "interior structure."

To Roth's credit is his avoidance of the sentimental stereotype of pastoral innocence (Austrian countryside, flowers, Genya, good) versus urban corruption (New York City, cellars, rats, evil). Genya, it should be remembered, met her faithless gentile lover among the blue cornflowers; Albert allowed his father to be gored by a bull in a field. In the complicated texture of Roth's novel, as in real life, country and city, light and dark, good and bad are intertwined. For example, flowers, normally associated with summer, life, beauty, growth, and vitality, play an important role in David's introduction to death. When David sees a wreath on a tenement entrance, "The green leaves were half concealed in snow; even the purple ribbon was covered. The poor white flowers looked frozen" (58). In one of the most beautiful anecdotes in the novel, Genya tells David about her grandmother when he asks if she has ever seen a dead person:

> Now long ago, she had a little garden before her house. It was full of sweet flowers in the summertime, and she tended it all by herself. My grandfather, stately Jew, could never understand why she should spend a whole spring morning watering the flowers and plucking off the dead leaves, and snipping here and patting there, when she had so many servants to do it for her. (65)

The grandmother promotes the growth of new blossoms by pruning the dead leaves and branches, but she cannot avoid the inevitable. Genya explains that "As she grew older, she grew very strange. . . . When autumn came and everything had died—" Her sentence is unfinished as David, frightened by his own mortality, interrupts her and asks, "Died? Everything?" Genya first eases his fear by explaining that only the flowers died, but then continues her story telling how the grandmother would not leave her house for days, not until the first snowfall. One day, late in the fall, "dressed in her prettiest Sabbath clothes" and the pearls her husband had given her as her first present, the grandmother told Genya the story of Petrush Kolonov, an elderly peasant who when he grew very old, "would sit on a stone and look at the mountains" (67). When David asks his mother why the old man sat like this, Genya can only laugh and point out that three generations have now asked the same question. Here, through a pregnant silence, Roth succeeds in conveying the eternal mystery of death and the existential need of each individual to accept it on his own terms. Genya then describes metaphorically her grandmother's final acceptance of her own death: "And so we walked and the leaves were blowing. Shew-w-w! How they lifted, and one blew against her coat, and while the wind held it there, you know, like a finger, she lifted it off and crumbled it." That winter she died.

Animal imagery is even more extensive than flower imagery in Roth's novel. Lyons suggests that fire images in Albert's curses "and the contrasting animal imagery seem to reflect Albert's vision of the universe: one is either a destructive, burning figure of wrath or a victim."[11] When Albert curses Luter and vows to destroy him for having turned against him at work, he warns Genya, "I'm no lamb" (126), but after his hand is mangled by a machine at the shop, he humbly admits, "they led me out like sheep" (135). Later, when Genya fears Albert's being injured while crossing over tenement roofs on his new job as a milkman, he curtly dismisses her fears: "I don't pretend to be a mountain goat" (210).

Lamb, sheep, mountain goat—all are more appropriate as symbols of David, who is more sacrificial victim than victimizer. David's wonderful sensitivity is seen in his compassion for his father's horse Tilly, who falls down one winter afternoon on her way back to the stable. Roth describes Tilly poetically as having "one eye the cloudy color of singed celluloid, or a drop of oil on a sunless puddle. She would stand patiently, even when children were pulling the hairs out of her tail to plait rings with. And yet she seemed no weaker and no worse than most of the horses who passed through Ninth Street" (208). Even young David is aware that his father's complaints about Tilly are justified and that Albert wants "tremendous power in the beast he handled just as he himself seemed possessed of tremendous power." David pities the beast, but hopes that the company will give Albert a "livelier" one. Apparently his wish comes true, because in chapter 2 of "The Rail," while David sits in the shade of the hallway waiting for his father, Roth describes the new horse as follows: "Just outside the doorway and under the fierce glare, the horse, black flanks rippling like water, flashed out viciously with hoof and tail at the glinting flies" (268).

Since the Freudian symbolism of the horns and the identification of Albert Schearl with bulls have already been discussed by the critics mentioned earlier, only a few brief examples here should suffice. When Genya asks Albert what he would prefer after he insults her picture of the Austrian cornfields, he answers, "Something alive. . . . A herd of cattle drinking such as I've seen in the stores. Or a prize bull with a shine to its flanks and the black fire in his eyes" (190). In one of the earlier chapters, Albert tells Luter at dinner how he used to tend black and white prize bulls in Austria. Luter prefers the amenities of urban life and dislikes the country-side. "I don't like the earth," he tells Albert. "It's for peasants . . . "(31). In a rare mood for him, Albert laughs and replies:

> I *think* I do. I *think* when you come out of a house and step on the bare earth among the fields you're the same man you were when you were inside the house. But when you step out on pavements, you're somone else. You can feel your face change. Hasn't that happened to you? (31–32)

Through such passages Roth portrays Albert as an Esau figure incapable of adjusting to life in New York. Luter tells Genya that Albert is a strange man, with his love of cattle. As he leers at Genya, Luter says seductively, "Now when I think of Europe, and of my hamlet, the first thought that comes to me, just as his first thought is a cow or a prize bull, my first thought is of the peasant women" (43). After his argument with Luter and the injury in the printing shop, Albert tells Genya bitterly that from now on he wants to work "out doors — alone if I can. but out doors always . . . I'll not let myself be hemmed in by ink and iron any more. I don't want any foremen for my friends. I don't want anybody. I — I have no fortune with men" (137).

It is in chapter 6 of "The Rail" that David discovers the new whip and magnificent mounted bull's horns that his father has bought. The horns suggest "terrific power" (298), and Genya explains that they do not come from a cow: "A bull. . . . They were monstrous [in Austria] — walls of flesh and strength." David cannot believe that his father bought his trophy just for memory's sake.

> Somehow looking at the horns, guessing the enormous strength of the beast who must have owned them, there seemed to be another reason. He couldn't quite fathom it though. But why was it that two things so remote from each other [a beaten thief and his mother's look of contentment, apparently after sex with Albert] seemed to have become firmly coupled in his mind? It was as though the horns lying on the washtub had bridged them, as though one tip pierced one image and one tip another — that man outstretched on the sidewalk, that mysterious look of repose in his mother's face when he had come in. Why? Why did he think of them one and the same time. He couldn't tell. He sensed only that in the horns, in the poised power of them lay a threat, a challenge he must answer, he must meet. But he didn't know how.(299)

Here is the classical Oedipal conflict, with the son in competition with the powerful father for the possession of the mother. Redding, in her fascinating but not always convincing analysis of agricultural myths in *Call It Sleep*, recalls David's clutching at knives in his dream of his father's approaching steps. When Albert tells Genya how he stood by and let the bull kill his hated father many years before, Redding concludes that "The bull image, the concept of a tool or weapon (here, the 'stick') shared by the father and son, the patricidal scene, and the betrayal of the son by the mother all have specific counterparts in various myths of rebellion among the classical deities."[12] Redding also discusses European agricultural myths in which a goat, bull, or ox represents the corn-spirit, this animal being killed in actuality or effigy, with children participating in the ritual. Redding connects the myths to *Call It Sleep* by pointing out that "The horns of the cuckold motif and the theme of the inept workman afford further dimensions to Roth's delineation of Albert and his many job failures."[13]

One other nature image identified with Albert in Roth's novel is worth mentioning in passing — volcanoes. The most important volcano reference appears at the beginning of chapter 16 of "The Cellar" when David observes his father's growing anger at Luter, who has not returned. The sight of Albert's wrath terrifies him.

> Never, not even the night he had beaten David, did he radiate, so fell, so electric a fury. It was as though his whole body was smouldering, a stark throbbing, curdling emanation flowed from him, a dark, corrosive haze that was all the more fearful because David sensed how thin an aura it was of the terrific volcano clamped within. (127)

In this passage the volcano image blends effectively with David's usual view of his father as a Jehovah figure with his raised hammer and lightning bolts, dealing out swift punishment to objects of his wrath.

The character in *Call It Sleep* most like Albert Schearl, despite their constant dislike of one another, is his sister-in-law, David's Aunt Bertha. Animal imagery is a delightful part of Bertha's characterization, supplying some of the novel's earthy humor. Like Albert, Bertha has a sharp tongue and uses it to lash at the objects of her scorn. Indelicate, crude, incendiary, she is the peasant immigrant trying to adjust to urban America. Unlike Albert, she is learning to cope with this strange but exciting new land, and by book 4 she has a husband, two stepdaughters, a candy store, and a baby on the way. For her, the American Dream is coming true.

Whereas both Albert and Genya remember their Euopean past with more nostalgia than regret, Genya's longing for the blue cornflowers of Austria, as Lyons point out, "is in direct opposition to Aunt Bertha's hilariously vulgar conclusion about their village: 'Veljish was still as a fart in company. Who could endure it? Trees! Fields! Again trees! Who can talk to trees?'" (153).[14] Walking toward the Metropolitan Museum with her nephew, Bertha marvels at the lack of children on the street: "Bah! It is quiet as a forest here. Who would want to live in these houses?" (147). Once inside the museum, Bertha, afraid of getting lost, instructs David to keep one eye on the statues and paintings, the other on a couple they are following: "We must cleave to them like mire on a pig!" (149). When Bertha and David collapse from exhaustion back at the Schearls' apartment, Bertha explains that they are so late because they could not find their way out: "Ach, green rump that I am, the dirt of Austria is still under my toe-nails and I plunge into museums" (150). She admits that in America she works "like a horse and I stink like one with my own sweat. But there's life here, isn't there?" (153).

In one of the best comic scenes in the novel, Bertha's peasant naturalness is temporarily defeated by Albert's cantankerous propriety. Showing her sister at the dinner table the package of large white bloomers she has just bought, Bertha rapturously demonstrates how, if held in a certain way upside down, "they look like peaks in Austria" (157). A furious Albert orders Bertha to desist, but she taunts him with crude insults: "Is he so pious, he can't bear to look at a pair of drawers? Does he piss water as mortals do, or only the purest of vegetable oil?" The scene climaxes with Albert's ripping the garment apart and flinging the halves scornfully at his sister-in-law: "Here are your peaks!" (158). For her sister's sake, Bertha makes an uneasy truce with Albert, telling Genya, "He's a mad dog. . . . He has to run. There's nothing to do but keep out of his way" (159).

Where Albert is identified with bulls and mad dogs, Bertha and Genya are identified with harmless calves. Bertha claims that all the German romances Genya read in Austria filled her with "strange notions" (165). Genya, she complains, is now "too calm, too generous. . . . perhaps you've forgotten what a mopish calf-eyed creature you are." Nervous about her forthcoming marriage to Nathan Sternowitz, Bertha says she feels "like a calf being led to the shambles" (167). Natural images involving farm animals, snakes, and insects flow freely from her tongue and Albert's. When a customer is surprised that Bertha's daughters are still in bed and asks, "Your fledglings are still in the nest?" (310), Bertha says that Polly and Esther are "Lazy as cats," but when no one is around, she calls them "Bedbugs foul!" and "stinking heifers" (308), "cattle" (309), and "sows" (310). Later, cursing Nathan in the store, she says may he "Be a scape-goat for dogs! . . . And for rats! and for snakes!" (381). When Albert hurls her aside despite her being pregnant, she calls him "Monster! Mad dog!" (399). Albert matches her curse for curse, calling her "that red cow" (388, 391), "that she-ass" (397), and "You treacherous cow!" (398). Much earlier in the novel, a slightly calmer Albert simply calls his foul tongued sister-in-law a "wasp" (189). All of these examples and many others add a tartness, an earthy realism, a barnyard humor to a tense, nervous, psychological novel.

Bird images are also important in *Call It Sleep,* though not appearing as frequently as images of other animals. They occur most often in relation to David, but occasionally to Genya[15] and her grandmother. In *Rites and Symbols of Initiation: The Mysteries of Birth and Rebirth*, Mircea Eliade explains that "bird symbolism is always connected with an ascension" and "the ascent to heaven symbolized by the flight of birds is characteristic of archaic culture."[16] Following Eliade's lead, Lyons, in her book on Henry Roth, relates the yellow bird images in *Call It Sleep* to the theme of resurrection and rebirth, but before going into this connection, it is helpful to consider first some other bird images, and to remember that Roth, in passages discussed earlier, also uses bird images to depict a frightening world of vulturism. Eliade's generalizations are very useful, but they need qualification in view of the complicated intermixture of good and evil in Roth's novel.

One of the earliest bird images appears in a nightmare David has had after his sexual experience with Annie in the closet. Genya, while she dresses him, reminds him of the details of the dream, trying to help him face his fears: "A woman with a child who turned loathsome, and a crowd of people following a black-bird. I don't understand it. But my, how you screamed!" (57). Since Genya never learns of the Annie episode, she cannot identify the blackbird in David's nightmare. More characteristic of Roth's use of bird imagery is the scene in chapter 7 of "The Picture" when David goes down to the street and imitates the sound of a caged parrot and canary which he usually finds on the first floor fire escape. Typical of the bilingual child is his wonderful curiosity, as he wonders whether these two birds understand each other's sounds. Triggering these thoughts was his inability to understand Genya's revelations to Bertha in Polish:

> Secrets. What? Was wondering. What? Too cold now. Birds go south teacher said. But pigeons don't. Sparrows don't. So how? Funny, birds were. In the park on Avenue C. Eat brown. Shit green. On the benches is green. On the railings. So how? Don't you? Apples is red and white. Chicken is white. Bread, watermelon, gum-drops, all different colors. (174)

When, almost twenty years later, J. D. Salinger uses the ducks-going-south motif in *Catcher in the Rye*, it helps characterize a sensitive sixteen-year-old who is having a nervous breakdown, fearing his return home after expulsion from yet another prep school. David's problems are, to him, no less acute, but it is hard to take them very seriously with the addition of Roth's scatalogical humor mixed with the child's curiosity.

In chapter 12 of "The Cellar," David is indirectly identified with a flock of sparrows resting on the wires overhead. Desperately trying to find his way home at dusk after running away from the terrors of the neighborhood boys and the cellar, he notices that "a small flock of sparrows, beading the wires between two telegraph poles, tweaked the single dry string of their voices" (95). Observing them quietly from "the railing of a porch, a grey cat stopped licking a paw and studied them gravely, then eyed David as he passed." Without the focus moving from cat and birds to cat and David, the reader might see this brief scene only as urban realism, but with the shift, Roth subtly reinforces the child's increasing fears of a hostile, predatory world.[17] A related sparrow image appears in chapter 7 of "The Coal," when David insists on burning the *chumitz* (food not suitable for Passover) in the street to avoid a sin. As he passes the tenements, the blacksmith's, the seltzer bottlery, and the stable, this is what he observes: "grey sparrows by puddles pecked at the yellow oats among the cobbles, among the cobbles miraculous blades of grass" (245). Though not as important an image as the piece of metal which is the only thing left of the plastic doll (207) burned earlier in the street by some neighborhood boys, the miraculous blades of grass growing among the cobbles, and the sparrows feeding on the oats left by passing horses, reinforce the theme of survival and the resiliency of man and nature. Fifteen pages later, the positive connotations of bird imagery are seen again as David returns home after traumatic experiences at the streetcar tracks and then the cheder. On the eve of the first day of Passover, "Deliverance was in the air . . . deliverance from Egypt and from winter, from bondage and death!" (260). David feels "only a deep untroubled gentleness . . . a wordless faith, a fixity, mellow and benign," as he reaches his tenement and hears the canary and the parrot whistling. David's confidence is at its highest point as "The Coal" ends. The hallway is no longer as dark as it used to seem. He is no longer afraid and realizes that many of his fears are simply in his head. Naively, he concludes, "Can't never be scared. Never. Never. Never . . ." (261).

One of the novel's most poetic bird images appears in an anecdote told by Genya. Albert has just complained bitterly about his milkman's job and wasted life. He would like his youth back, but Genya disagrees. She says she would like to be a grandmother, and remembers how her grandmother once told her how fast her life went by: "I stepped into the sun, I took one breath and suddenly I was a grandmother—Throw clocks away!" (266). To her, "They measure nothing. . . . Only the swing of cranes in the tides of their flight is worth reckoning. The rest is rattle on Purim— deliverance from Haman long hanged!" Redding points out that the crane has long been a symbol of longevity and is also related to the corn myths. With Frazer as her source, she explains that "in autumn, Greek farmers interpreted the trumpeting of the cranes as signals that the rains would soon arrive, and that it was time to plow; meanwhile, they prayed to Zeus and Demeter for a heavy corn crop."[18]

The yellow bird images, which, as Lyons observes, "are memory images from the scene in 'The Coal' in which David experiences a fleeting epiphany while watching the sun move across the river,"[19] are, in the tradition mentioned by Eliade, related to the themes of rebirth and redemption. The yellow birds first appear in David's stream-of-consciousness as he is given first aid and is coming out of shock after almost electrocuting himself. David has a vision of the Christ-like man on the tugboat who stood in the bright sunlight the day he (David) almost fell off the pier, hypnotized by the brilliance of the light reflected off the water. In his vision, the man *"grinned and whistled and with every / note yellow birds flew to the roof"* (425). David then sees this man appear in the telegraph wires. *"The wires twanged brightly. The blithe and golden cloud of birds filled the sky"* (425–26). Temporarily the birds vanish when David next envisions his father delivering milk, jumping from rooftop to rooftop, brandishing a hammer like a whip. But they return once more triumphantly as an *"exalted"* David cries out, "Whistle, Mister! Yellow birds!" (431). Thus the yellow birds, both in their ascent and color, are identified with fertility (the sun and the corn) and with God's power to renew life (the radiance and light).

Since both Lyons and Redding discuss the red cock image that appears in "The Rail," only brief mention of it need be made here. As David moves in a trance toward the car tracks seeking purification, among the various street people a radical soap-box orator refers to the symbolic red cock of the revolution. Lyons sees three kinds of redemption suggested in this chapter: sexual, political, and Christian. David's insertion of the ladle in the lips of the track has obvious sexual undertones. The consequent shock will be his equivalent of Isaiah's purification from the coal. The political radical speaks of the coming revolution ("when the red cock crows" [417]), which will free all of the workers from economic slavery. And third is the New Testament allusion to the cock's crow when Peter denies Christ three times ("How many times'll your red cock crow, Pete, before y' gives up? Tree?" [418]). Lyons concludes that "in the climactic moment of David's vision, the three analogues, the sexual, the political, and the Christian, completely combine as the red cock stands for the penis, revolution, and the Biblical cock. . . ."[20] Redding, in her exploration of agricultural myths in Roth's novel, describes how a cock is sacrificed in Galicia as part of the corn-spirit ritual. "Since the corn-spirit in the form of the cock is destroyed at harvest, but returns to life in spring, we must consider it to be still another death-and-rebirth pattern typical of corn-myths in general."[21] Thus both Lyons and Redding interpret the red cock references as part of David's rebirth and transcendence at the end.[22]

Although such an optimistic interpretation is tempting, Roth never makes it that easy for his readers. He refuses to see life in simple black-white, country-city, and good-evil antitheses. In the thick texture of *Call It Sleep*, opposites are often combined. Snow and rain images supply countless examples. Lyons almost falls into a trap when she claims at first that, after his sexual experience with Annie, ". . . David experiences a self-purification in the snow. . . . the snow represents whiteness, light, and purity. He plunges into the snow thinking 'how miraculously clean it was, all about him, whiter than anything he knew, whiter than anything, whiter.'"[23] Lyons is only partially right. The snow in the passage from which she quotes also suggests David's solitude, his preferring to avoid the company of other children, his being different from them. Here are his thoughts just prior to the passage Lyons quoted:

> Must cross. Before him at the corner, children were crossing a beaten path in the snow. Beside him, the untrodden white of the gutter. He stopped. Here was a place to cross. Not a single footprint, only a wagon rut. Better not. The ridge of snow near the curb was almost as tall as himself. But none had crossed before. It would be his own, all his own path. (59)

As the other children jeer at him, David jumps and lands in deep, wet snow. The farther he goes, the more the snow on the city streets loses its purity: "Sidewalk snow, riddled with salt, tramped down by the feet of the children, reddened with ashes, growing dirtier as it neared the school." Then David sees some boys laughing as they urinate in the snow. "The water sank in a ragged channel, steaming in the snow, yellowing at the margins." Roth's point of view merges with David's as he concludes, "Sidewalk snow never stayed white." This simple observation serves as an objective correlative for the whole novel: the child's bonding to the mother will not last forever; the purity he craves cannot be found on earth. Everything changes.

A good example of this constant blending of opposites[24] in *Call It Sleep* is seen early in the novel as a curious David watches the snowflakes on his way to school:

> The silent white street waited for him, snow-drifts where the curb was. . . . Black overhead the flakes were, black till they sank below a housetop. Then suddenly white. Why? A flake settled on his eye-lash; he blinked, tearing with the wet chill, lowered his head. Snow trodden down by passing feet into crude, slippery scales. (58)

In a similar description two pages earlier, David watches the snow from his window. He "stared a while at the sinking patterns of the flakes. They fell with slow simplicity if you watched them, swiftly and devious if you looked beyond" (56). Black becomes white, gentle snow becomes treacherous ice, slow movement seen from up close is swift movement from a distance. The child is awed by the miraculous changes taking place before his eyes. The effect is almost mystical intoxication: "Their monotonous descent gave him an odd feeling of being lifted higher and higher; he went floating until he was giddy. He shut his eyes." David innocently wishes that people would never shovel the snow. "He would rather the snow were on the ground all year."

To the child, snow is usually pleasurable; to the adult it can symbolize boredom and death. Genya tells Luter, "Nothing ever came to my hamlet except the snow and the rain" (33). To David she tells the story of her grandmother's last autumn. The old woman in her shroud looked "like early winter snow. . . . And I thought to myself even then, let me look deeply into her face for surely she will melt before my eyes" (68). But even David is learning — in his mind he juxtaposes images of snow with the confetti he saw thrown at newlyweds leaving a wedding, and he notices at a funeral that the bereaved's white handkerchief with its black border looks "white as snow" (61). Running for comfort to his mother after witnessing the beginning of a funeral procession, David calms down and looks out the window: "A fine rain had begun to fall, serrying the windows with aimless ranks. In the yard the snow under the rain was beginning to turn from white to grey" (63).

Rain imagery in *Call It Sleep* has the same mixture of positive and negative connotations as the snow. When Genya finishes her story about her grandmother, David is in a "dreamlike" (68) state and wishes that he could always be alone with her: "He was part of her. The rain outside the windows set continual seals upon their isolation, upon their intimacy, their identity."[25] Yet when David's father makes him go out in the same rain to get a newspaper, the rain falls on his face and neck "with icy fingers" (78), and the "rain-swept" streets are empty and frightening. David falls on a grate because of the icy slush and loses some pennies in "numbing snow" (79). At the end of chapter 10 of "The Rail," as David departs from Leo after promising to take him to see Polly and Esther the next day, in return for the broken rosary which he craves for good luck and protection, he thinks, "And either he found a solvent for his fears or he was lost. He walked into the dreary rain as into an omen. . . . " (328, Roth's ellipsis). Here the ominous rain foreshadows the events to come. And finally, when David wants to ask Rabbi Pankower about the Isaiah passage that obsesses him, violent thunder and lightning interrupt, causing the frightened rabbi to pinch his star pupil, as the old man says, "Lightning before the Passover! A warm summer" (234), to cover his embarrassment. Mixed with the humor is Roth's important juxtaposition of divine force with the power of cleansing and redemption.

Unfortunately, Roth has a tendency sometimes to overwrite in some of his descriptive passages. The prose, trying to become poetry, strains too hard and becomes affected, pretentious, literary in the worst sense. One such passage is a description of April rain as David runs towards the cheder:

> Ahead of him, flying toward the shore beyond the East River, shaggy clouds trooped after their van. And across the river the white smoke of nearer stacks were [sic] flattened out and stormy as though the stacks were the funnels of a flying ship. In the gutter, wagon wheels trailed black ribbon. Curtains overhead paddled out of open windows. The air had shivered into a thousand shrill, splintered cries. . . . The black sidewalks had cleared. Rain shook out wan tresses in the gathering dark. Against the piebald press of cloud in the craggy furrow of the West, a lone flag on top of a school steeple blew out stiff as a key. (223–24)

Fortunately, Roth manages most of the time to control his fondness for "shaggy clouds" and the rain's "wan tresses." For example, in chapter 11 of "The Rail," he carefully avoids the pathetic fallacy in his description of David observing his mother sitting on a sill, washing the outside of the windows. He fears for her safety so high above the street, but "The sky above the housetop, rinsed and cloudless, mocked him with its serenity" (329). An especially effective passage much earlier in the novel captures the mixture of awe and fear in the child's mind, as he runs far from his neighborhood and gets lost in an ominous, fairytale-like landscape of "yeasty snow," menacing trees, a clucking rooster, broken sidewalks, and "wintry bleakness":

> On either side of the street, splotches of yeasty snow still plastered the matted fields. On ledges above the rocks, the black talons of crooked trees clawed at the slippery ground. At the doorway of a chicken coop, behind a weathered, ramshackle house, a rooster clucked and gawked and strutted in. The level sidewalks had ended long ago; the grey slabs underfoot were cracked and rugged, and even these were petering out. A sharp wind was rising across open lots, catching up cloaks of dust, golden in the slanting sun. It was growing colder and lonelier, the wintry bleakness of the hour before sunset, the earth contracting, waiting for the night. (94)

One last example of Roth's effective use of the weather to express mood and the psychological state of his young protagonist[26] is particularly interesting as it illustrates his success in conveying David's sense impressions and thought processes as though he were seeing things slightly out of focus, in a dream-like state. According to Theresa R. Mooney, David's imagination presents three worlds: objective reality, his dream world "of reveries that intimate transcendence, and a world of fear and guilt."[27] The following passage describing David's observations and feelings as the rain begins to fall portrays the first and third worlds mentioned by Mooney and gives an idea of the intentionally blurred focus of much of the novel. The key word is "indeterminate":

> Umbrellas appeared. The black shopping bags of hurrying housewives took on a dew-sprent [*sic*] glaze. Inside their box-like newstands, obscure dealers tilted up shelves above the papers. As the drizzle thickened the dull façades of houses grew even drabber, the contents of misty shop-windows indeterminate. A dense, soggy dreariness absorbed all things, drained all colors to darkness, melted singleness, muddied division — only the tracks of the horsecars still glistened in the black gutter as whitely as before. He felt disgusted with himself [after his futile attempt to get roller skates from his cousins Polly and Esther]. (316)

Sometimes Roth's water images are drawn from his apparent love of the ocean, as when he describes emotions in terms of waves of anger or terror. Other times, the ocean suggests in the inquisitive mind of the child the eternal mystery of existence, the mystical presence of a world the senses can only infer, the home of powerful, divine forces, with powers of retribution and salvation, of immeasurable pain and blinding radiance. To a curious, imaginative child like David, the ocean contains a dynamic, transcendent world of constantly shifting, sometimes beautiful, more often threatening, but always hypnotic forces.

One of the earliest examples of Roth's use of the pleasant, trance-inducing rhythm of the ocean to suggest his protagonist's peaceful state of mind is found at the end of chapter 1, when David listens to the girls in the street singing their song about Walter Wildflower: "His body relaxed, yielding to the rhythm of the song and to the golden June sunlight. He seemed to rise and fall on waves somewhere without him" (23). When, a few pages earlier, David runs outside to get quickly past the threatening cellar door,

> He jumped from the last steps and raced through the narrow hallway to the light of the street. Flying through the doorway was like butting a wave. A dazzling breaker of sunlight burst over his head, swamped him in reeling blur of brilliance, and then receded . . . A row of frame houses half in the shade, a pitted gutter, a yawning ashcan, flotsam on the shore, his street. (20)

Here even urban blight is softened, transformed by the beauty of the ocean imagery, as it is when, in chapter 2 of "The Coal," Roth describes "the naked wind . . . spinning itself a grey conch of the dust and rubbish scooped from the gutter" (222). In chapter 9, after his first terrifying experience at the rail, ocean imagery is used to express David's nervous exhilaration when Rabbi Pankower allows him to read aloud the Isaiah passage. The faster David reads, the funnier the Hebrew words sound to him. "The ripples had swelled to breakers. Immense hilarity battered against his throat and sides. . . . The surges of laughter, plunging within him, were so overwhelming . . . " (258).

Roth's water images do more than express the intensity of emotions. They also hint at the mystical world that David longs to be a part of. One of the best examples can be found in chapter 7, when David sits contemplatively on the wharf for a few minutes, even though his mother has warned him of the danger of this place. "Out here the wind was fresher. The uncommon quiet excited him. Beneath him and under his palms, the dry splintering timbers radiated warmth. And beneath them, secret, unseen, and always faintly sinister, the tireless lipping [sic] of water among the piles" (246–47). David is always crious about the "secret" and "unseen" forces around him, but the phrase "always faintly sinister" hints at the implicit danger of water, the underside of life. Roth's identification of the ocean with the cellar and all its negative connotations reinforces this threat and becomes part of the "interior structure" of the novel. The two strands are interwoven in book 1, "The Cellar," when David momentarily overcomes his fears and hides in the cellar after having knocked down a boy in the street. Roth writes, "From the impenetrable depths below, the dull marshy stench of surreptitious decay uncurled against his nostrils. . . . The rats lived there, the hordes of nightmares, the wobbly faces, the crawling and misshapen things" (92). It is appropriate that when David watches Genya light the Sabbath candles after their discussion of death, funerals, and eternal years, Roth uses ocean imagery to hint at David's unconscious fear of his mother's death: "Across the short space of the kitchen, his mother's face trembled as if under sea, grew blurred. Flecks, intricate as foam, swirled in the churning dark" (70). It is as though the child's imagination pictures his mother lost to him in the eternal deep.

This image of Genya's drowning is part of the nightmarish world of Roth's young protagonist. In subsequent chapters, the victim will be David himself, not his mother. Like both Malamud and Wallant, Roth was fascinated by the Fisher King legend: a vegetation myth of a sacrificial death by drowning to restore potency to the sick monarch and fertility to the parched land. Roth has subtly adapted this legend from Sir James Frazer's *The Golden Bough* and T. S. Eliot's *The Waste Land* as he plots David's initiation to life in the streets of New York. The guilt-ridden, fearful child is constantly trying to reconcile the painful world of reality with his longing for a world of pure ideality. David's sleepwalking state as he moves from his parents' apartment to the city streets is beautifully depicted in images of swimming under water. In his initiation rite he must plunge deeply beneath the surface and figuratively drown before he can be reborn. Like Ishmael in the Sea of Japan and Huck Finn in the Mississippi, David must return to the surface, only in his case the submersion is entirely meta-phorical. As David survives near electrocution, the policeman who resuscitates him explains to the gathering crowd, "'Foist aid yuh gits 'em hea.' His bulky hands all but encompassed the narrow waist. 'Like drownin', see?' He squeezed . . . " (423).

A close look at the "interior structure" of *Call It Sleep* confirms Roth's statement to Lyons that the artistry was consciously controlled, that he conceived of the novel "musically." In the Prologue, which Roth wrote last, after the book was finished, an angry Albert rips the blue straw hat from his son's head and skims it across the water in the harbor. "In the silvery-green wake that curved trumpet-wise through the water, the blue hat still bobbed and rolled, ribbon stretched out on the waves" (15). This is the first indication of the father-son conflict which intensifies as Albert beats David more than once in the novel and even draws blood. In the Prologue, only the hat is thrown into the water, but the antagonism, the murderous intent, and the child's consequent fear are clearly established. The figurative death by drowning (electrocution) in the climax is foreshadowed.

There are several underwater images throughout *Call It Sleep*, but only three more of the most important will be cited. At the beginning of chapter 4 of "The Rail," after his father has whipped him for allowing two men to steal milk from his wagon, David's confused mind tries to understand his victimization:

> Something, something had happened. . . . Nothing was left but a grey and vacuous idiocy, a world bewitched and hollow. It was as though he heard all sounds through a yawn or with water in his ears, as though he saw all things through a tumbler. When would it burst, this globe about his senses? (283)

Much later, when Aunt Bertha tries to save him with a lie, David, growing dizzy, reaches for his mother's dress. "And as though he had been struggling under water until this moment, David gulped down breath, heard sounds again, voices" (396). Most impressive is the third example, which appears in chapter 20 of "The Rail," as David flees hysterically through the streets at dusk and heads for the streetcar tracks after the dramatic confrontation with his aunt and uncle and Rabbi Pankower in the Schearls' apartment. Even in flight David is fascinated as he watches people pass the photography shop and its eerie "bar of green light." As the people passed,

> leisurely, self-absorbed, and as they entered the radius of the light, it fixed there, but drifted by with too buoyant and too aimless a gait for his own misery, drifted by with bloated corroded faces, as if heaved in the swell of a weedy glare, as if lolling undersea. Too sick to endure it, he looked away, looked up. (404)

The "bloated corroded faces," which in David's psychological state seem to be floating in undersea weeds, bathed in a deathly green light, expressionistically render the nightmarish descent of the child's mind into the abyss of fear. According to Mooney, David's reveries give him the feeling of separation from the real world. "His imagination suspends him in a sleep-like trance in which mental reality overshadows physical reality."[28] What he must do is "integrate the world of his mental realities with the world of his physical senses."[29]

Roth's orchestration of the water motif builds to a crescendo as David moves to the tracks and his symbolic death. The first of the italicized stanzas presenting David's fragmented thoughts begins:

> *Resounded, surged and resounded, like*
> *ever swelling breakers:*
> *— Double! Double! Double dared me!*
> *Where there's light in the crack,*
> *you dared me. Now I gotta.* (410)

David hears the sounds of a passing boat on the river and smells the salt in the water as he uses his foot to push the milk dipper into the crevice to cause the short circuit. After the brilliant explosion, "The crowd swirled about in a dense, tight eddy" (421). When the motorman pushes the mangled ladle from the rail, there is "A quake. As if leviathan leaped for the hook and fell back thrashing. And darkness." In front of the ambulance which arrives, "The crowd split like water before a prow, reformed in the wake. . . . Conch-like the mob surrounded, contracted, trailed him within the circle, umbiliform . . . " (429). As the doctor resuscitates David, the child's mind returns from the shock of oblivion, from the vast darkness into which he had plummeted. In David's semiconscious state, he envisions Isaiah's coal, not extinguished like the hissing brand in water ("*out / of the darkness, one ember / . . . flowered, one ember in a mirr- / or, swimming without motion in the motion of its light)*" (430). To Lyons, David has returned from his mythical descent to the underworld, and "the joyful imagery of the closing section of the vision . . . signifies a resurrection from the death-like state."[30]

Even more important than water imagery in the interior structure of *Call It Sleep* is light imagery, particularly sunlight. In many of the passages already quoted in the chapter, there have been repeated references to sunlight, reflecting on the East River, the ocean, hot city streets, or newly fallen snow. Sometimes it is part of what Lyons called "a resurrection from the death-like state." Frequently, in the imagination of David, it is identified with God. And even though many years after finishing *Call It Sleep*

Roth said of the book's ending that, despite David's sense of triumph, "I don't know what he feels triumphant about,"[31] the context of the novel supports a mutedly optimistic interpretation. David has had a profound illumination, a vision that has brought light from the dark. As Carol A. Binkert has so aptly suggested,[32] David's sleep at the end, his lapsing into a kind of forgetfulness, is in its way as significant as Dante's, when at the end of the final canto of "Paradise" he has seen the Trinity and the union of God and man and describes himself

> As one, who from a dream awaken'd, straight
> All he had seen forgets; yet still retains
> Impression of the feeling in his dream;
> E'en such am I: for all the vision dies,
> . . . ; and yet the sense of sweet,
> That sprang from it, still trickles in my heart.
> ("Paradise," Canto xxxiii, 11.55–60)

Even though Roth told Lyons that the light of the electrical current was a symbol of destruction rather than creation, although destruction of what he did not know,[33] Binkert sees David as evolving into the "existential man who finds meaning for himself in himself, who through a series of thwarted religious experiences and frightening everyday occurrences perceives no universal aesthetic, ontology, or metaphysic."[34] David learns to reject simplistic light-dark dichotomies and discovers "shades of one in the other." Roth may claim in hindsight, after almost four decades of writer's block, that creativity was destroyed in the boy, but the indeterminate ending does not support such a claim. Readers of the novel who have not read Roth's comments and are unaware of the critical debate on this matter might feel that David's intuitiveness, intellectual curiosity, perception, and questing spirit are undiminished as he sees his father from a new perspective and begins to learn to overcome his many fears and guilt feelings. David has looked into a dark abyss and found courage. Still unable to reconcile his mental images and feelings, he concludes that "He might as well call it sleep," the "it" referring to life's mixture of light and dark, good and evil, pleasure and pain. In the words of Baumgarten, David "does not simply light out for the wilderness; rather, he confronts the pain and suffering of Brownsville in order to discover new possibilities in Manhattan."[35]

Gary Epstein, in what is probably the most controversial new reading of *Call It Sleep* in the last ten years, sees the ending as David's defeat. Epstein agrees with Rabbi Pankower that "God's light is not between car-tracks" (257). David's mystical quest is short-circuited. Epstein sums up his argument as follows:

A) that David finds nothing but electricity, symbolic of nothing but brute, dumb force, in the rail, B) that David then abandons his search as well as that element within him that impelled him to search, C) that the "sleep" of the novel's title is symbolic of a spiritual death, and has been so identified in the novel, and D) that the ending of this novel, carefully read, may go a long way in explaining Roth's future inability to complete another one.[36]

Epstein claims that "The overriding symbolism of this novel rests on the light-dark dichotomy," and that all the examples of light counterpointed against the darkness of the cellar "prove evanescent or deceiving, or . . . disastrous." Thus he rejects Lyons's optimistic interpretation.

Epstein's provocative analysis of *Call It Sleep* raises some interesting points, but he might benefit from the advice of the Post-structuralist critics to always question the idea of an absolute, inflexible notion of dichotomy in fiction. A close examination of some of the light imagery in Roth's novel will support Epstein's observation that it is sometimes "deceiving," but that does not mean that it proves ultimately to be destructive. What Epstein has done is valorize the negative, whereas Lyons valorizes the positive. The truth may very well lie somewhere in between the binary opposition.[37] Since some of the critics have already discussed the light-dark dichotomy at considerable length, the focus here will be on only a few of the major sunlight passages to show how nature goes beyond mere embellishment to provide insight into the complicated meaning of the novel.

"The Rail" begins with an excellent example of Roth's lyrical treatment of sunlight. The imagery is somewhat blurred, inexact, connotative — giving the feeling of intense, overwhelming light and heat, yet a heat that can be tolerated. David is temporarily relaxed, at ease with the world, and feels both secure and happy this summer.

> It was a day in that season when the sun bolsters a fallen wing with a show of soaring, a day of heat and light. Light so massive stout brick walls could scarcely breast it when it leaned upon them; light that seemed to sliver windows with a single beam; that crashed against the careless eye like rivets. A day when clouds played advocates for pavements, stemming the glare on tenuous bucklers, growing stainless with what they staunched. A day so bright that streets would slacken when shaded momentarily, façade and wall would slump as if relaxing, gather new strength against new kindling. It was late July. (262)

The above passage is an example of what Roth must have meant when he told Lyons that *Call It Sleep* does not "lend itself to film. . . . In *Call It Sleep* there is more strees on a lyric quality or a poetic quality than in 99% of novels."[38] Roth's passage starts out with the positive connotations of the verb "bolsters" immediately followed by the negative implications of brick walls crumbling from the powerful force that can "sliver" windows and "crash" against the eye. But clouds relieve the aching pavements and walls of tenements, giving them new strength for the next onslaught, which they have survived before.

Just a few chapters later, David has the courage to climb out on the tenement roof for the first time. The dazzling light of the sun — described as "the disk and trumpet, triple trumpet blaring light" (296) — is adulterated by the black spots in the child's eye that cannot stare at it without flinching — "the eye sowed it with linty darkness, sowed it with spores and ripples of shadows drifting. (— Even up here dark follows, but only a little bit)." Two other intrusions of dark in this passage are the result of David's smelling the faint odor of ashes (with the connotation of cellars) and the flock of pigeons he sees in the sky, giving him the impression of "never-raveling smoke," though when seen "nearer at hand and higher, they glittered like rippling water in the sun." Thus Roth constantly interweaves the light and dark images like an Impressionist painter, as he depicts the fluid states of David's mind, his reverie, and his observations of the world around him. In the words of Carol Binkert, Roth develops "a continual string of images which refer to the light and the dark, but threaded in each are qualities of the other. In the darkness, there is light and in the light, darkness."[39]

David's temporary feeling of security and happiness on his summer vacation is soon replaced by his old fears when he has to accompany his father on the milk route. In the subtle modulation of light and dark imagery, the psychological change is seen as Roth probes David's subconscious thought. Observing with growing interest two boys about to fight, David is rudely interrupted by his angry father who, "dazzling in the light" (273), raps "the butt-end of his whip against the wagon."

> Whether it was that he had been staring down into the cellar too long, or whether because his fear of his father clouded and distorted all the things he saw, he could not tell. But he felt as though his mind had slackened its grip on realities. . . . The sunlight that had been so dazzling before was mysteriously dulled now as though filtered by an invisible film. (273–74)

The cellar-sunlight dichotomy is becoming fused in David's mind as he struggles throughout the novel to comprehend reality. Just one chapter after the above passage, David, who has witnessed his father whip and beat the man who had stolen the bottle of milk, is terrified: "For a moment longer, David's father towered above him, rage bellowing from him, shimmering in sunlight almost, like an aura . . . " (281). Thus, Roth associates light imagery with the Jehovah-like Albert to suggest, from David's perspective, power, retribution, punishment. Lyons carries this identification an important step further. When the cruel, anti-Semitic boys in the street force David to insert the sword in the tracks,

> the images used to describe the experience invoke power and sexuality as well as light. David must come to accept power as a correlative of mystical light just as he must accept the power of his father's horns as generative sexuality as well as violence. Addition of images of sex and power to light imagery gives the vision a new depth and completeness. . . . [40]

David, says Lyons, "is beginning to reconcile good and evil and to see God's light everywhere."[41]

The most important sunlight image in the entire novel, the last example to be analyzed in this study, appears in chapter 7 of "The Rail," the morning of the first night of Passover. It is David's mystical experience sitting on the pier on the East River, which identifies him most closely with the boy Wordsworth in "The Prelude," a comparison first made by Irving Howe in his well-known review of the 1964 paperback reissue of *Call It Sleep.*[42] David watches the activities on the river and is hypnotized by the sun dancing on the water. His mind wanders as he tries to suppress dirty words and thoughts suggested by the phallic smokestacks. "His gaze shifted to the left. As the cloud began to pass, a long slim lathe of sunlight burned silver on the water—" (247)

> A plain, flawless, sheer as foil to the serried margins. His eyes dazzled.
> —Fire on the water. White.
> His lids grew heavy.
> —In the water she said. White. Brighter than day. Whiter. And He was.
> Minutes passed while he stared. The brilliance was hypnotic. He could not take his eyes away. His spirit yielded, melted into light. In the molten sheen memories and objects overlapped. Smokestacks fused to palings flickering in silence by. Pale lathes grew grey, turned dusky, contracted . . . in the swimming dimness. . . . (247)

As he remembers his mother's description of God's radiance—"Brighter than day . . . Brighter . . . Sin melted into light . . ."—David is saved from falling into the water by the sound of the motor of a passing tugboat and the Christlike figure of the pilot who yells to him, "Wake up, Kid . . . 'fore you throw a belly-w'opper" (248).

Echoes of Gerard Manley Hopkins's sonnet "God's Grandeur" ("The world is charged with the grandeur of God. / It will flame out, like shining from shook foil. . . .") can be heard in the lyrical presentation of David's stream-of-consciousness, with its repetitions and alliterative pairs. Where Hopkins finds comfort and hope in the pervasiveness of God, if men would only turn to Him, David craves the purification that only God can give. As he slowly comes out of his trance, he feels as though he has been weeping.

And with the suddenness of snapping fetters the spell broke, and he stared about him too unsteady to rise. What was it he had seen? He couldn't tell now. It was as though he had seen it in another world that once left could not be recalled. All that he knew about it was that it had been complete and dazzling. (248)

David's epiphanic experience in this brilliant scene foreshadows the epiphany he has at the book's climax. Rabbi Pankower is wrong when he laughs at the child and admonishes him that "God's light is not between car-tracks" (257). The rabbi could have learned from his star pupil that God is everywhere, whether in "the glint on tilted beards, . . . the uneven shine on roller skates, . . . the dry light on grey stone stoops, . . . [or] the oily sheen on the night-smooth rivers . . . " (441). Perhaps David's "triumph" is that in sleep, "every wink of the eyelids could strike a spark into the cloudy tinder of the dark, kindle out of shadowy corners of the bedroom such myriad and such vivid jets of imges . . . " (441). The concluding fusion of the light-dark dichotomy in this passage, the final paragraph in the novel, is the beginning of what Roth himself called that "slow, laborious development" by which one attains unification in this world. The child does not become a man overnight. The pain in his scorched foot is part of the price he has paid for trying to reconcile the ideal and the real. The electricity in the track may not be Isaiah's coal—David is not allowed to talk to God—but he does hear his father, for the first time, acknowledge paternity of the child when answering the policeman's questions. David and his father may never become friends, but the intentionally indeterminate ending allows for the possibility of hope. Even in the darkness of his dreams, David is able to find light.

Chapter 4

"Detroit's Diff'rent": Nature versus the Machine in Harriette Arnow's *The Dollmaker*

I n 1955, when the National Book Award for fiction was given to William Faulkner for *The Fable*, the runner-up was Harriette Arnow's *The Dollmaker*, a remarkably sensitive and moving novel about the difficulties of a Kentucky farm family adjusting to life in Detroit during World War II. In Arnow's depressing portrayal of life in a large American industrial city in the early forties, the protagonist's deep feelings for the natural beauty of the Cumberland area contrast sharply with her dislike of the ugliness of a wartime housing development in Detroit. It is her vivid memory of the former that enables Gertie Nevels to survive the latter, and it is the cost of this survival which is the theme of Arnow's novel.

Approximately the first quarter of the book (chapters 1–9) deals with the life of Gertie Nevels and her family in Ballew, Kentucky, a life filled with struggle and hardship, but one in which Gertie lives in relative harmony with the natural world around her. She is like the tough old hickory tree scarred by lightning but still able to provide seed and nuts for squirrels and children.[1] Chapters 10 and 11 are transitional, the first dealing with the Neveleses' arrival at their new home in the government housing project ironically called Merry Hill. The remaining twenty-eight chapters chronicle the drabness of existence for the Neveleses and their neighbors who produce the arsenal that wins the war, but lose their souls in the process.

Whether Arnow ever read "The Ax Helve" (1923) is relatively unimportant, but Robert Frost's poem sheds some interesting light on her craftsmanship in *The Dollmaker*. In Frost's poem, Baptiste, a French Canadian lumberjack, intrudes upon the persona's cutting logs one day and criticizes his ax:

It was the bad ax-helve some one had sold me —
"Made on machine," he said, plowing the grain
With a thick thumbnail to show how it ran
Across the handle's long drawn serpentine,
Like the two strokes across a dollar sign.[2]

Later, when the persona accepts Baptiste's invitation to visit his cabin, he
is presented with the gift of a handmade ax-helve and is given a brief
lecture on the superiority of the handcrafted artifact over the factory
product:

He showed me that the lines of a good helve
Were native to the grain before the knife
Expressed them, and its curves were no false curves
Put on it from without. And there its strength lay
For the hard work.

"Baptiste," Frost explains, "knew how to make a short job long / For love
of it, and yet not waste time either." Like Baptiste, Gertie Nevels, the Kentucky dollmaker, knows how to carve figures "native to the grain" with
"no false curves." On the train to Detroit, when she finds a hickory nut
in the wastepaper basket and takes out her knife, she explains to a frightened
black mother how she loves to carve. Deftly she shapes "a split basket,
the splints marked clearly in the hard nutshell, the handle smooth, curving at the top as the nut had curved, while the sharp peak at the bottom
of the nut grew smooth and became the bottom of the basket" (144–45).
Gerties makes "the basket markings fine and tiny so that the work might
last a long while" (145).

Whether Gertie is carving ax handles, baskets, dolls, or crucifixes,
it is soon evident that Arnow is using carving as a metaphor for writing fiction. Arnow, too, follows the native grain of her characters in shaping their lives in the transition from farmland to housing development,
from Kentucky to Michigan. Each small stroke of her pen adds realistic
(though occasionally excessive)[3] detail that authenticates setting and enriches characterization, giving the characters that extra dimension found
only in the best of fiction that "might last a long while." When toward
the end of the novel Gertie's husband, Clovis, and his friends have rigged
up a jigsaw so that she can mass produce any pattern she wants — "a
Christ — a fox — anything; they'll all be flat, a course, but you can round
em off with yer knife an they'll look genuine hand-carved, an'ul take less'n
a fifth a th time" (457), Gertie at first refuses. A true artist, she hates
the jigsaw, "an ugly little thing; it was like a monster from some fairy tale
that, instead of grinding salt, spewed ugliness into the world" (465), but

with the factories laying off the workers, the war having just ended, and with a family to support, she reluctantly sacrifices her artistic integrity. This is the cost of survival. Fortunately, however, Gertie's creator, Harriette Arnow, who took five years to write *The Dollmaker*, according to Glenda Hobbs,[4] opted for the slow, painstaking craftsmanship that produces round, not flat characters, the contours of art, not the curves of dollar signs.

In *The Dollmaker* Harriette Arnow works within a tradition Leo Marx has aptly described as "a new [appearing after 1844] distinctively American, post-romantic, industrial version of the pastoral design."[5] Arnow's novel is a striking example to support Marx's claim that "it is difficult to think of a major American writer upon whom the image of the machine's sudden appearance in the landscape has not exercised its fascination."[6] Using as his touchstone Hawthorne's description of the intrusion of a train whistle into the idyllic quiet of Sleepy Hollow in the woods of Concord, Massachusetts, Marx explains how "the disturbing shriek of the locomotive changes the texture of the entire passage. Now tension replaces repose: the noise arouses a sense of dislocation, conflict, anxiety." To Marx, the experience is "nothing more complicated than noise clashing through harmony," but "Like the focal point of a complicated visual pattern, this elemental, irreducible dissonance contains the whole in small."[7] It would be difficult to find a more appropriate figure than Marx's "machine in the garden" to characterize Gertie Nevels's "sense of dislocation" and consequent "anxiety" in her move to Detroit. It is the intrusion of the car, the airplane, and, above all, the train, which violates the pastoral quality of Gertie's life and brings her to grief.

In the novel's stunning opening scene, Arnow introduces her machine-garden antithesis with Gertie astride her mule, Dock, near the Cumberland National Forest, carrying her very sick child to the highway where she plans to hitch a ride into town to the nearest doctor. The mule shies away from the blacktop, preferring to walk on the thick pine needles covering the ridge top next to the road, but Gertie calmly maneuvers the balky animal into the path of an oncoming military car, which consequently skids into a thicket of pines on the edge of a bluff. Although the car draws blood from the animal (the cruel, angry officer ignorantly calls the mule a horse), a determined Gertie ignores injury and insult to take charge of extricating the vehicle and getting it back on the road. That Arnow goes beyond realism and conceives of her protagonist as a kind of legendary figure is evident as Gertie uses the great strength of her Amazonian frame to push the car to safety, and then stays "a moment in the mud, her knees doubled under her, her hands dropped flat on the earth, her drooping head between her arms, her whole body heaving with great gasping breaths" (14). Gertie is like Antaeus, her strength coming from the Kentucky soil, the rich black earth deposited annually by the Big South Fork of the Cumberland River on her father's riverbottom fields. It is this tellurian strength that gives her the courage and confidence to perform a tracheotomy on Amos, her sick child, with a sandstone shelf and a stone pillow for an operating table. While the "chicken-hearted" officer faints, Gertie explains to his driver: "Once I saved a cow that was choked — an in her windpipe I put a piece of cane" (19). Within minutes, Gertie has cut and hollowed out a small piece of poplar and inserted it in Amos's throat. Even the doctor is amazed at this woman's bravery and skill in saving her child. This initial episode, however, is the only example in the novel of the triumph of the organic and pastoral over the mechanical and urban.

In Kentucky, Gertie Nevels frequently feels a transcendental oneness with her natural surroundings. Once she even feels guilty at her own happiness, proudly observing that all her family's food at the supper table, "everything, even the meal in the bread, was a product of her farming" (86). No watch or calendar is needed for her to tell the hour or month; her activities are guided by the position of the sun and the seasonal cycles, measured by such things as dogwood blooming and molasses-making time. At night she loves to wake up in the loft of the shanty she and Clovis rent and see the stars or hear the rain on her roof. The morning star is her guide as she makes her way in the dark to the spring which seeps into a hollow basin at the bottom of the ledge,

> and without being able to see where stone ended and water began she squatted by the pool and dipped the bucket in, then lifted it and drank easily and soundlessly from the great thick rim as others might have sipped from a china cup. The water, cold with faint tastes of earth and iron and moss and the roots of trees, was like other drinks from other springs, the first step upwards in the long stairs of the day; everything before it, was night; everything after, day. (76–77)

Again there is a hint here of the mythicizing of Gertie's character, with her drinking from the bucket as if from a Holy Grail.

Spending a night at the Tipton Place, which Gertie is buying with the money she has saved and from the money that her brother Henley left her when he was killed in the war, Gertie leaves the children inside studying their book lessons while she walks outside in the rain and fog. Even though nature does not always welcome her ("Saw briers pulled at her skirt, and rain-drenched sumac and sassafras sprouts slapped at her . . . " [129]), her happiness is undaunted and she continues "to smile as she plodded on up through the old cornfield. Now and then she would stop to cut a sprout or a grapevine, whispering to it, laughing a little. 'Jist you wait till I git started. Away you'll all have to go to make way for my grass and clover an corn.'" As she looks for a tree to cut down for saw handles and a maul to make rails, she carefully selects one that is blighted. She has as much compassion for trees as she does for animals and people:

> It was with a little sigh and a fleeting look of sorrow that at last she chose her tree. There was more than enough tough straight trunk for the big maul and handles, but some winter weight of snow, some accident with man or animal or weather, had crooked the top so that it could never grow into a fine upstanding tree. (129)[8]

Little does Gertie realize that a tragic accident not too far into her future will prevent her favorite child from growing into adulthood. Gertie's move to Detroit, giving up the Tipton Place to join her husband, will lead to her disillusionment, tragic loss, and personal corruption.

Arnow uses the Tipton Place symbolically the way Steinbeck uses the much talked about and dreamed of farm the itinerant hands hope to purchase some day in *Of Mice and Men*, but Gertie comes close to achieving her dream. The Tipton Place really exists. "Twice she stooped and scratched at the earth with her fingers. Each time she smiled, for the soil was black and loose still, almost as good as fresh new ground" (49). Gertie as Earth Mother figure can be seen in the way she tries to preserve the land's fertility. On the deserted Tipton Place she finds some

> ancient black-trunked dying apple and pear trees, almost lost in the sumac and scrub pine that were smothering the growth of sage grass. One tree with a few knotty red apples still clinging leaned tipsily like a tree not quite blown down, but on going closer she saw the gully, deeper than she was tall, a red wound in the hillside stealing the earth from the tree. (50)

Gertie throws a few dead apple limbs into the gully and some rocks, saying to herself: "That'll hold back a little dirt, an keep the hillside from bleeden to death." To Gertie's delight, in a sheltered area near the gate, despite the lateness of the season, she finds "a great bunch of yellow chrysanthemums, so sheltered here on the southern slope that they were blooming still, like the artichokes that grew higher than her head by a porch corner." Just as the mentally retarded Lennie in *Of Mice and Men* urges George to tell him about the farm that they hope some day to own, the five-year-old sprite-like Cassie begs her mother to repeat how they will store apples and pears in their cellar where there is also a smokehouse. They will pick their own blackberries and have fat hogs and chickens. To Gertie the romantic dreamer, the Tipton Place is her "Promised Land" (103), a place in which it "was forever spring" (53). Arnow summarizes Gertie's religious belief when she writes: "Her foundation was not God but what God had promised Moses—land . . . " (121).

As Gertie's children are quick to point out when they arrive in Michigan, "Detroit's diff'rent" (148). Enoch scouts the new territory outside the railroad station and reports back to Gertie: "I seed Dee-troit, Mom. It's snowen like I ain't never seed. The snow in Detroit don't fall down. It goes crosswise. . . . An, Mom, I seed a million cars" (151). The wind blows off Gertie's hat and "as if it had fingers, unbuttoned the new coat that billowed first behind her, then whipped about her legs as if in this place all directions were north" (153). The snow whirls like white sand.[9] "A gust of wind, wild as March and cold as if the sun had died, whirled words and cries away" (154). The cab driver is the mythical ferryman who informs the Nevels that Detroit is not like the city pictured in the children's easy readers. He has picked up arriving southerners for forty years, and they all want to save their money to buy a farm and go back. Ominously, "Gertie scratched a hole in the frost on the window, but when the frost had swallowed the hole she did not scratch again" (157). As they drive to their new home on Merry Hill, they are introduced to the sounds of the city, "sounds such as they had never heard; sometimes a broken clanking, sometimes a roar, sometimes no more than a murmuring, and once [as they pass a pressing plant] a mighty thudding that seemed more like a trembling of the earth than sound" (158). They see red lights, smoke, blurred buildings, smokestacks, trucks, and trains, "as if all these were alive and breathing smoke and steam, as in other places under a sky with sun or stars the breath of warm and living people made white clouds in the cold." The passing cars seem to be "empty of people, driving themselves as through a world not meant for people." Despite all the noise, the buildings "seemed empty of life." A shipment of tanks looking like giant insects goes by on railroad cars. In the distance are the steel mills, and Gertie sees "a faint reddish light . . . as if somewhere far away a piece of hell had come up from underground" (159). As the cab ride completes the last part of the journey from Kentucky to Detroit, the cab driver delivers the Nevels to the land of the living dead.

Wilton Eckley writes of Harriette Arnow that "the predominant influence, the one that 'more-or-less colored all the rest of my life,' was her early life on the hill; and more than ever she was drawn to write of the hills."[10] In Kentucky Gertie frequently turns to the hills as a source of solace and strength, in both a religious and a natural sense. Merry Hill, however, built close to the steel mill, is different. As they get close, Enoch says, "I hope it's a high hill . . . where I can see all over the country" (159). The naive Gertie assures her son that it will be a real hill, "covered with cattails and weeping willows." But even young Enoch is country-wise and corrects his mother: "Weepen willers don't grow on hills." The cab driver's wisecrack foreshadows the misery ahead: "Detroit's willers grows on Detroit's hills. . . . " The color symbolism reinforces his point: "The frost on the car windows was at times a reddish pink, as if bits of blood had frozen with the frost." The only hills the Nevels will see in Detroit are huge piles of coal. As Gertie looks at the wasteland around her new home, an airplane taking off from the nearby airport roars overhead. She stares

> past the dirty alley snow, littered with blowing bits of paper, tin cans, trampled banana skins, and orange peels, at a high board fence. Past the fence she saw what looked to be an empty, brush-grown field; but while she looked a train rushed past. Everything was blotted out in the waves of smoke and steam that blew down; tiny cinders whirled with the snow against the windshield, and the smell and taste of smoke choked her. The noise subsided enough that she could hear the driver say, "Well, this is it." (160)

The rhythm of *The Dollmaker* is now produced by the repeated contrast Arnow draws between Gertie's memories of her rural past and the actualities of the urban present. The vibrant sensuosity of Arnow's prose is marked by her recording on every page the different sounds, sights, and odors of country versus city. When Gertie has trouble falling asleep, she listens to the night sounds of Detroit, the mechanical humming of the refrigerator (appropriately called an Icy Heart) and the ticking of the clock. She wishes that she could hear instead the movement of water over stones, the wind in the pines and poplars, the baying of the hounds in the woods, or the cry of an owl. As she tries to relax by carving a figure from a piece of maple scrap wood, the glare of the naked light bulb hurts her eyes.

> The night sounds of Detroit came between her and the thing in the wood, but worse than any noise, even the quivering of the house after a train had passed, were the spaces of silence when all the sounds were shut away by the double windows and cardboard walls, and she heard the ticking of the clock, louder it seemed than any clock could ever be. She had never lived with a clock since leaving her mother's house and even there the cuckoo clock had seemed more ornament than a god measuring time; for in her mother's house, as in her own, time had been shaped by the needs of the land and the animals swinging through the seasons. She would sit, the knife forgotten in her hands, and listen to the seconds ticking by and the clock would become the voice of the thing that had jerked Henley from the land, put Clovis in Detroit, and now pushed her through days where all her work, her meals, and her sleep were bossed by the ticking voice. (198–99)

Clovis gets up when the alarm wakes him at six to get ready to leave for the factory. The next hour and a half are still as dark as night, and Gertie lies awake remembering "the warm feel of a cow's teats or the hardness of a churn handle, or better beyond all things, the early morning trips in starlight, moonlight, rain or snow, to the spring—the taste of spring water, the smell of good air, earth under her feet" (198). In the city, she walks on ice and concrete to get a bucket of coal. She does not bother to look for stars, since there are none unless it is very windy, "and even in winds so bitter they brought tears, the alley smelled still of smoke and fumes."

The "nasty" odors inside the Nevelses' unit inform Gertie's sensitive nose that it is the time of day she used to love the most but now hates. In her fantasy she sees the sun set "behind the hills across the river. The cedar trees above the creek whispered among themselves in a rising night wind. The new milk was cooling on the porch shelf" (251). Gertie's reverie continues, but it is shattered by the arguing of the children over use of the radio and by the voice of the newscaster describing the destruction of a tank battalion in Europe and the grisly details of a recent murder. She even hates the sound of her own voice screaming at the children, but that is quickly drowned out by another plane overhead. "The plane, like the man's voice, the trains, the heat, the smelly sticking fish, the damp grease-gommed snow pants [which had fallen off the clothesline over the stove], seemed inside her, clawing through her head, tearing her into pieces with gripping, many-fingered hands" (252).

More than anything, Gertie misses trees. She is upset that there are no trees near the ugly temporary portable school buildings put up to accommodate the many children of the war workers. To Gertie, "There must be a tree. One tree for the children to see come spring, some flowering bushes, like the mock orange they'd set by Deer Lick School when she was a girl, some flowers, something" (188–89). She tries to get the sulky Reuben to go outdoors instead of watching the endless coal trains bringing Kentucky Egg to the factory and steel mill. Through the "steamy, smoke crusted" windows they can see "the strip of earth between their building and the next . . . forever empty save for the two scraggeldy [sic] little half dead maples that stood with the forlorn air of things transplanted into unkind earth" (314). It takes a youngster's imagination to transfigure such barrenness into something tolerable. When Maggie Daly visits the Nevelses and looks out "the half of the kitchen window left from the icebox, she exclaims: 'Yu know, if yu don't look high up yu can think yu gotta tree there an notta telephone pole'" (171). At Christmas, Gertie is saddened by "the dried-out Christmas tree that had no smell except one that made her think of shoe polish, for Clytie had sprayed it with artificial snow. It held no memory of earth or wind or sun or sky; a tree grown in a field, Clovis had said, just for Christmas. Lifeless it was, as the ugly paper wreath Clytie had bought" (261–62).

Even when spring comes to Merry Hill there is not much improvement.

The hard-packed ice and snow changed soon into black water that, held up by the deeply frozen ground beneath, lay in a sheet, sometimes inches deep, over all of Merry Hill. There floated on it, mercifully hidden until now by the layers of ice and snow, all the debris of the winter—newspapers, paper wrappings, orange rinds, and other garbage, lost and broken toys, and the frozen feces of the many wandering dogs and cats. There was even one dead dog around which a bevy of mud-splattered children congregated, but it, like everything else after the long burial in the sooty snow, was sooty gray. (357)

Several chapters later, on a hot summer day, Enoch wants his mother to go with him to a scrap-wood place to hunt for boards for Gertie to use with the jigsaw Clovis has bought to mass produce Gertie's wood carvings. Enoch says that they will take a shortcut through a vacant lot, because "it would be cool by the pools of water and through the little trees" (465). Gertie corrects him: "Brush and scummy ponds, not trees and pools, son." When they reach the vacant land beyond the railroad tracks, Amos follows "a skinny, big-eyed frog . . . across piles of rusty tin cans and rotting papers until it jumped into a puddle of black swamp water" (466). At first Gertie derives no comfort from the natural surroundings. "The mosquitoes were bad and so were the flies, and the whole place smelled like a garbage can on a hot day when the collectors were a week overdue." Then she gathers a bouquet of red flowers growing near the foul smelling black water and stands awhile under a blighted cottonwood sprout. "[I]f she kind of shut her eyes and forgot the smell, it was a little like having a whole tree between her and the sky . . . " (466–67).

Reuben and Cassie Nevels are like the novel's two struggling maples "transplanted into unkind earth." Reuben hates the new school, especially Mrs. Whipple, his hostile homeroom teacher. One day he is punished for having broken the rules by cutting "through the swampy vacant land by the railroad tracks instead of sticking to the patrol route . . . " (325). His new classmates do not believe that he owns a real gun. Clovis, angry with his rebellious son, slaps him hard and warns: "You've got to walk where they tell you to walk" (326). Gertie tries to comfort the hurt Reuben and draws upon nature for a meaningful analogy, but her voice lacks conviction. She reminds him of the creek back home where he had once seen a bear.

> "Recollect how them rocks way up high, by the bluff at the beginnens uv th creek, was rough an all shapes an sizes? An recollect th little round rocks down at th mouth by the river? They was mighty nigh all alike an round an smooth. They got thataway abangen agin one another a comen down th creek in th fallovers an . . ." She choked—she was no rabbit to beget rabbits. . . . "Nobody asked them rocks did they want to be smooth an all alike. You might like playen with a toy gun. Try it." (329–30)

In chapter 23, when Reuben runs away from Detroit and goes back to his grandfather's farm, Gertie goes out on a cold, windy night to search for him. In the deep snow in the vacant lot, "She tripped over tin cans, struggled through piles of rubbish, and slipped, falling at times, when she stepped into one of the many little frozen ponds. Willow and alder brush and strange trees with unfamiliar twigs slapped across her face and tore at her clothing" (341). Away from the steel mill the stars are thicker. "Detroit seemed far away. If Reuben were close by, he would be in such a place, as far away as he could get from the city." With the tall brush above her head, Gertie feels that "if a body stood still and didn't listen too hard, it was like being in a little woods where twigs instead of smoke-stacks and telephone poles stood between her and the sky." However, as soon as she shines her flashlight and sees the garbage, she knows that Detroit is still there.

In some of the passages already quoted, there have been references to the sounds of airplanes taking off from and landing at the airport near the housing project. Two additional passages need mentioning as important examples of the airplane as intruder, violating the garden of Gertie's mind and its many tranquil images of her former life in Kentucky. In one scene, as the women are talking in a neighbor's apartment, the roar of the engines of a particularly low flying plane frightens Amos, who runs to his mother. She presses him to her bosom and clasps her hands over his ears, but "she herself was never able to keep from cringing and shivering at the sounds" (222). More significant is the scene at Cassie's funeral. At the cemetery, "the grass showed green under thin scatterings of April snow. She [Gertie] had wanted very much to see the earth, something real—but there was a green thing like paper spread over all the good earth" (404). To Gertie the casket looks cheap, the wood sappy. "She wanted to cry out, to tear off the cloth, see the wood, touch the earth; but. . . . " Clytie cries as the casket is lowered. "Then everything was drowned, blotted out by an airplane coming in low and loud, for, as Clovis had promised, the cemetery was close to the project." The artificial turf, from which Gertie will not escape even in death as long as she lives in Detroit, and the abrasive sound of the plane overhead, are the objective epitome of all that Arnow hates in the big city.

The most ominous of all the machines that befoul the garden image in Gertie's mind is the same one that disturbed Hawthorne's repose at Sleepy Hollow, the train. It appears repeatedly in *The Dollmaker*, from chapter 10, Gertie's departure from Kentucky, to the horrible tragedy in chapter 26, when Cassie loses first her legs and then her life to a train; and it reappears sporadically until the end, like the aftershocks of an earthquake.

On the crowded, noisy, smelly train to Detroit, Gertie daydreams about the clean odors she has left behind: "She'd go outside and smell the good clean air; there would be a melting snow smell and a pine smell on the ridge tops, and by her own house the smell of cedar through the creek fog" (139). The present smells of vomit from the babies and young soldiers, the thick cigarette smoke, and the odors of stale foods in the hot car make Gertie want to throw up. In the Ladies Room, "She flung up the toilet seat, knelt, and vomited. Cold air like water bubbling from a spring came through the open hole. She knelt a long while, savoring the rushing air" (140).

In the restroom on the train, Gertie observes "a smear of reddish mud" on a sleeping woman's shoe. She has never seen this kind of soil before: "redder than any earth she could remember, and sandy. . . . " Gertie cannot resist rubbing it between her fingers, discovering how "Sandy and poor it was; scrub pine and saw briers would grow in it, but so would sweet potatoes" (140–41). The black woman, the first one Gertie has ever seen, confirms her view, and Gertie says, "I wonder . . . what the ground around Detroit is like? Will it grow sweet taters?" (141). The friendly black woman, as naive as Gertie, optimistically predicts that "Detroit's goen to be nice" (142). Her husband has found a place for them to live called Paradise Valley. To Gertie, "Paradise" is "a pretty word. . . . When the woman spoke it in her soft rich voice, it made her think of peaches, pure gold on one side, red in the gold on the other, soft, juicy, warm in the August sun, warm-tasting like the smell of muscadine above the river in October." There is a touch of sadness in Arnow's irony. Gertie will soon discover the sterility of the earth around Detroit. It is not fit to nourish children like Cassie and Reuben. The black woman will discover the anxieties of life in a ghetto that is no paradise. Gertie's compassion for her fellow man is evident when she adds, "I'll allus think that a body oughtn't to die first to git it—that is, at least a little paradise on earth" (143).

The first night Gertie and her children sleep in Detroit, Clovis falls asleep quickly, but Gertie lies in bed trying to blot out the smell of the gas and water and remembers the sound of the talking pines back home. "The talking rose, became the roar of a fast through train, its screeching whistle rising above the roar as it neared the through street. This was followed at once by the tumultuous sound of its passing, so close it seemed in the very house" (179). Sixteen chapters later, the scene is repeated like a refrain. Grief stricken over the loss of Cassie, Gertie tries to picture the Kentucky sky and clouds, the wild pansies and tall pines, the red blooms on the sugar maples, the pure black earth and the white water—but her concentration is broken by the loud sounds as "A fast train roared by, and she sat bolt upright. Telephone poles, a row of chimneys, smoke, and an airplane tore apart her sky" (114).

Later that winter, Gertie sadly watches Amos playing indoors, sailing his two carved boats in the wash basin or toilet bowl. Not wanting him to forget the Kentucky outdoors, she asks him, "You recollect back home, th trees, an runnen through the woods with Gyp, an a runnen down the hill to the spring" (246). Apparently he has already forgotten his dog and the Kentucky farm. Their conversation is interrupted by a train whistle, "sharp, hard jabs of sound followed by the roaring rush that rattled the windows and set the house atremble." When Amos says, "That train carried people," Gertie sadly replies, "You're learnen your trains, son. . . ."

Arnow's Thoreauvian distrust of the train becomes ominous foreshadowing in her description of the children going to the ugly, crowded portable school for the first time. As Gertie watches anxiously, "The children were piling up like leaves against a cedar tree, and the cars and trucks were stretching out as far as a body could see, but the train stood there puffing like some great iron beast with no skin to hurt in the cold" (185). The organic image of the leaves and tree in contrast with the mechanized monster is characteristic of Arnow's techinque throughout the novel. Her intent is sometimes too explicit, as when she adds, "The children stood without complaining, accepting the train and the cold and the smoke and the smell of the cars as if they were a natural part of God's world, all but Cassie, who stood with trembling chin and brimming eyes."

The most tragic example of the train as mechanical monster involves Cassie. After Gertie Nevels, Keziah Marie (Cassie) would have been Hawthorne's favorite character in *The Dollmaker*. Cassie is Arnow's Pearl, Hester's elf child. This mischievous, imaginative, creative sprite prefers the companionship of her imaginary playmate—Callie Lou, "the strong-willed witch child" (49)—to that of other children. Happy in and at one with the fields and hills of Kentucky, she is miserable in the housing project in Detroit. In Kentucky she flits about like a wild bird (39). In chapter 3, for example, Gertie reaches in vain "for a cocklebur on the child's dress tail; but Cassie had darted out of arm's reach, and was now tiptoeing for a late-hanging crimson saw-brier leaf near the tumble-down rail fence by the lane" (47). In one scene she appears near the country store "waving a bunch of red dogwood berries" (97). She hides in the brush and loves to climb the pine trees. Once when she falls over a walnut root and hurts her mouth, her mother cleans the wound with cold spring water (51), after which both mother and daughter drink from the same cup. Gertie and Cassie have a special bond, and when Cassie sees Gertie cry for the first time, she clasps her arms around her mother's neck, "choking her, while

the child shivered and trembled like a young lamb in a January rain . . . "
(71).

Cassie is good at memorization but does not know her letters and cannot learn to read. As the Nevels children have their reading lesson, Cassie
is the only one not paying attention. She will not even try to read the
primer and, lying on a sheepskin, explores the mouth of the family's patient dog. The dog "would have clamped his teeth hard on a hand of any
of the others could they have managed to get so much as a finger into his
mouth, but for Cassie, whether wandering through the woods or lolling
in the house, he was ever a patient, smiling friend, even when she put her
bonnet on his head and called him Callie Lou's granma" (89).

Like her mother, Cassie loves the sky at night and asks Gertie if "them
men that ride them airplanes . . . ever hit the stars?" (117). "Nobody can
hurt the stars, honey," Gertie comforts her, "they'll allus be there." When
Cassie asks her what the stars say, Gertie explains that they say

> Different things to different people; fer one thing they say, "We'll never change,
> and we'll never go away—all the nations on this earth with all their wars,
> they cain't cut us down like we was trees." And they say to Cassie Marie, "Lit-
> tle girl, if'n you lost yer friends an kin you'd still have us an th sun and th
> moon." (118)

In this manner Gertie not only instills a love of nature in Cassie, but gives
her a religion more attractive than the hell and brimstone Protestantism
of her maternal grandmother. When Cassie asks why Gertie likes to look
at the stars, Gertie quotes the Bible: "The heavens declare the glory of
God; an the firmament showeth his handiwork" (117). Unfortunately,
Clovis does not share this natural religion with his wife and daughter.
While Clovis is in Detroit before his family arrives, Gerties wishes that
he were looking at these same stars, "But Clovis had never been a body
to fool with the stars or the moon" (115).

Cassie is much closer to her mother than she is to her father, and thus
finds it much more difficult to establish roots in Detroit. She even shares
her mother's love for the piece of wild cherry wood from which Gertie
is carving a figure of a laughing Christ and urges her mother to bring it
to Detroit. "Only Cassie had begged for the wood, hugged it as if it had
been human" (141). Glenda Hobbs makes the perceptive observation that
"Callie Lou is as real and as important to Cassie as the laughing Christ
in overalls is to Gertie."[11] To the child, says Hobbs, Callie Lou is more
"than an imaginary friend: she betokens Cassie's individuality, her ebul-
lient creativity, and her love for Kentucky, where Callie Lou was born."

In Detroit, Cassie is a disturbed, withdrawn, unhappy child; "More
lost and lonesome than afraid, she always seemed like a child away from

home" (199). Her picture hanging on the kindergarten wall depicts "a green hill with a black tree" (200). Enoch tells his mother that the other kids are calling her "cuckoo" because she always talks to the imaginary Callie Lou. Clytie complains because Cassie cut up the beautiful blue dress on her store-bought Christmas doll and transferred it to the little hickory doll that Gertie had carved for her in Kentucky. Glasses for her poor eyesight are the recommendation of the well-meaning kindergarten teacher. Clovis insists that his daughter stop talking to the imaginary Callie Lou to facilitate her "adjustment" to Detroit, but Gertie convinces him to give the child a little more time, until spring. "The real spring with grass and flowers and budding trees would come and Callie Lou would have to go away, but let her live now in this short false spring" (358). Little does Gertie realize how short a time Cassie has left. When Gertie's friend Mrs. Anderson joins the chorus of voices urging her to help the child grow out of her dream world, Gertie's growing frustration and worry lead her to drive Cassie outside to play with the other children, for the first time denying the reality of Callie Lou. Since the mother has lost her brother, Henley, in the war and Reuben, who has run away back to Kentucky, Cassie, too, must learn that in life people have to give up things they love. But at the same time that she orders the child outside, "She was breathing hard, choked up inside, fighting down a great hunger to seize and hug and kiss the child, and cry; 'Keep her, Cassie. Keep Callie Lou. A body's got to have somethen all their own'" (366).

As Cassie seems to be adjusting to the loss of Callie Lou, Gertie discovers that her daughter has not given up her imaginary playmate but relocated her among the trees across from the railroad tracks. Relenting and deciding to let Cassie keep Callie Lou at home, Gertie goes to look for Cassie, who has run away from the children making fun of her. The intrusion of the machine in the garden culminates in one of the most powerfully tragic scenes in all of American fiction. As Gertie goes to the railroad tracks and finds the monstrous engine asleep, she suddenly hears Cassie call out Callie Lou's name. "Memories of old tales of witches and warnings of names called down from the sky or up from a river came back to her. The wind, she'd always said, for the wind in leaves and by water had many voices. There was a little wind today, but the brassy-voiced Detroit wind could never whisper so" (388). Gertie sees Cassie on the other side of the fence near the trains, but the sound of an airplane drowns out her warning. Cassie shields Callie Lou's imaginary body with her own from the sound she hates and then hastily seeks shelter against the great wheel of a box car as she sees the through train approaching. When the box car suddenly moves, Cassie is mutilated before her mother's eyes.

The death of Cassie Nevels after the train severs both her legs is the heart of Arnow's novel. Just as Cassie's life is lost, so are Gertie's dreams. But *The Dollmaker* continues for another twelve chapters, almost one-third of the book. Gertie's aching loss is unbearable; however, she is tough and she survives. After a long period of withdrawal and phenobarbitol-induced numbness, she pulls through. The challenge of the unfinished carving of the wild cherry wood is one source of her salvation; her children's need for a mother is a second. The rhythmic contrast of the natural life of Kentucky versus the mechanized bleakness of Detroit continues to be the author's central technique, but one special pattern of nature imagery demands attention in the novel's last section—flowers. Arnow uses flowers, like many authors before her, to analogize human life. Certain flowers and plants become symbols of Gertie Nevels, but above all, Arnow uses flowers to symbolize an ineluctable life force, a cyclical growth and change that cannot be denied. "Nothing gold can stay," Frost once wrote, but the perennial return of the flowers in the spring gives hope for survival, for the triumph of life over winter/death, even if there is no rebirth for Gertie in the spiritual sense.

The first day that Gertie is willing to leave the house, weeks after Cassie's death, in order to see Mrs. Daly's new baby, Arnow's protagonist is like the wild, transplanted violets that Mrs. Schultz never expected to make it through the winter. The triumphant Mrs. Schultz calls to Gertie's attention "the violet leaves, still blue and rolled against the cold; but living leaves" (434). She explains, "I put that rock around them to keep the children from squashing them after they'd brought them to me from that vacant land on the other side of the railroad tracks. And now they've pulled through. . . . " Actually, a more appropriate symbol for Gertie is the hardy cactus that is mentioned on the bottom of the same page. A heavy, ugly woman, "bent lovingly over a crepe-paper-swathed pot in which a dusty gray and prickly cactus stood," smiles at Gertie and says, "A whole new leaf it gives, since Christmas. . . . " It is this same woman who, in the last chapter of the novel, her husband having been blinded in an industrial accident and her family now being evicted from the project, sees Gertie again and says, "Ain'tcha du one wot grows such pretty flowers? I been t'inking—couldcha keep mu cactus? I've had it su long; it's older'n mu kids. Yu'd understand wot it needs better'n most around" (566).

Though flower and plant imagery appears most frequently in the last quarter of the novel, especially after the management of the housing project gives out free grass seed and fertilizer and loans out garden tools, Arnow introduces an important plant image in chapter 4, long before Gertie leaves Kentucky. This plant becomes identified with Gertie herself in conflict with her narrow-minded mother, whose religiosity functions as a life-denying force. To Gertie, her mother's face is "pale beyond any face she knew, almost never touched by sun or wind, seeming always close to death and God" (58). Mrs. Kendrick's potted geraniums and begonias seem as bound up, as constricted, as their constipated owner. They "were blooming, but in a sad, half-hearted way, as if they were tired of the red clay pots, tied with crepe paper, that cramped their roots like too tight shoes" (63). On a dais built by Gertie's father are many more plants, the "king" of them all being a huge maidenhair fern that visitors are afraid to get too close to. Gertie vividly remembers many trips into the woods to dig up "the black rich earth from generations of leaves dying on limestone ledges, for the dirt must be scraped from a damp limestone ledge where other ferns grew, so that every few years the plant had to be re-potted and divided, with rooted fronds going out to all the neighbors." Shortly after her marriage to Clovis, "her mother had given her a good-sized piece of it, rooted in a large red pot. She had on the way home stopped by a limestone ledge above the creek and there set the fern where it belonged. . . . " Gertie, too, has roots deep in the rich Cumberland soil and she will soon be choked by the constricting environment of Detroit, with no one to rescue her as she had freed the plant.

It is the lure of growing things that finally helps bring Gertie out of her long, self-imposed alienation after the trauma of Cassie's death. At first, doped up with phenobarbitol, she is indifferent to Enoch's laborious digging of postholes and his putting up a makeshift fence with the help of their neighbor Victor, who also loves flowers. Victor's wife, Maxine, pleads with Gertie to come outdoors, telling her, "You'll smother in this room, kid. The sun's took a a notion to shine, an considering it's Detroit it's doing pretty good. You need a little air" (412). Gertie is gradually attracted to the earth at the bottom of Enoch's posthole, and though it has more sand in it than the earth back home, to her surprise it does have the same clean smell. As Mrs. Schultz begins to plant her petunias and pansies, Gertie is ashamed that "she was the only woman in the alley who had no growing thing" (430).

Flowers are also identified with Cassie, as when Gertie shows interest in the plants that the Italian fruit and vegetable man brings on his truck. "Among them were some tiny lavender flowers such as Gertie had never seen. They make her think of the wild sweet Williams back home — something wild for Cassie's grave . . ." (438). This use of a flower image to invoke in Gertie a thought of Cassie is natural and spontaneous, as is Arnow's subtle symbolism in Gertie's response to the gift of a free box of damaged pansies and the lavender flowers she had admired: "the flowers were only a little battered, a little wilted; the roots were damp and living" (439). This organic image beautifully follows the grain of Arnow's materials and hints at Gertie's eventual recovery. The contrast between the flora of Kentucky and Detroit continues, with a small but significant change. When Clytie brings home some lilacs from the huge bush growing next to her girlfriend's house, Gertie at first claims that the wild plum trees and honeysuckle vines back in Kentucky have a stronger odor, but a few days later she changes her mind. The lilac's sweet odor even takes away the smell of the gas and the chlorine in the water. After the neighborhood children bring home pieces of lilac bushes growing next to the rusty lamp-posts in the development, "the sweetness hung over the alley like the steel-mill smoke" (444). In fact, the lilac smell lasts as long as the train grease on Gertie's hands from Cassie's death. With this ambiguous juxtaposition of the pastoral and the industrial, a standoff of sorts, Arnow seems to be hinting at the subtle change taking place in Gertie, preparing the reader for the symbolic action that ends the novel nine chapters later.

Flower symbolism also effectively reinforces characterization and theme when Maxine decides to run away from Victor and heads for the coast to fulfill a lifelong dream to see the sea. Before she departs, she gives Gertie twenty dollars to buy flowers. Victor expresses his rage and hurt by throwing his beloved lilacs into the garbage can. When the neighborhood children take Victor's lilacs from the garbage and try to make a garden of them, Gertie is tempted to explain that grass cannot grow on trampled ground, but she says nothing: "Children needed earth as well as grass and flowers" (447). Despite Gertie's premonitions, the grass does grow, but the children trample her petunias and pull up her marigold beds. Thus Arnow's signals are mixed — Gertie shows signs of recovery, of survival and even adjustment to a hostile environment, but there is an aesthetic loss.

Arnow's use of flower imagery to analogize human conditions is not always effective. Sometimes she lapses into sentimentality, as in the scene when Gertie weeds the nameless white flowers growing against the wall of their unit. Many of them are "so trampled by the children their stems lay on the ground, but still they opened their little spires of pure white bloom above the cindery earth. She wished she could call such valiant creatures by name . . . " (463). Another example of this kind of saccharine excess is found in Gertie's response to her friend Sophronie's praise of her garden. The analogy to the human condition is too emotional, too strident. When Gertie smiles on "the dwarfish, child-battered plants covered with their many petaled flowers all shades of gold and bronze and brownish red," she feels that

> There was something frantic in their blooming, as if they knew that frost was near and then the bitter cold. They'd lived through all the heat and noise and stench of summertime, and now each widely opened flower was like a triumphant cry, "We will, we will make seed before we die." (495)

Arnow is much more effective when she combines three main strands of imagery — flowers, technology, and the Bible — to produce the following poetic description of the steel mill, the night Gertie is searching for her missing son, Reuben. Her

> eyes were like they had used to be when she looked too long at a bright sunset. Though now instead of suns before her eyes there were streams of steel bright as the sun but not sunlike, more like a fiery fountain out of Revelation, springing in the land where might have walked the angel with the feet of burnished brass and the golden girdle, and above it the angel might have stooped to gather flowers. For out of the beds of flame and smoke the flowers came; long gracefully drooping stems would for an instant hang out of the kettle, lean earthward, blooming on the end into the blood-red flower, blooming, dying all in an instant, their seed a tiny lump of smoking steel. (344)

In this alliterative paean to the production of steel, Arnow suggests awe, spirituality, power, gentleness, beauty, hurt, birth, and death — a kaleidoscope of conflicting images and emotions that stir Gertie's artistic response, just as the scene inspired the frustrated painter Lena Anderson, who on her return to Merry Hill for a visit in the novel's last chapter tells Gertie: "I liked to look at it [the steel mill] and dream sometimes of painting it at twilight when the red was like blood on the children" (560). *The Dollmaker* is the painting Lena Anderson never put on canvas, the carving of a laughing Christ turned Judas, which Gertie never finished.

Gertie Nevels is one of life's survivors, but she is like one of the potato bugs that Enoch describes when the neighborhood children are having an argument over whether the victims of an atom bomb cry afterwards. Enoch says:

> I figger that ole bomb just kills th ones real close right away; them on u edge gits bad burnt an crawls around awhile — Mom, recollect back home when we'd git rid a th tater bugs by knocken um off into a can with coal oil in it, then when we'd git a lot we'd drop a lighted paper inu can? You allus wanted a big fire an burn em all up right quick; but no matter how big a fire we'd have they'd be some that jist git scorched, and they'd crawl like crazy ever which away till they died. They'd be bad swinged, but they couldn't die — not right away. Now, I figger them Japs around u atom bomb is kinda like them bugs. (474)

Gertie, too, is scorched, but she is one of the lucky ones. Arnow's compassion for the Japanese, after the apocalypse of Hiroshima and Nagasaki, is expressed most fittingly through the natural symbolism of flowers. Mrs. Schultz asks Gertie for a bouquet to give to their crying Japanese neighbor, Mrs. Saito, when the news comes of the dropping of a second atom bomb and the Japanese surrender. To the bigoted Mrs. Daly, the

Japanese are not as good as white Christians, almost as bad as Communists, but "'yu still gotta say, people is people'" (476).

As *The Dollmaker* ends, Gertie smashes the unfinished cherry wood carving that has been the novel's master symbol. Walter Havighurst, writing of Arnow's book in the *Saturday Review of Literature*, concludes that "This final symbolism is cloudy and inconclusive. . . ."[12] Joyce Carol Oates sees Gertie's commercialization of her art as a betrayal, proof of her defeat. Gertie is "determined to be Judas, to betray the Christly figure in the piece of wood she never has enough time to carve out, and the Christly figure is at once her own and that of the millions of people, Americans like herself, who might have been models for Christ."[13] To Oates, "Man is both Christ and Judas, the sacred, divine self and the secular, betraying human self. . . . " Dorothy Lee, on the other hand, refuses to see the smashing of the piece of wild cherry wood as "final" defeat. She argues that the novel ends on a note of transcendence. Gertie "has always had compassion for others, but her vision now is less provincial. She recognizes suffering of a broader scope and understands the unity of all men who share it."[14] The knowledge she has gained of the City of Hell is "spiritually freeing." To Lee, "Gertie's final act is more analagous to Christ's: self-sacrifice for the redemption of others."[15] Gertie "has finally recognized the duality of existence. Judas, after all, facilitates Christ's sacrifice. The face of Christ must both laugh and suffer if it is to reflect reality. To transcend Hell, one must first *know* it."[16] Glenda Hobbs agrees and finds *The Dollmaker* ultimately on the side of affirmation. "However much sorrow pervades the man in the wood and the book in which he lives, both works are life-affirming. For all the sadness and spoiled hopes, both testify to the power of the female imagination and to the common humanity that binds us all."[17] To support her interpretation, Hobbs quotes Arnow, who in 1963 explained that she originally contemplated giving *The Dollmaker* the title *Dissolution*, but decided "it would not do. A combination of war and technology had destroyed a system of life, but people were not all destroyed to the point of dissolution."

Lee's, Hobbs's, and Arnow's statements to the contrary, it is difficult to find much affirmation in the conclusion of *The Dollmaker*. Lee finds Gertie's movement from pastoral innocence to urban experience an educational journey, but she overlooks the fact that even in Kentucky Gertie had foreknowledge of her defeat. Arnow writes: "maybe she had always known those other trees [on the Tipton Place] would never be her own — no more than the fireplace with the great slab of stone — just as she had always known that Christ would never come out of the cherry wood" (137). Furthermore, late in the novel Arnow identifies Gertie herself with the suffering figure in the unfinished wood carving. As she turns to it for comfort when she hears a train whistle and relives the final moments of Cassie's mutilation, "gradually her own torture became instead the agony of the bowed head in the block of wood" (427). Whether it be Christ or Judas, this figure's hands are giving something up, "holding tightly a thing they could not keep. The head was drooped in sorrow, looking once at the thing it had to give away" (427–28). One of the things Gertie had to give away is her beloved children, Reuben and Cassie, who have slipped through her hands in Detroit. Many chapters later, when she is working on the separate fingers, Gertie wonders: "What did the hand hold, heaped so high, so full it slipped between the fingers? Sandy earth from her father's river-bottom fields?" (502). Thus Reuben and Cassie and the Cumberland earth are one, and Gertie loses all of them, along with her dreams.

When, on the final page, Gertie brings the heavy hammer down on the wedge in the crack in the resistant cherry wood, the image is devastating: "The wood, straight-grained and true, came apart with a crying, rendering sound, but stood for an instant longer like a thing whole, the bowed head, the shoulders; then slowly the face fell forward toward the ground, but stopped trembling and swaying, held up by the two hands" (571). Even Gertie's final statement that many of her neighbors could have been the model for Christ's face does little to soften the impact of her destructive act.

In the clash between the pastoral and the technological, the machine has won. The creative, individualistic, and the natural have lost out to the rigid, conforming, and mechanical. In Arnow's *The Dollmaker*, what Leo Marx called "this elemental irreducible dissonance" is the dominant note. Wilton Eckley might claim that nature is "the ultimate reality" in Arnow's fiction,[18] but he is wrong. Nature is a pristine standard against which to measure the ugliness of urban existence, but "the ultimate reality" in *The Dollmaker* is the tragedy of change. One of Gertie's favorite books, Ecclesiastes, expresses it best: "For man also knoweth not his time: as the fishes that are taken in an evil net, and as the birds that are caught in the snare; so are the sons of men —" (41). Gertie's expulsion from Eden is no fortunate fall.

CHAPTER 5

"April Is the Cruellest Month":
Nature in Bernard Malamud's *The Assistant*

I n a personal essay written three years before his death, Bernard Malamud reminisced about moving his wife and infant son in 1949 from
New York City, which "had lost much of its charm during World War II,"
to the Pacific Northwest, with the beauty of its "vast skies, forests, coastal
beaches, and the new life it offered. . . ."[1] During this period of teaching
English at Oregon State in Corvallis, Malamud found himself reflecting
on his "father's immigrant life, how he earned his meager living [as a gro-
cer] and what he paid for it, and about my mother's, diminished fear and
suffering. Their lives were 'perhaps' matter for my fiction." The qualifier
"perhaps" should not be surprising since it simply reveals the author's
wish to discourage a strictly biographical approach to his fiction. He then
quickly admitted that it *was* his parents he had in mind when he "invented
the characters who became their fictional counterparts" (for example,
Morris and Ida Bober in *The Assistant* [1957]).

Although Malamud experimented with different forms and styles in
his short stories and novels, through four decades he never moved far
from one central theme — what it means to be human in an inhuman world.
One of the most explicit statements of this theme appears in a scene from
a projected play, "Suppose a Wedding," published as part of Malamud's
second collection of short stories, *Idiots First* (1963), in which an old, retired Jewish actor, Maurice Feuer, is talking to his prospective son-in-law,
Leon, whom he does not like. Like Morris Bober in a dialogue with Frank
Alpine in *The Assistant*, Feuer says, "I suffer for those who suffer. My
heart bleeds for all the injustice in this world."[2] When Leon tries to impress Feuer by describing his feeling of catharsis on seeing a tragic play,
the older man rudely interrupts: "Don't quote me your college books. A

writer writes tragedy so people don't forget that they are human. He shows us the conditions that exist. He organizes for us the meaning of our lives so it is clear to our eyes." With this statement Feuer expresses the credo that was to govern Malamud's writing during his entire literary career.

One of Malamud's ways of organizing his fiction to probe the meaning of life was to link it to myth. Carl Jung explained the effect of this connection best when he wrote:

> The man who speaks with primordial images speaks with a thousand tongues; he entrances and overpowers, while at the same time he raises the idea he is trying to express above the occasional and the transitory into the sphere of the ever-existing. He transmutes personal destiny into the destiny of mankind, thus evoking all those beneficent forces that have enabled mankind to find a rescue from every hazard and to outlive the longest night. That is the secret of effective art.[3]

It has become a commonplace of contemporary criticism to mention Malamud's use of myth in his stories and novels. One of the first critics to write about the important use of the changing seasons in *The Assistant* to provide the "timeless and placeless New York landscape with a kind of metaphysical climate,"[4] was Jonathan Baumbach in *The Landscape of Nightmare: Studies in the Contemporary Novel*: "The novel starts in early November and ends in mid-April, symbolically covering the Fall, the Death, and the Redemption of Man. The seasons mirror the inner conditions of the central characters." Another critic, James M. Mellard, has written extensively on Malamud's use of the pastoral mode, arguing that it appears even in his urban fiction through his use of lower-class, proletarian characters and his "pervasive use of nature imagery."[5] In *The Assistant*, says Mellard, the nature imagery "suggests that the narrative center of the novel lies in the pastoral vegetation myths, rituals, and ceremonies that celebrate the cycles of death and renewal in nature." Sandy Cohen sees Malamud as using both "the fertility cycle myth and the American Dream" to reveal "the relationship between man and this world. . . . Both represent standards: the former systematic and immutable, the latter modish and vague."[6] As the seasons change in a predictable way, an author like Malamud can correlate and measure "the changes taking place in his characters and the changes taking place in the seasonal cycle. . . ." Unfortunately, Cohen's theory becomes simplistic and proscriptive as he argues that

> the seasonal cycle is the norm, the ideal pattern for character development. Ideally a character in a Malamud novel should progress as do the seasons and their mythically associated moods (bleak November, lusty May, and so on). How well a character resembles the systematic and immutable fertility

cycle indicates how well adjusted he is mentally, ethically, socially, physi-
cally, and aesthetically.[7]

More specifically, Mellard sees Frank Alpine functioning as the mythical
son-hero transforming the wasteland: " . . . Frank's role is to replace the
'scarecrow' father and to bring to fruition the 'flower-like' daughter if the
human wasteland is to be revitalized along with nature."[8]

Although this myth approach to interpreting Malamud's fiction works
well with his first and last novels (*The Natural*, 1952, and *God's Grace*,
1982), and some of the fiction in between, if pushed too hard it leads to
a distortion of the tone of *The Assistant*.[9] To see Frank as transforming
the wasteland, as Mellard does, is to magnify the character's limited ability
and to find major change where there is only possibility of fulfillment.
To emphasize Frank's role as ritual hero is to blur his movement from
schlemiel to shlimmazel. What Mellard overlooks is that the change of
the seasons, the circular movement that leads to Frank's replacing Morris,
also results in the new grocer's inheriting the old man's future. This is not
to deny the important transformation of Frank's character from immoral
drifter to moral benefactor, but despite the possibility of hope, there is
the equal chance of failure. As Malamud once wrote in an unpublished
letter in response to a question about the ending of "The Magic Barrel":
"There's no proof Leo will be destroyed by Stella. Kaddish may express
a hope as well as a mourning. I like the juxtaposition."[10] The comparison
is self-evident.

The myth approach to *The Assistant* has thrown considerable light
on the thematic intent of Bernard Malamud, but a return to the text for
a close study of the author's nature imagery and symbolism contributes
to a fuller understanding of his complex art. Nature in this novel provides
a major pattern of imagery that functions not only to supply a mythic
substructure to universalize a contemporary story and to support theme
and characterization, but also, as was true in the novels of Dos Passos,
Farrell, Roth, and Arnow, to reinforce mood, provide comic and ironic
undertone, and to serve as a link between the worlds of dream and reality,
fantasy and fact. As it functions in all of these ways, one should keep in
mind Sidney Richman's admonition that "Nature in *The Assistant* offers
less release than in *The Natural*, and the anti-romantic irony haunts the
experience of all the characters — no matter how romantic their sensibili-
ties."[11] Richman suggests that Malamud's criticism of the Romantic "myth
of nature, or at least his insistence that the hero must triumph over nature" stems from his religious heritage — "the tradition of a people whose
distrust of nature was always intense."[12]

Metaphorically, there is no summer in the present existence of Malamud's characters — only what they dimly remember from their youth when things seemed to be better. "If a temporal universe even exists in *The Assistant*," says Richman, "it is hard to discover. Night gives way not to day but only to a night less dark, and the seasons play endless variations on a perpetual winter."[13] The daily events in the lives of Malamud's characters are reflected in the hard brown earth, leafless trees, bitter wind, yellow slush, and dark, cold rain. This correlation can best be seen in the hard life of Morris Bober, the sixty-year-old grocer whose life is a dismal story of repeated failure. When Morris, out of desperation, decides to ask for a cashier's job in a supermarket now owned by his former partner who once cheated him out of a promising business, Malamud writes that the weather, "though breezy, was not bad — it promised better, but he had little love for nature. It gave nothing to a Jew. The March wind hastened him along, prodding the shoulders. He felt weightless, unmanned, the victim in motion of whatever blew at his back. . . ."[14] Though Morris may feel that nature is no friend or comfort to him, only another force contributing to his victimization, to Malamud, nature imagery and symbolism supply a motif that greatly enriches the texture of his story and becomes part of its interior structure.

Malamud carefully prepares his reader for the drama that is about to unfold. The opening sentence of the novel announces that "The early November street was dark though night had ended, but the wind, to the grocer's surprise, already clawed" (3). Wind imagery is associated mainly with Morris. Depressed, unable to fall asleep, he thinks of his grocery store as "always a marginal one, up today, down tomorrow — as the wind blew" (10). In summarizing his life story for his new assistant, Morris tells how as an immigrant he was preparing to become a pharmacist by going to night school. One of his favorite poems, which he still remembers, began, "'Come,' said the wind to the leaves one day, 'come over the meadows with me and play'" (83). It did not take Morris long to recognize the difference between the romantic sentimentality of the verse and the harshness of earning a living in America. Marriage made him impatient with the school and hastened his entrance into the world of business. Now, as he contemplates selling the unsuccessful store, he pictures himself in the cold "without a roof over his head. There he stood in all kinds of weather, drenched in rain, and the snow frozen on his head" (5).

From the window of his store, Morris looks out at the street and remembers how, as a boy in Russia, he loved the outdoors; now, "the sound of the blustery wind frightened him" (5). Not for a long time "had he lived a whole day in the open. As a boy, always running in the muddy, rutted streets of the village, or across the fields, or bathing with the other boys in the river; but as a man in America, he rarely saw the sky. In the early days, when he drove a horse and wagon, yes, but not since the first store. In a store you were entombed" (5–6). Iska Alter, in a study of Malamud's social criticism, makes the perceptive observation that "The memories that haunt Morris are not, ironically, of an American paradise but of an Eastern European one. . . . The world of persecution has become a remembered Eden of open space, while America, the new land, is a closed box, a coffin."[15]

In late March, when Morris returns from the hospital after his inept attempt to commit suicide, his self-pity is interlaced with the pathetic fallacy. From his bedroom window he watches winter's reluctance to surrender to spring:

> There was at least more light in the day; it burst through the bedroom windows. But a cold wind roared in the streets, giving him goose pimples in bed; and sometimes, after half a day of pure sunshine, the sky darkened and some rags of snow fell. He was filled with melancholoy and spent hours dreaming of his boyhood. He remembered the green fields. Where a boy runs he never forgets. His father, his mother, his only sister whom he hadn't seen in years, gottenyu. The wailing wind cried to him. . . . (194)

Both the self-pity and pathetic fallacy recur when Morris reflects on the irony of life. *His* grocery store is undamaged by the fire *he* tried to start; Karp's liquor store is accidentally burned to the ground by Ward Minogue, and the lucky owner collects the insurance. The day is overcast, "and there were snow flurries in the air. Winter still spits in my face, thought the weary grocer. He watched the fat wet flakes melt as they touched the ground. It's too warm for snow he thought, tomorrow will come April" (219).

Morris thinks that his luck has finally improved as Karp accepts the inflated figure the old grocer asks for his store and apartments. Morris's rare happiness is once again identified with his boyhood in the Russian outdoors:

> The spring snow moved Morris profoundly. He watched it falling, seeing in it scenes of his childhood, remembering things he thought he had forgotten. All morning he watched the shifting snow. He thought of himself, a boy running in it, whooping at the blackbirds as they flew from the snowy trees; he felt an irresistible thirst to be out in the open. (221)

At this point Malamud introduces the major ironic twist of the plot. Feeling the urge to shovel the snow for the gentiles who will be walking to church, ignoring Ida's warning that "It's winter," not spring, he waits until the evening before going outside. Clouds of snow are blowing through the streets. "To his surprise the wind wrapped him in an icy jacket, his apron flapping noisily. He had expected, the last of March, a milder night. The surprise lingered in his mind but the shoveling warmed him. He kept his back to Karp's burned hole, though with the black turned white it wasn't too hard to look at" (222). Morris recalls the hard winters of his first years in America, followed by a milder cycle. But now the harshness has returned and he is worn out from his exertion. Still, he won't give in to Ida, who calls him to stop. "For twenty-two years," he shouts to her, "stinks in my nose this store. I wanted to smell in my lungs some fresh air" (223). Morris's body, however, cannot take the shock, and that night the pneumonia sets in that kills him. The poor schlemiel-shlimmazel cannot understand why nature has played such tricks on him: "So he had shoveled snow in the street, but did it have to snow in April? And if it did, did he have to get sick the minute he stepped out into the open air?" (225)

Three days after April Fool's Day, Morris dies. Nature plays its last trick on him, an irony that he would have appreciated: "In the cemetery it was spring. The snow had melted on all but a few graves, the air was warm, fragrant" (230). Here the voice is Malamud's — matter-of-fact, unemotional. The pathetic fallacy is conspicuously missing, the irony quietly effective.

One pattern of nature imagery subtly used by Malamud to add a quite different, almost surrealistic touch to the story, what Dos Passos in *Manhattan Transfer* called a "blurred perspective," involves the sea and marine life. Through his use of underwater images, Malamud suggests, sometimes comically, sometimes seriously, the dark, submerged quality of the life of the Bober family and some of their neighbors. A hint at this pattern of imagery can be found in the names of the characters – Karp, Pearl, Minogue[16] – but more conclusive is the passage revealing Frank's thoughts after his remorse over the rape of Helen. Taking advantage of Ida's desperation over Morris's illness, Frank, despite his having been fired by the grocer, moves back behind the counter. He is tortured by the sight of the grocer's daughter: "All this time he had snatched only glimpses of her, though his heart was heavy with all he hoped to say. He saw her through the plate glass window — she on the undersea side. Through the green glass she looked drowned, yet, never, God help him, lovelier" (184).

The image of drowning and the undersea quality of life in and around the store are also implied in passages describing Morris. Early in the novel, as he counts the day's receipts that come to only ten dollars, "He thought he had long ago touched bottom but now knew there was none" (24). A few pages later, as he is numbed from the blow from Ward Minogue during the robbery, he thinks how little America has given him. He has defrauded Ida and Helen, "he and the bloodsucking store" (27). Much later, when he cannot stand the dishonesty of trying to sell a worthless store to an unsuspecting buyer, Morris blurts out the truth that the store is run down, but that a young, energetic owner might be able to save it. Ida tries to prevent him from ruining the sale, "but Morris kept on talking till he was swimming in his sea of woes . . ." (203).

Of the various marine or fish images seen in the characters' names,[17] Nat Pearl's is the most ironic. This sexually aggressive law student falls far short of Helen's romantic dreams. Baumbach sees Nat as "the spiritual heir of his father, a good but materialistic man, whose livelihood comes from selling penny candy. That Helen's dream of a better life might be satisfied by marriage to Nat Pearl suggests the inadequacy of her aspirations."[18] Nat, in short, is no pearl.

The most interesting fish name in the novel is *Karp*. In the first description of the liquor store owner, the fish image is cleverly implied. Helen observes "paunchy Julius Karp, with bushy eyebrows and an ambitious mouth, blowing imaginary dust off a bottle as he slipped a deft fifth of something into a paper bag, while Louis, slightly popeyed son and heir, looking up from clipping to the quick of his poor fingernails, smiled aimiably upon a sale" (16). The fat body, mouth puckered as it blows air, and the "popeyed" son — all suggest the fish analogy. More significant is Morris's dislike of this man, who, supposedly his friend, has allowed another grocery store into the neighborhood to compete with the struggling Bobers. To make a profit, Karp is willing to betray friendship and loyalty, and he lacks the compassion Malamud considers the essence of a person's humanity. Karp's name is well chosen, as this fish lives off the bottom of the lake and destroys the eggs and nests of more valuable fish. The angry Morris, while convalescing, discovers that he dislikes the greedy Karp "more than he had imagined. He resented him as a crass and stupid person who had fallen through luck into flowing prosperity. His every good fortune spattered others with misfortune, as if there was just so much luck in the world and what Karp left over wasn't fit to eat" (118). It is Karp who escapes from his store when the robbers drive around the block and then decide to rob Morris's instead. It is Karp who owns the empty store across the street from Morris's and breaks his word, renting it to another grocer. It is Karp whose store is destroyed by fire while Morris's attempt at arson fails. When Karp offers to buy Morris's store, "Morris couldn't believe his ears. He was filled with excitement and dread that somebody would tell him he had just dreamed a dream, or that Karp, fat fish, would turn into a fat bird and fly away screeching, 'Don't you believe me,' or in some heartbreaking way change his mind" (220). Morris's skepticism foreshadows his disappointment, as once more dream turns into nightmare. Karp has a heart attack, survives, but is no longer interested in buying out Morris. The fat fish-fat bird will retire, living comfortably off the insurance money, leaving Morris to his doom.

Malamud also makes extensive use of nature imagery in developing the character of Morris Bober's daughter, Helen. The barrenness of nature reflects the bleakness of her life. When she appears in the opening chapter, Helen gets off the subway two stops before her home and walks through the park "despite the sharp wind. . . . The leafless trees left her with unearned sadness. She mourned the long ago before spring and feared loneliness in winter" (15). Like her father, Helen spends hours "at the window, looking out at the back yards. The remnants of last week's dirty snow. No single blade of grass, or flowers to light the eye or lift the heart. She felt as if she were made of knots . . ." (118). Thus the grayness of fall and winter and especially the leafless trees become the objective epitome of Helen's existence.

Helen does not know what she really wants. A romantic dreamer, she is reading *Don Quixote* on the subway at the novel's beginning. Embarrassed by the presence of Nat Pearl, to whom she had lost her virginity the previous summer, she tries to hide "her thoughts behind the antics of a madman until memory overthrew him and she found herself ensnared in scenes of summer that she would gladly undo, although she loved the season; but how could you undo what you had done again in the fall, unwillingly willing?" (14).

Helen sentimentally equates summer with romance, love, friendship, and happiness. Nostalgically, she remembers her past fun, "spending every day of summer in a lively crowd of kids on the beach" (42). Malamud writes that Helen's "summer face was gentler than her winter one" (239). Early in the novel, Louis Karp takes her for a walk one dark windy night on the Coney Island boardwalk. As Helen gazes enviously at the large homes facing the ocean, she notices how deserted the island is. Only an occasional hamburger stand or pinball concession is open. "Gone from the sky was the umbrella of rosy light that glowed over the place in summertime. A few cold stars gleamed down. In the distance a dark Ferris wheel looked like a stopped clock. They stood at the rail of the boardwalk, watching the black, restless sea" (42). Helen's life is on hold and she longs for "the return of her possibilities" (43), perhaps some vaguely realized dream of rosy lights, spinning Ferris wheels, and romantic attachment. Instead, she has to suffer the crude, animalistic advances of Louis Karp, who is bored by her philosophizing about her youth and complains of the cold: "Jesus, this wind, it flies up my pants. At least gimme another kiss" (44). She removes his hands from her breasts and rejects his marriage proposal. The pathetic fallacy effectively expresses her mood as "She listened to the wind-driven, sobbing surf," but Malamud deflates the romantic with the realistic as Louis replies, "Let's go get the hamburgers" (45).

Repelled by Louis Karp, Helen wishes that Nat Pearl would call, but she is disappointed. Malamud continues his pattern of seasonal symbolism:

> December yielded nothing to spring. She awoke to each frozen, lonely day with dulled feeling. Then one Sunday afternoon winter leaned backward for an hour and she went walking. Suddenly she forgave everyone everything. A warmish breath of air was enough to inspire; she was again grateful for living. But the sun soon sank and it snowed pellets. (88–89)

Here is a subtle foreshadowing of the affair she will soon have with Frank Alpine, her father's assistant.

As Helen's feelings for Frank slowly blossom, Malamud has the couple move from the prison-like confinement of the store to the openness of the local park. Their favorite trysting place is "in front of the lilac trees" (160). It is in the park where they embrace for the first time. Helen is fascinated by the mysterious Italian, but he falls considerably short of her romantic ideal. Sickened by the drabness of her life, she cannot envision this man leading her out of her past. All of her dreams are summed up in her wondering, "Would it never come spring?" (131). As the frequency of their meetings increases, they go from cold park bench to street corners. "When it rained or snowed, they stepped into doorways, or went home."

Because of the bad weather, the couple are forced to return indoors. At first Helen refuses to come to Frank's room, but seeing his disappointment, she relents, after two dreary days of cold rain. Allowing him only limited sexual play, Helen insists that he discipline his emotions until she is sure of her love for him. Lying on Frank's bed, Helen listens contentedly "to the quiet sound of the rain in the street, making it in her mind into spring rain, though spring was weeks away; and within the rain grew all sorts of flowers, in this flowery dark—a sweet spring night—she lay with him in the open under new stars and a cry rose in her throat" (138). The romanticism of this passage is, of course, all in her imagination, and Malamud uses this misleading sentimentality to contrast vividly with the ironic plot development that follows.

Arranging their next meeting in the park because she has something nice to tell him, Helen rushes to Frank after an earlier date with Nat. Frank is sure that Helen is willing to sleep with him now. The bittersweet quality of the scene is hinted at when Malamud describes the girl's mood: "The night's new beauty struck Helen with the anguish of loss as she hurried to the lamplit park a half-hour after midnight" (163). Other young lovers sit embracing "in the dark under budding branches," but eventually they depart and Helen is left alone. Combining the ominous with the hopeful in the kind of ambiguity that Malamud loves in establishing mood and creating suspense, he describes the girl's emotions as follows: "She felt the stars clustered like a distant weight above her head. Utterly lonely, she regretted the spring-like loveliness of the night; it had gone, in her hands, to waste. She was tired of anticipation, of waiting for nothing" (165).

It is at this point that the Malamudian irony is particularly effective. Ward Minogue attacks Helen in the park, ripping her clothes and banging her head against one of the trees. As she tries to fight off the rapist, Frank arrives just in time, like the hero he wishes he were, and drives the anatagonist away. The couple kiss "under the dark trees," but Frank shows none of the discipline Helen had insisted on, drawing "her deeper into the dark, and from under the trees onto the star-dark field" (167). As they sink "to their knees on the winter earth," Helen pleads with Frank to wait, but he cannot. With romantic love almost within his grasp, the schlemiel ruins his chances by completing the rape that Ward had started.[19] Chapter 6 ends with an outraged Helen calling her rapist a "Dog — uncircumcised dog!" (168).

With the naturalistic themes of the struggle for survival and the victimization of man in an unsympathetic world, one might expect to find considerable animal imagery in *The Assistant*, but there is far less comparison of people with animals, for example, than one finds in Edward Lewis Wallant's *The Pawnbroker* or Saul Bellow's *Mr. Sammler's Planet*. The explanation can perhaps be found in the discussion between Morris and Frank of what makes a Jew. When Morris ultimately explains his view that the essence of Jewishness is being righteous, honest, and good to other people, he concludes: "We ain't animals. This is why we need the Law. This is what a Jew believes" (124). Frank immediately points out that the same virtues can be found in other people as well, but Morris's statement is not undercut by irony.

Malamud does use a few miscellaneous animal images to describe some of his characters, but most are insignificant. The milkman hurries into the store like "a bull" (6), and Frank jokes about Morris's haircut, telling him that he looks "like a sheep that had the wool clipped off it" (127). When Nat calls Helen for a date and she gives him a hard time, he answers, "I'm not exactly a pig, Helen" (110). Only slightly more important are those animal images associated with Frank. Early in the novel Frank tells Morris how all his life he has worked "like a mule" but always messes things up (36). Waiting for Helen to come home from the library, Frank stands "like a crippled dog as she passed him" (238). Malamud writes that Frank "was always tired. His spine ached as if it had been twisted like a cat's tail" (241). Guilt-stricken after the rape of Helen, he is terribly depressed. "The self he had secretly considered valuable was, for all he could make of it, a dead rat. He stank" (175).

Three other more important patterns of nature imagery closely identified with Helen and Frank are moonlight, flowers, and birds. The way
Malamud blends all three in *The Assistant* reveals a craftsmanship that
depends more heavily on the imaginative than the mimetic. It is a technique that calls for the evocative, poetic, and legendary rather than the
actual. It is this Chagall-like technique of Malamud's by which he trans-
mutes the mundane into the bizarre that has led critics like Alfred Kazin
to call him a "fantasist of the ordinary."[20]

A good example of this hallmark of Malamud's in *The Assistant* can
be found a few days after Christmas on a night with a full moon. Dressed
in his new suit, Frank overtakes Helen on the way to the library and suggests that they walk in the park. There he begins to tell her a beautiful
story about his idol, St. Francis of Assisi. Thinking about the wife and
family he could never have, Francis became despondent and was unable
to fall asleep one winter night. He "got out of his straw bed and went outside of the church or monastery or wherever he was staying. The ground
was all covered with snow. Out of it he made this snow woman, and he
said, 'There, that's my wife.' Then he made two or three kids out of the
snow. After, he kissed them all and went inside and laid down in the straw.
He felt a whole lot better and fell asleep" (95).

The moonlit park is a most appropriate setting for the telling of this
story.[21] This is the first time Helen and Frank have been alone together
very long, and she is beginning to see a side of him of which she has been
unaware.[22] The sweet sadness of the saint's story reflects her own mood
after a drab day as secretary in an office. She senses that her father's
strange assistant has something in common with her. When he sighs and
she asks if anything is wrong, the following exchange takes place:

> "No, just something popped into my mind wen I was looking at the moon.
> You know how your thoughts are."
> "Nature sets you thinking?"
> "I like scenery."
> "I walk a lot for that reason."
> "I like the sky at night, but you see more of it in the West. Out here the
> sky is too high, there are too many big buildings." (99)

In this open setting, nature is more than mere scenery. Malamud uses
it skillfully to create mood, develop character, and express theme. Frank
is encouraged to tell Helen about a previous romance that ended in a
tragic automobile accident. The whole pattern of his sad, lonely life is revealed. For such people the sky is always too high, beyond their reach.
As Helen ponders Frank's stories in bed that night, she realizes that "She
had had her own moonlit memories to contend with" (101). Unable to fall

asleep, "she regretted she could not see the sky from her window in the wall, or look down into the street. Who was he making into a wife out of snowy moonlight?" (102).

The most obvious identification of Frank with St. Francis[23] occurs shortly after the above scene when a depressed and restless Helen walks in the park and watches a man (actually Frank) "feeding the birds. Otherwise the island was deserted. When the man rose, the pigeons fluttered up with him, a few landing on his arms and shoulders, one perched on his fingers, pecking peanuts from his cupped palm. Another fat bird sat on his hat. The man clapped his hands when the peanuts were gone and the birds, beating their wings, scattered" (118). This passage echoes one much earlier when Frank, hanging around Sam Pearl's store after robbing Morris, looks at pictures in a magazine and is excited to see one of St. Francis of Assisi, "standing barefooted on a sunny country road. His skinny, hairy arms were raised to a flock of birds that dipped over his head. In the background was a grove of leafy trees; and in the far distance a church in sunlight" (30).[24]

In preparing his readers for the growing relationship between Frank and Helen, Malamud also introduces bird images in his description of the grocer's daughter. The first is seen through the eyes of her doting father: "She looks like a little bird, Morris thought. Why should she be so lonely? Look how pretty she looks. Whoever saw such blue eyes?" (20). The second bird image related to Helen is a cliché, as Frank longs for the grocer's daughter while he works in the store: "She was in her way a lone bird, which suited him fine, though why she would be with her looks he couldn't figure out" (63). The most important of the three images is the comparison Frank draws as he spies on Helen in the bathroom: "Her body was young, soft, lovely, the breasts like small birds in flight, her ass like a flower" (75). Here Malamud brings together two of the main patterns of imagery associated with Helen and Frank—birds and flowers.

To throw some light on the complicated flower symbolism that follows, it is helpful at this point to summarize a legend about St. Francis even though Malamud does not explicitly refer to it in *The Assistant*. According to Nikos Kazantzakis, who gives his version of the story in his biography *Saint Francis of Assisi*,[25] Sister Clare sent word to the sick Francis asking him to visit her and the other sisters at the convent of San Damiano. Francis tells the messenger, Father Silvester, that he will come "when the road from the Portiuncula to San Damiano's is covered with white flowers" (129). Cynical Father Silvester takes this indirect answer to mean "never," but the more trusting Brother Leo, the narrator of the story, rushes outside to see whether God has performed a miracle. As he reaches the road this very cold morning, he is overjoyed to find the entire way, "hedges, stones, dirt . . . blanketed everywhere with white flowers, as far as the eye could see!" Pulling up a handful, he rushes back to the bedridden Francis and tells him what he has found. Thanking God for this miracle, Francis places the white flowers on his bloody eyelids and the wounds on his temples. Then he delivers a little sermon to his companions on the miracles of all nature: "Just look at the humblest leaf of a tree, just look at it in the light—what a miracle! The Crucifixion is painted on one side; you turn the leaf over on the other and what do you see—the Resurrection! It is not a leaf, my brothers, it is our hearts!" (130). At this point St. Francis gives Father Silvester the bloodied flowers to take with his message to Sister Clare as a sign that God wants him to visit her. Father Silvester is to tell her that "When they touched the earth they became all covered with blood." Although Francis's knees buckle as he is taken outdoors, he is able to reach the road, where the flowers have now vanished: "it was as though they had been a layer of winter hoar frost melted by the rising sun" (131). Francis calls their disappearance another miracle: "The flowers came down from heaven, delivered their message, and then returned. They did not want human feet to step on them."

Whether this particular story was known to Malamud is not important. It is characteristic of the many legends told about St. Francis, combining the fanciful with the ordinary in a manner that would have delighted Nathaniel Hawthorne, who also loved the twilight zone of the imagination. Perhaps, the storyteller hints, there never were any flowers. Perhaps the hoar frost excited the imagination of the friars, who saw what they wanted to see. In either case, a pleasant, entertaining story is told, evolving a thoughtful moral. The juxtaposition of the white and red, the beautiful and the painful, the real and the imaginary, instructs the reader in the need for faith, for a belief in miracles that can turn crucifixions into resurrections.

With this story in mind, with its patterns of flower-frost imagery, its theme of suffering and rebirth, its mixture of hope and skepticism, one can better understand Malamud's unusual use of rose symbolism, which first appears in a strange dream Farnk has in his troubled sleep after raping Helen:

> That night he dreamed he was standing in the snow outside her window. His feet were bare yet not cold. He had waited a long time in the falling snow, and some of it lay on his head and had all but frozen his face; but he waited longer until, moved by pity, she opened the window and flung something out. It floated down; he thought it was a piece of paper with writing on it but saw that it was a white flower, surprising to see in wintertime. Frank caught it in his hand. As she had tossed the flower out through the partly opened window he had glimpsed her fingers only, yet he saw the light of her

room and even felt the warmth of it. Then when he looked again the window
was shut tight, sealed with ice. Even as he dreamed, he knew it had never
been open. There was no such window. He gazed down at his hand for the
flower and before he could see it wasn't there, felt himself wake. (185)

Through this dream Malamud is contrasting the romantic sentimentality
of the St. Francis–Sister Clare legend with the harsh reality of the Frank-
Helen affair. The spiritual relationship of the first couple is changed into
the carnal relationship of the second. Frank Alpine is doomed to play the
role of the schlemiel; for him, no flowers will miraculously appear in the
snow.

Malamud extends this pattern of rose imagery in a fascinating way.
One day, Frank finds a board in the basement of Morris's store and starts
carving it to pass the time.

> To his surprise it turned into a bird flying. It was shaped off balance but with
> a certain beauty. He thought of offering it to Helen but it seemed too rough
> a thing — the first he ever made. So he tried his hand at something else. He
> set out to carve her a flower and it came out a rose starting to bloom. When
> it was done it was delicate in the way its petals were opening yet firm as a
> real flower. (192)

Frank considers painting it red but leaves it unpainted, wraps it in store
paper, prints Helen's name on the package, and leaves it taped to the
mailbox. When Helen unwraps it, the wooden rose reminds her of her
unhappiness. She throws the gift away, and "In the morning, as he aimed
a pail of garbage into the can at the curb, Frank saw at the bottom of it
his wooden flower" (193).

The rose as a symbol of love is seen again at Morris's funeral. As Morris's coffin is lowered into the ground, "Helen tossed in a rose" (231). A
characteristic Malamudian irony follows: Frank leans forward to watch
it land and falls into the grave. Poor Morris Bober cannot even be laid
to rest in peace. This Chaplinesque humor, the mixture of the ludicrous
with the pathetic,[26] is Malamud's perfect touch to lighten the heavy-handed
symbolism of the identification of Frank with Morris. The store-as-grave
symbolism is now complete. Frank's future is sealed.

But Malamud makes one last extension of the rose–bird–St. Francis
pattern of imagery, ending his novel on that note of ambiguity which he
loves so well. In a final imaginative flourish, he combines the ordinary
with the fanciful, the serious with the comedic, and the depressing with
the hopeful. Frank, exhausted from working two jobs to support Ida and
Helen, suddenly has a remarkable rebirth. The internal warfare between
his good and evil impulses abruptly ends, and he stops both his dishonesty
in the store and his voyeurism. Helen has sensed the change that has taken

place in her benefactor but rejects his generous suggestion that she transfer from evening college to day classes. Afraid of rejection if he asks her to renew their relationship, Frank turns to the Bible to calm his nerves:

> As he was reading he had this pleasant thought. He saw St. Francis come dancing out of the woods in his brown rags, a couple of scrawny birds flying around over his head. St. F. stopped in front of the grocery, and reaching into the garbage can, plucked the wooden rose out of it. He tossed it into the air and it turned into a real flower that he caught in his hand. With a bow he gave it to Helen, who had just come out of the house. "Little sister, here is your little sister the rose." From him she took it, although it was the love and and best wishes of Frank Alpine. (245–46)

Here Malamud has dipped once again into his magic barrel to provide hope for the frustrated grocer. If the Helen of his fantasy accepts the rose of love from St. Francis, perhaps she will eventually accept it from him. James Mellard prefers the happy ending to support his analysis of the vegetation myth underlying the novel. To him, Helen's acceptance of Frank's offering proves "that Frank's sterile lust has now become life-giving love."[27] To Mellard, Frank's reverie shows that the grocer has at last "succeeded not only with Helen but in gaining a measure of control over his fate, however savorless that fate might be to most of us. Through the ritual participation of man in nature's cycles, man has been able to unite eternal and temporal, desire and necessity, creativity and creation, art and life."[28] But with this partial truth Mellard misses the purposeful ambiguity that is so characteristic of Malamud's craftsmanship. True to his literary creed, Malamud ends his novel on a note of uncertainty. "It's part of life," he once wrote in the late sixties. "I want something the reader is uncertain about. It is this uncertainty that produces drama. Keep the reader surprised. That is enormously important to me."[29] As the drama of Morris Bober and his assistant closes, the only certainty Malamud allows his reader is the pain of suffering. The St. Francises and Morris Bobers of this world have taught their disciples well. The test of man's humanity is to suffer for one's fellow man, be he Christian or Jew. As the novel ends, an exhausted, frustrated, but determined Frank Alpine, right after the Passover celebration of freedom from bondage, accepts the martyrdom of suffering as a sign of his redemption, and becomes a convert to Judaism.

Chapter 6

The Mistral of Sol Nazerman:
Nature Imagery in Wallant's *The Pawnbroker*

In the opening scene of Edward Lewis Wallant's *The Pawnbroker*, Sol Nazerman, a forty-five-year-old refugee who has survived the gas chambers and crematoriums of Nazi Germany, walks heavily across the hard sand along the Harlem River, heading for his shop in the city. The sound of the pawnbroker's crunching footsteps, writes Wallant, "could almost have been the pleasant sound of someone walking over clean white snow,"[1] but the qualifier *almost* alerts the reader to the difference between the ideal and the actual, the world as it could be and the world as it is. As Sol draws closer to the grimy city, the novel's major setting, he wonders, "What was there here, in this shabby patch on his journey to the store each morning, that eased him slightly?" (5), and he concludes that "this brief part of his walk was a bridge between two separate atmospheres, a bridge upon which he could readjust the mantle of his impregnable scorn." The "two separate atmospheres" are the past and the present, Eastern Europe and New York City, the late 1930s and the postwar period; and Sol's mantle of scorn is his protection against the horrors of both. But the mantle slips and is in constant need of readjustment as Sol painfully discovers that he is not Ethan Brand, not Captain Ahab, and that a man without a heart is not alive. For all his imperturbability, Sol derives some comfort, some temporary relief, from the world of nature, his bridge between past and present.

Wallant's use of nature imagery is an integral part of his characterization of the novel's protagonist. It is nature that provides this man-of-the-book, now living in an environment of "filth-encrusted sidewalks and gutters" (249), one of the few pleasures left to him in this world. But even here the cynical pawnbroker is cautious, because he is well aware that nature can be ominous and hostile to man, as on the Thursday evening when after a hot, cloudy day, "the sun came out with a cruel brilliance that seemed to curl up the bits of rubbish in the streets. This satire on sunsets struck like flame against the weary old people sitting on steps and goaded the children to excesses of noise and violence" (190). And then there is the sultry August day when "The air was thick and hot, worse even than the inside of the store. . . . There was no relief in sight. He looked up; the sky stared down at all the stone and brick, a pale-blue monstrous eye that lumped him and all the other ridiculous creatures with the filthy city" (109).

What is even worse, of course, is nature's supreme indifference to man. Sol painfully remembers the sight of his friend Rubin, trapped by the Nazis' dogs against the wire fence of the concentration camp, "*Their snarls . . . wetly muffled by what they were doing. All the men in the column were bony-gray profiles, death masks coated by the faint dustiness of the air. A pigeon appeared on one of the sludge-colored barracks roofs; not quite sure of its roost, it fluttered its wings as it stood; then rose again and disappeared over the monotonous horizon of the camp*" (100). Chapter 26 begins on the day of Sol's nightmarish anniversary of his wife's death: "There was a shine to even the grimy landscape of the city, and the air was possessed of the clarity that frequently follows heavy rain" (248). New York City has "a quality of richness, as with old bronzes in sunlight." There is no pathetic fallacy here.[2]

The degradation and murder of his family and the Nazi surgical experiments on his body have left Sol with a "face of gray Asian stone" (17), and this hard substance provides a pattern of imagery that Wallant repeatedly uses to describe the pawnbroker's impassivity. In chapter 12, for example, when Sol returns home from work to find his sister Bertha and her friends clumsily trying to play marriage broker, he is rude and uncooperative. "For a few minutes they talked carefully around him, and he sat like a stone in their chatter" (130). Several chapters later, as Tessie offers her breasts to Sol, he is impassive and just sits there "stonily" (193). The most important stone image appears in chapter 6 and foreshadows the change that will come over the pawnbroker at the climax of the novel. The Negress Mrs. Harmon has returned to the shop to pawn three suits to pay some bills. When she describes her lot in life and laughingly questions the ability of human endurance to withstand God's tests, Sol offers her a meager five dollars but feels a surge of the old compassion for human suffering which he thought he had buried forever. This feeling "sent a streak of apprehension through him; he recalled the power of a few blades of grass to grow through and split solid stone" (76).

Sol considers it essential to his survival that he stifle such feelings. A hard world must be met with equal hardness. Once again he must "readjust the mantle of his impregnable scorn." The people who cross his path daily he considers no better than animals or insects. When Sol wakes up in Tessie's apartment after a brief nap, he hears the sounds of life coming from many different apartments: "All around him life of various sorts, stone hollowed out and filled with the insect life of humans, the whole earth honeycombed with them" (60). The Jesus Ortizes, George Smiths, and Murillios of the world are "insects ruining the sweet, silent proportions of the earth. . . . Where was the gigantic foot to crush them all?" When Tessie bemoans her hard life and past, telling Sol that she feels like screaming to death all day, Sol coldly replies, "But you don't and I don't and the old man doesn't. We live and fight off the animals" (62). To Sol, people like Murillio, Jesus, Bertha, and Selig are all "'Some more animals. What is there to say! The whole world is a big zoo. Maybe I will go to Alaska, to the North Pole,' he said with glassy humor. 'The polar bears should be amusing company'" (193)[3]

Sol's Darwinian concept of the struggle for survival is reinforced by the cannibalism of Bertha and her family, with whom he lives. The victim of Bertha's cannibalism is her artistic son, Morton, who is not as Americanized as her husband and daughter. To the assimilated Bertha, Morton is more like a European ghetto scholar. As she looks around the dinner table, "Suddenly her eye fell on her son, still eating silently and voraciously. She turned a half-guilty cruelty toward him, as though with some compulsive pecking-order instinct, she knew he was the only victim for her there" (34–35). Criticizing his eating habits, she yells at him, "Look at you! Like an animal wolfing the food, scowling" (35). When his father and sister join the mother in the sport of baiting Morton, he stomps out of the room to his mother's cruel remark, "Ah, there's a runt in every litter." Bertha's attempt to enlist Sol's support in their little game fails; the memory of Nazi dogs snapping at Rubin's heels as the fleeing prisoner clung desperately to the barbed wire fence of the concentration camp is too painful. Sol's parting curse puts them in their place: "Eat each other up, for all I care, but do not bother me!" (36)

The imagery of predatory animals and their prey, which suggests the vulturism of the world and man's inhumanity to man, runs as a leitmotif throughout the novel and becomes an important part of its interior structure. When Tangee, Buck White, and Robinson try to pawn a stolen lawnmower, "There was, in their idle patience, the murderous quality of hunting dogs so sure of their prey that they rest, panting, in a confident circle around it" (23). At a Sunday morning breakfast, Bertha, Selig, and Joan start snapping again at Morton, who "snarled miserably, like a trapped animal" (95). Sol tries to shut himself off from the sound: "The voices of his relatives snapped in a closing circle around the ugly weakness of their prey, but he heard them only distantly, like the sound of some faroff hunt." When Murillio becomes annoyed by Sol's stubborn refusal to accept money that has been collected in the gangster's whorehouse, "His eyes darkened, and the irritated cougar showed from under the neat, human face" (159). Sol tries to "ignore the black-and-white beast planted motionlessly in the far corner of his eye. Slowly, casually, he scanned the soft buff walls. You must make no sudden moves with certain wild things; sharks were said to strike if you make a commotion in the water" (160). Murillio, beginning to lose his patience with this strange antagonist, "studied Sol's face with inhuman curiosity, like a great cat watching with unblinking interest the reactions of its prey when it cuffs with covered claws" (162).

One of the characters most frequently identified with an animal in *The Pawnbroker* is Jesus Ortiz. Wallant compares him to some member of the cat family, usually a leopard, and the effect of the imagery is to suggest his gracefulness, curiosity, and potential danger. The first time he appears, Wallant describes him as "moving with that leopard-like fluidity, that made it hard to say where bone gave way to fine muscle" (8). He has a "smooth tawny face" (41), and as he listens attentively to the pawnbroker, his mentor, "his eyes [are] as clear and receptive as those of a cat searching the dusk for nourishment" (52). After his lesson he saunters out of the shop "with his leopard walk" (53). At the violent climax of the novel it is his agility and speed that lead to his death, as he intercepts the bullet intended for the pawnbroker.

When Wallant uses animal images to describe Sol, the effect is to emphasize his heaviness, his size, his entrapment in a hostile world. In the pawnshop, "His ponderous body moved swiftly as a penned elephant behind the counter" (219). The agile Ortiz sidesteps Sol's rushes like a matador. When the determined Sol tries to break up his partnership with Murillio, the pawnbroker suffers the indignity of having a gun shoved into his mouth. Murillio orders him to "stand there like that a while, taste the bit. See, you're just like a horse. Get a little balky and we pull the reins. Get real wild . . . well, you know what they do to horses" (163). Another comparison with one of nature's creatures reveals Sol in all his terrifying grotesqueness. As Murillio offers Sol a new business arrangement not involving money from the brothel, "Sol's face registered the slow descent from bewilderment to anger. He opened and closed his mouth on his indignation a few times like a fish not sure of its atmosphere" (161). The most frightening of all these images, and one highlighting the theme of cannibalism, appears in Sol's nightmare when he remembers the Nazi surgeons experimenting on his body: "'WHAT ARE YOU TAKING OUT OF ME?' *he screamed, seeing himself 'boned' like some beast being prepared for someone's meal"* (131).

Sol's reaction against the carnivorousness of life is to insulate himself from its daily horrors, to stifle all feeling, to remain as uninvolved with people as possible in urban America — an impossible challenge to a man who helps support at least six different people. When he explains to the emotionally upset Tessie his stoic creed, he is subconsciously trying to convince himself that he is more uncommitted than he is. Sol tells his mistress to forget the past. "Don't think, don't feel. Get through things — it is the only sense. Imagine yourself a cow in a fenced place with a million other cows. Don't suffer, don't fear. Soon enough will come the axe. Meanwhile, eat and rest. Don't pay attention, don't cry" (229). As Sol methodically makes the funeral arrangements for Tessie's dead father and hands her the signed blank checks that she will need, she says, "Sometimes I do not think you are human at all" (230). Sol, of course, is well aware of his seeming inhumanity and realizes that there is more life in the grieving Tessie and her dead father than in himself. Incapable of feeling "pain or grief," he sees himself "like a creature imbedded in a plastic block."

Three chapters later Wallant echoes the image of the animal imbedded in a child's toy block and reinforces the themes of isolation, insulation, coldness, and hardness. It is the twenty-eighth of August,[4] the horrible anniversary he has been dreading. In a brilliant image that suggests Dante's Devil imbedded in ice slowly being melted by the inferno in the lowest pit of Hell, Wallant adds a sense of the timelessness of suffering and death with a picture of a frozen, prehistoric monster: "Fifteen years ago today his heart had atrophied; like the mammoth, he had been preserved in ice. What did he fear then? If the ice finally melts, the meat of the entombed creature merely rots. One could only die once," Sol reasons. "He had been extinct for a long time, and only the carcass remained to be disposed of" (249).

A considerable part of Wallant's success in this novel is his transcending the confinement of time and suggesting, as in the mammoth image above, the agelessness of the pawnbroker and his suffering. The clocks in Sol's store all tell a different time. "The false measure of time clicking from the many clocks offered him nothing. The hours were too slick to seize and led nowhere anyhow. His body smelled like clay, faintly damp, sunless, old" (117). In a conversation with the social worker Marilyn Birchfield, Sol tries to give her the impression that he is a survivor of the Paleolithic Age, and that his memories of life's horrors go back to prehistoric times. "There is a world so different in scale," he tells her, "'that its emotions bear no resemblance to yours; it has emotions so different in degree that they have become a different *species*!' He tilted his face up toward the sky in a pose of a sunworshiper, but his eyes were malevolently open.'*I am past that by a million years!*'" (146).

The two references to the sun in the above passage underscore another pattern of imagery of major import in *The Pawnbroker*. Sol's first name is the first clue to Wallant's artistic intention. The irony is heavy-handed, as it is soon obvious to the reader that there is very little sunshine in this man's life. Yet it would be as fallacious to conclude that his life is entirely "sunless," as it would be to call him "a sunworshiper." Morton's charcoal drawing of his uncle sitting in the backyard has sensitively portrayed the man as the novelist conceives him:

> The scene sparkled, seemed to be in a crsip twilight, and the roofs and branches were sure, steady shapes in a subtle pattern that hid under the obvious one. In one corner of the picture was a shapeless figure in a garden chair, and all the twilight led to it, so there was a brightness of sky and a brightness around the man and great darkness between. (166)

Morton has seen the inner light and goodness of this deformed man beneath the stony facade, beneath the protective insulation. Separating Sol from the serenity and peace of the sky is "the great darkness" of his past, his physical and psychic scars. It is this alienation that makes Sol a tragic figure; it is this darkness that must be breached to make him a whole man again.

Throughout the novel Sol takes excursions into the sunshine, but the block of ice in which he is encased does not melt easily. On one Sunday morning, as he and his nephew sit apart in the backyard of their Mt. Vernon home, "the soft summer sounds fell over him with the sunlight, as unfelt as the lightest rain of pollen" (98). Wallant underscores the resemblance between the two isolates when he describes Morton "as alien with his sallow face in that cheery sunshine as his uncle."

Sol is more at home in the dark and dreary pawnshop where he spends his long days behind the counter. "The store was dim even with the lights on, so it seemed the quality of light was at fault, not the intensity. Outside, the evening sun made the street shimmer in a golden bath through which the passers-by moved like dark swimmers in no hurry to get anywhere" (26). Even such small details as the sunlight glinting off Leopold Schneider's recently pawned gold-plated Daniel Webster award are significant. The plaque "caught a tiny dart of sunlight, and it disturbed Sol's corner vision. He picked the award up and shoved it into a low, dark shelf where the light never reached" (15–16). This action is Sol's sarcastic commentary on the absurdity of gold-plated oratory awards in a depraved world. At the same time it suggests Sol's own cynical desire to isolate himself from the hundreds of thousands of Leopold Schneiders, aspiring poets, playwrights, and idealists who hope to make this a better world. Sol refuses to loan more than one dollar on the award, and when the desperate Schneider asks, "Haven't you got a heart?" Sol quietly answers, "No . . . No heart" (15).

In chapter 14 the romantic and compassionate Marilyn Birchfield persuades Sol to eat lunch with her by the river. Begrudgingly he admits that "it will do [him] no harm to sit quite idly in the sun for a short time" (141). When Marilyn teases him about her seeing him smile for the first time ("I'm beginning to think you're hiding a human being under your cold manner," ([142]), Sol, "taking a little deeper breath of the tarry air," warns her: "This is pleasant. . . . I feel it rests me a little. Do not spoil it with silly analysis." Marilyn, of course, is right, and Sol knows it. The sunshine is necessary to thaw the ice and renew life. As the couple head back to the city streets and Marilyn tells Sol that as a woman, she likes him and would like to see him again, he puts her card in his pocket, "his vision . . . darkening already in expectation of the fluorescent dimness of the pawnshop" (149).

Sol's hellish nightmare gets worse as the day of his anniversary gets closer. He is afraid to sleep in the dark and keeps himself up so as not to dream. He lies awake in bed "until the sun came into this room like a trustworthy guard. And he slept a little while then" (131). In chapter 17 Sol again derives comfort from sunlight after the steady stream of customers has given him an excruciating headache. "He felt driven to scream, and even opened his mouth; but suddenly he found quiet and emptiness. One late beam of sunshine cut through the dust of the recent stampede. He looked at it for a long, numbed minute" (178).

The most dramatic sun image appears in an incident that occurs on the Sunday morning before Sol's anniversary. Early in the morning he drives away from the house to avoid all contact with his relatives. "Already the cicadas had set up an intense and threatening buzz, which reached up to the hot blue sky" (204).

> He drove with both hands tight on the wheel, as though he had just learned to drive. All the bright light threatened him like a single massive flame. And he was filled with mysterious dread for the unusual emotion he now seemed to recognize—a sudden and unbearable loneliness. He saw himself as the last living creature on a burning orb. He had known many solitudes before, but the sense of isolation he had now made all that had come before seem only like a bad dream there had been hope of waking from. (205)

Sol wants to cry but has forgotten how. He pulls off the road and sits "with his mouth open. The heat collected around him, as he stared at the parched grass that edged the road. Nothing, nothing." Then Sol does a strange thing. Finding a flashlight in the glove compartment,

He took it out and flicked the switch on; he could just about see the pallid glow of the tiny bulb's filament. Then he aimed that infinitestimal illumination at the immense cauldron of white sunlight; it made him shake his head, and once he had begun it, he found he could not stop. The heat rose to the temperature of an oven, and he sat breathing heavily through his mouth, a gray figure in the motionless car, on the desolate landscape.

The blazing heat in this remarkable passage suggests both the Nazi crematoriums and hell's flames. The burning sun stands for all those cosmic forces that beat down on man impersonally. But man somehow resists. Somehow he finds the courage and strength to say no to destruction.[5] Although he knows not why, he cannot accept the meaninglessness of life, his insignificance in the universe. As Sol aimlessly fingers the odds and ends in his pocket, he finds Marilyn Birchfield's card and decides to accept her offer to go with him on an excursion on the Hudson River. His loneliness is more than even he can bear.

Marilyn Birchfield's role in *The Pawnbroker* is hinted at by her last name. She is a foil to Sol Nazerman, and where he has the ashen gray color of death, she has the healthy pink of life. Like the Lena Groves and Hilma Trees of earlier American fiction, she is a fertility figure whose function is to bring about regeneration. Throughout the novel she is identified with the beauty, vigor, and cleanness of natural things.[6] In chapter 3, where she first appears, both Ortiz and Sol intuitively sense that this will be a quiet day in the shop. To Sol, "there were things you anticipated with illogical confidence. . . . You walked down a certain road and as you approached a farmhouse you *knew* there would be a smooth-skinned beech tree heavy with leaves" (41–42). Minutes later, Marilyn Birchfield, "a heavy-set woman, in her early thirties" (42), walks into the pawnshop "with an adolescent awkwardness, a sort of touching, coltish animation quite different from the movements of a stout matron." Sol sees her as "a medley of sunlight and twany pink skin" (43). "You couldn't imagine anyone who looked like that ever dying."

The next time Sol sees Marilyn is six chapters later. As she enters the dark shop, the brightness of the sun is behind her. "A cool refreshing breeze seemed to have followed her into the store . . . " (102).[7] The little sunburn on her face has come from her eating lunch by the river, and before she leaves she gets the rude pawnbroker to agree to join her for lunch the next day. When she reappears in chapter 14, she appears to Sol "like a substantial vision of cleanliness," and as she waits for Sol to accompany her on her luncheon date, "He was astounded by her smile and her brightness and for a moment he wondered what she had to do with him" (137).

Chapter 14, the picnic lunch by the Harlem River, is the prelude to chapter 21, the excursion on the Hudson River. Sol is skeptical, fascinated by the frank and aggressive Marilyn, but suspicious of outward appearances. He is too wise to be deceived by the apparent beauty of the scene.[8] "A few feet below was the greenish-brown water, from which the sun managed to bring shimmering sequins: out of all the muck an illusion of brightness" (139). As he gazes at the coalyard on the opposite bank, he watches some boys leaping into the "greasy river and then climbing back up to jump again. It was amazing how fresh the water looked when they splashed it up into the sunlight."

It is in this setting that Marilyn asks Sol why he is so bitter. In the silence before his answer, "Sol studied a pair of gulls gliding vigilantly over the dark water, dipping now and then as though they had discovered life in that unrevealing flow, only to rise up with hardly a movement of their wings when they discover their mistake" (145–46). The implication is clear. Sol's bitter experiences in Europe have protected him against the continual disillusionment of the foolish gulls. To Sol, all of existence is a polluted river; only the gulls like Marilyn Birchfield have not yet made this discovery. Sol calls her "touchingly naïve" (146) and cruelly makes fun of her supposed knowledge of loneliness and suffering. Marilyn stubbornly insists that she is aware of the darker forces of life and is not "the dewy-eyed fool" he thinks she is. ". . . I have hope for everyone," she tells him. "Even for myself" (145). When Sol denies that he is bitter and argues that all he wants from life is "peace and quiet," Marilyn asks him why he has not found what he craves. "'Isn't it possible your philosophy, or lack of philosophy, or whatever you live by, is in error?' she said, trying to bring the sweet smell of her own history to an ugly Jewish man on the banks of a filthy river; for she had a heritage of missionaries, and like her ancestors she was willing to brace a variety of wildernesses" (147).

When Wallant describes Marilyn in chapter 21, the Hudson River excursion, he subtly introduces an image that helps link her with Sol's wife, father, and children on a prewar picnic, which is described four chapters later. Marilyn is smiling as she greets the pawnbroker this Sunday morning, "and her face seemed appropriate to the wide, sun-filled vista. She wore a yellow dress which cast up a buttery glow under her chin, and her eyes were soft with contentment or some other odd joy" (207). The bright sun and the "buttery glow" tie in closely with Sol's dream of Ruth, who on the picnic, stuck dandelions in her *"black shine of curls,"* giving the impression of *"little yellow suns in the night of her hair."*

In Sol's dream, the only pleasant one he is to have in the two-week period prior to his anniversary,

> He walked up the gentle slope with the jar of milk and the bottle of white wine cold and wet from the brook where he had cooled them. Butterflies an-

> ticipated his route, swirling up from the high grass in palpitating clouds of color; there was the hot, peaceful din of insects all around, a drowsy twittering of sun-weakened birds. The smell of the ground made him breathe heavily, as from an intoxicant, humid and sweet. (241)[9]

This sentimental idyll, the only such picture of Sol's happy, pre-war life that Wallant gives the reader, is saved from triteness by the tragic framework of the story. It appears three-quarters of the way through the novel, and the reader already knows the extent of Sol's suffering. The alluring peace and beauty of nature make Sol's loss all the more poignant, his cynicism and skepticism all the more understandable. How can he trust the natural warmth, beauty, and goodness of Marilyn Birchfield when the world has shown him how ephemeral such appearances are? Even in his dream[10] he is not reunited with his loved ones, but stopped short as they run to greet him. "And he was paralyzed too, forever out of reach of the dear faces, frozen a few feet short of all he had ever loved. And then it all began dimming; each face receded, the sunny afternoon turned to eternal twilight, dusk, evening darkness!" (242).

On the Hudson River excursion boat Marilyn tells Sol nostalgically how often her family used to picnic "on a lake, spend the whole day in the sun and air."

> People's voices sound so different in the country, happier, easier. My father used to say that people had to get off the concrete of sidewalks sometimes just to remember what the earth is like underneath. He liked to sound like a homespun, country philosopher. Of course, he was born in the heart of Boston, but he was a big weekend nature-lover. He'd take us for long walks, identifying birds and trees. "Breathe deeply," he'd say. "Smell the air the way it's supposed to be, untarnished by soot and smoke and carbon monoxide." (207–8)

Marilyn is good for Sol, reminding him that there are happy memories as well as sad, that there is natural beauty in life as well as cruelty, that man cannot be indifferent to the world around him, that he cannot live in isolation no matter how deeply the world has hurt him. Her story about her father's nature hikes reminds Sol of a trip on the Vistula he took with his mother when he was a boy. He vividly remembers watching the scenery move by the portholes of his stateroom, eating their kosher food on the deck of the ship, and observing the Russian peasants. Sol relaxes, even compliments Marilyn, who has complained about her weight, and then says:

> One forgets how attractive America must be . . . Most of my time has been spent in the city. Of course, I live in Mount Vernon, which I suppose is an attractive enough town. But I derive no pleasure from it. There must be

thousands of miles of lovely countryside, and I have heard that some of the mountains are very impressive. Often I have thought I would like to go up some very high mountain. I have the idea it would be very beautiful and peaceful. The world might look quite worth while from those heights. You would not see people or dirt or. . . . (209–10)[11]

Marilyn tries desperately to prolong this mood of quiet reverie and says, "Wouldn't it be wonderful . . . if this trip could last for a long, long time? To think of nothing except what pretty scene might appear around the next turning. To talk and eat when we were hungry and sleep when we were drowsy. And then to wake, as you did when you were a child to see the woods and fields going by and know how much went by while you slept" (210). Even Sol is touched by the simple hedonism of this paradisiacal dream and wistfully admits, "That would be nice—if it were possible." When Marilyn says that they can try to pretend it is so, Sol replies that he is "not very good at pretending," but he is willing to try—a remarkable concession on his part. His innate love of nature begins to thaw feelings encased in ice all these years. "Hills scalloped the sky, and the sun covered the water with a multitude of tiny brilliants, which flashed in their faces and made them close their eyes and talk sleepily of small, almost intimate things" (210–11). For the first time in years, Sol is able to fall asleep without having to tire himself out by reading.[12]

The romantic idyll on the Hudson reaches its climax as the boat returns to New York City. Wallant uses bold, impressionistic strokes to describe the sunset as the couple face the west on their deck chairs: "The water was a pink-gold, the sky washed with vermillion and purple and orange. Each cloud was outlined with fire, and the hills of the earth were deep in shadow; it was as if the passengers floated on the edge of day and night and had the choice of either" (212). The choice, actually, is Sol's, between hope and cynicism, life-in-death and death-in-life. The scene is breathtaking, "But somehow," he tells Marilyn, "I do not trust its beauty, it is too blatant, too obvious." When Marilyn argues that "All appearances aren't deceiving," Sol answers, "Perhaps not, but it is safer to follow the old Roman law—guilty until proved innocent."

As the boat returns to the city, Sol tries to be his old cynical self. "I fear we must stop with the make-believe," he tells Marilyn. When she suggests that they can take this excursion into nature again, he can only reply, "Agh, how many times can you use a dream? It wears out so quickly against life. Never mind, it has been a pleasant, restful day. Perhaps I have regained some energy. I thank you very much. . . ." A couple of days later, when she reappears at the pawnshop and invites Sol to dinner, he is on the verge of a complete breakdown and cruelly warns her: "do not think of becoming intimate with me. For your own good I say this. . . . You would be guilty of necrophilia-it is obscene to love the dead" (219).

The theme of death-in-life running through *The Pawnbroker* has already been mentioned, but it is necessary to return to it at this point to explain Wallant's use of water imagery in his adaptation of the Fisher King myth. Like Henry Roth and Bernard Malamud, Wallant is fascinated by this old vegetation myth, but his direct source is probably T. S. Eliot rather than Sir James Frazer's *The Golden Bough* or Jessie L. Weston's *From Ritual to Romance*. Like the characters in Eliot's "The Waste Land,"[13] Wallant's characters await the rain which, along with a sacrificial death, is needed to bring fertility to a parched land. In a sense, Sol is the sexually maimed monarch whose potency must be restored. Wallant does not make use of the seasonal symbolism usually associated with the myth, since his story spans only the last two weeks in August in New York City, but he does emphasize the extreme dryness and then uses rain as a symbol to suggest the renewal of life.

The Saturday night before Sol's anniversary there is considerable heat lightning, but no rain. Sol awakens from his nightmare about the piles of naked corpses at the crematorium and is "all drenched with sweat and dry mouthed from gasping in dreams. He saw the sudden flash and heard the rumble of thunder and yearned for the cooling sound and feel of rain. But he had no hope for it. He lay for many hours without hearing any more thunder, and he was still awake when daylight came, clear and hot and dry" (203).

Sunday morning Sol escapes from the house before any of his relatives are awake. He is overwhelmed with loneliness as he drives aimlessly ahead, observing "the parched grass that edged the road" (205). "He yearned to cry but knew he was not capable of crying." It is in this scene that Sol, "a gray figure in the motionless car, on the desolate landscape," aims his flashlight at the merciless sun. Unable to stand the weight of the loneliness, Sol gets out of the car and walks "over the dry crackly August grass" (206) to a telephone booth to call Marilyn Birchfield and accept her offer to go on the Hudson River excursion.

By Wednesday morning, the day before his anniversary, the heat has become unbearable; "the sky was burned to the pallid blue of scorched metal" (226). The store, Sol's world, is even worse; "inside there was only the different, older heat of a closed dead place." It is in this chapter that Sol and Tessie find Mendel dead, and Sol, unwilling to let himself feel "pain and grief," refuses to come to the funeral. "The pawnbroker," says John G. Parks, "pays a great spiritual price for his survival in insulation from human involvement. The shell he erects to protect himself from human penetration also prevents him from feeling and taking responsibility for his feelings."[14] To the grieving and horrified Tessie, Sol has now lost his last touch of humanity. As he leaves Tessie's apartment after making the funeral arrangements, Sol hears "the very distant mumbling of thunder" (231).

That Wallant is a little uncomfortable about using the rainstorm as a melodramatic cliché can be seen in his description of the tenement dwellers: "People all around were picking up the newspapers they had sat on and preparing to go inside, glancing apprehensively at the occasional flashes of lightning which made the sky line appear to be a stage setting for a familar drama of violence" (236). Wallant uses this stage prop to reflect the inner turbulence of Sol, to foreshadow the violent robbery-murder on the next day, and to underscore the novel's mythical substructure. The one part of the ritual that is missing is the sacrificial death, and that will take place on Thursday as the grotesquely masked robbers act out their roles in the tomb-like pawnshop.

Wallant counterpoints the effect of the rain on the pawnbroker with vignettes of several other characters during the same storm. In this way the private hell of Sol Nazerman is extended to the periphery of the waste-land. Whereas in Sol's mind the rain is associated with thoughts of death[15] (the rain drums "outside his lighted room as though on a coffin" [242]; "the scale of notes the dripping made was an American dirge rather than a lullaby"), it takes on different meanings in the minds of others. The storm worries the lonely, nervous Jesus, who earlier in the evening had gone to church with his mother and scoffed at his white namesake on the cross, "Oh man, you don't know the half of it" (238). Walking home in the rain, he is "all hunched over, nailed heavily to the earth by the torrential downpour" (239). Back in his room, he watches "the rain trying to wash the old filth from the streets" (246–47), and his nerves are strangely soothed. Wallant thus uses the rain as a symbolic baptism for Jesus, who has less than twenty-four hours to live. Mabel, Jesus' girl friend, also finds the rain soothing and cleansing as she stares out of the whorehouse window and dreams of being a virgin again, walking down a church aisle in a white bridal gown with Jesus Ortiz by her side. All the while her next customer lies on top of her, "she listened to the sound of the rain and watched fur-tively the occasional flickers of celestial light" (243). The same storm in-tensifies the hellish loneliness of George Smith, the depraved black intellec-tual, who stands under a dripping awning wishing he could discuss the Marquis de Sade, Baudelaire's "Flowers of Evil," or Rimbaud's "The Season of Hell" with the cantankerous pawnbroker. Finally succumbing to the fierce urge to attack some unsuspecting little girl in the street, "He hoped the end was near." To the underworld boss Murillio, wistfully longing for in-tellectual and cultural companionship, the storm outside his penthouse window reminds him "of the poor Sicilian earth; he remembered how it looked, beaten by the rain" (245). And finally, Sol's nephew, Morton, who has just finished a charcoal portrait of his uncle in his hot sticky room, opens the window and stands "for a minute looking out at the invisible, heavily dripping darkness, the occasional shine of black leaves from unidentifiable light sources. The air felt cool and soothing on him" (246). Not in the mood to look at his new collection of pornographic pictures, he starts to cry, and "through his opened window, above the sound of the rain, he thought he heard, from the floor below, an echo of his crying."

What Morton hears is only a prelude to the flow of Sol's tears the next evening when the long drought is broken. At the climax of the novel, when Jesus intercepts the bullet meant for the pawnbroker, Sol's dry spell of self-imposed isolation and feigned indifference to others is ended. For the first time, in the presence of others, he begins to cry.

> And then the dry retching sound of weeping, growing louder and louder and louder, filling the Pawnbroker's ears, flooding him, drowning him, dragging him back to that sea of tears he had thought to have escaped. And he sat hunched against that abrasive roar, his body becoming worn down under the flood of it, washed down to the one polished stone of *grief*. (272)

This "grieving, loving identification with all mankind," says Max F. Schulz, is the result of Wallant's belief in "the Tolstoian ideal" that in order to "be human and whole, . . . we have no alternative to this redemptive anguish."[16]

The novel ends where it began, with Sol at the river. He can cry once again for all the victims of life, those dead and those still alive, the maimed and the sick. The image of the Harlem River flowing toward the sea expresses Wallant's awe at the vastness of life and the impenetrable mystery of death. Sol

> wiped his eyes clear again and . . . stood watching the river as it slid obscurely under the bridges toward the sea, bright and glittery in the boat lights on its surface, so vast in its total, never anything here and now, as it hurried slowly toward the obscurity of the salty ocean; so great, so touching in its fleeting presence. The wetness dried on his cheeks and a great calm came over him. (279)

The oxymoron "hurried slowly" effectively expresses the relentless movement of each man's life toward death, a passage that necessarily involves others who are on the same journey. As Sol prays for his dead to rest in peace, he takes "a great breath of air, which seemed to fill parts of his lungs unused for a long time. And he took the pain of it, if not happily, like a martyr, at least willingly, like an heir." With this epiphany of love, Sol heads for Tessie's apartment to join her in mourning for her dead.

CHAPTER 7

"More Green Growth Rising from the Burnt Black": *Mr. Sammler's Planet*

Though American authors were slow in responding to the immensity of the Holocaust, two major novels grappled impressively with the problem of Jewish survivors of Nazi atrocities. Both Wallant's *The Pawnbroker* (1961) and Bellow's *Mr. Sammler's Planet* (1970) have as their protagonists European scholars who have lost their wives to the Nazi murderers and who have themselves managed somehow to return from the dead. Both men now reside in New York City, but where Wallant's protagonist has built a wall around himself and become a caustic misanthrope, Bellow's older protagonist, now disillusioned with the scientific, humanistic optimism of H. G. Wells, has somehow maintained his love and compassion for his fellow humans, even though sorely tested by their eccentricities and imperfections. Where Sol Nazerman craves isolation and finds it painful to talk with relatives, customers, and strangers, Artur Sammler still enjoys the stimulation of discussing philosophical concepts with family, friends, and new acquaintances. Where the movement of Wallant's novel centers on Sol's eventual return to the mainstream of human relations, Bellow's Sammler, since the late fifties, has not been so isolated, so withdrawn into himself. Thus, in terms of plot, suspense, and character development, there is more interest and movement in *The Pawnbroker*; more introspection, more philosophical discussion, and more of a static quality in Bellow's novel. This does not mean that *Mr. Sammler's Planet* lacks conflict. On the contrary, the novel succeeds in creating considerable tension in its dialectical approach, its constant clash of ideas: the old versus the new, the real potency of thought versus the alleged potency of sex, the conservative versus the radical, the sane versus the insane, the stable versus the abnormal, and tempered optimism and hope versus bitter pessimism and despair.

Like Wallant, Bellow draws on many nature images to express these contrasts, to delineate character, to clarify theme, to lighten tone, and to enrich language. An example from the novel that accomplishes most of these objectives is the following passage, in which Artur Sammler, having observed the way Dr. Govinda Lal, the Asian biophsyicist working for NASA, has charmed Sammler, his daughter Shula, and his niece Margotte, realizes how different the two men are:

> But for himself, at this time of life and because he had come back from the other world, there were no rapid connections. His own first growth of affections had been consumed. His onetime human, onetime precious life had been burnt away. More green growth rising from the burnt black would simply be natural persistency, the Life Force working, trying to start again.[1]

It is this persistent "green growth rising from the burnt black" that Bellow celebrates in *Mr. Sammler's Planet*. However, early in the novel Sammler warns that one must be cautious in interpreting the symbols found in the natural environment. He remembers when he first "began to turn to the external world for curious ciphers and portents" (89). It was during the summer and autumn in wartime Poland when he had survived the Nazi extermination of the Jews and been hidden in a mausoleum that he became "a portent watcher," but he now considers this preoccupation "very childish, for many larger forms of meaning [for example, a belief in God and man's creation in God's image] had been stamped out . . ." (89–90). To a man hiding in a cemetery, every "straw, or a spider thread or a stain, a beetle or a sparrow had to be interpreted. Symbols everywhere, and metaphysical messages" (90). Mixed with Sammler's skepticism, however, is the hint that such potential symbols are hard to ignore.

Artur Sammler is no shallow optimist. He is a man who cannot "bear to face windows through which nothing but blue sky is visible" (295). When he smells the arrival of spring in the air, the sweet odors are a mixture of "Lilacs and sewage" (117). (Actually, "There were as yet no lilacs, but an element of the savage gas was velvety and sweet, reminiscent of blooming lilac.") Unlike Sol Nazerman, he is still capable of appreciating nature's charms and does not agonize over the deceptiveness of appearances. For example, while being driven to New Rochelle, he admires the Hudson River: "how beautiful, unclean, insidious! and there the bushes and the trees, cover for sexual violence, knifepoint robberies, sluggings, and murders. On the water bridgelight and moonlight lay smooth, enjoyably brilliant" (181). Over seventy years old, having been given a second life, he is still capable of feeling "Bliss from his surroundings!" (117). The sun feels good pouring through his gaps as if he were a Henry Moore sculpture (43). At first his Holocaust experiences made him resist "such physical impressions — being wooed almost comically by momentary and fortuitous sweetness. For quite a long time he had felt that he was not necessarily human" (117). During this period, he "Had no great use . . . for most creatures [and] very little interest in himself. Cold even to the thought of recovery."[2] This description of Sammler also fits Wallant's pawnborker — that is, until Nazerman's epiphany experience at the novel's climax. Artur Sammler's metamorphosis, on the other hand, occurred before the reader has even met him:

> But then, ten or twelve years after the war, he became aware that this too was changing. In the human setting along with everyone else, among particulars of ordinary life he *was* human — and, in short creatureliness crept in again. Its low tricks, its doggish hind-sniffing charm. So that now, really, Sammler didn't know how to take himself. (117)

"Doggish hind-sniffing charm"[3] is a most felicitous phrase to describe the animalism that Sammler has learned to tolerate as a necessary part of being human, of being alive. He is bemused by man's mixed nature, man's spiritual aspirations always in conflict with his animal needs. Sammler would like to be like God, disinterested, "free from the bondage of the ordinary and the finite. A soul released from Nature, from impressions, and from everyday life" (117). However, an old man who has learned "to be careful on public paths in New York, invariably dog-fouled, . . . the grass . . . all put out, burned by animal excrements . . ." (105), and who for convenience's sake sometimes urinates in the washbasin in his room "(rising on his toes to a meditation on the inherent melancholy of animal nature, continually in travail, according to Aristotle)" (15), is invariably reminded of his "creatureliness." Even though, says Bellow, one might expect that a Holocaust survivor "who has come back from the grave" (118) should be concerned only with the spiritual, "mysteriously enough, it happened . . . that one was always, and so powerfully, so persuasively drawn back into human conditions." Once again Bellow describes this duality in man, his shadow and substance, with imagery drawn from nature:

> So that these flecks within one's substance would always stipple with their reflections all that a man turns toward, all that flows about him. The shadow of his nerves will always cast stripes, like trees on grass, like water over sand, the light-made network. It was a second encounter of the distinterested spirit with fated biological necessities, a return match with the persistent creature. (118)

Echoes from Melville, one of Bellow's favorite authors, can be found in a later passage, in which Mr. Sammler realizes that he is no Captain Ahab pursuing a symbolic white whale. Sammler sometimes feels that he is now "*out* of it, *hors d' usage*, not a man of the times. No force of nature, nothing paradoxical or demonic, he had no drive for smashing through the mask of appearances. Not 'Me and the Universe'" (136). Where Ahab dealt only with absolutes and sought knowledge never meant for man, Sammler's "personal idea was one of the human being conditioned by other human beings, and knowing that present arrangements were not, *sub specie aeternitatis*, the truth, but that one should be satisfied with such truth as one could get by approximation." In short, Sammler's creed is "Trying to live with a civil heart. With disinterested charity. With a sense of the mystic potency of humankind. With an inclination to believe in archetypes of goodness." Unfortunately, life in New York City in the 1960s is a constant challenge to such beliefs. Goodness is hard to find.

America in the 1960s is in a constant state of turmoil. The civil rights movement, student protests, rampant crime and violence, a sexual revolution, and American involvement in an unpopular war are all part of a national turbulence that provides the backdrop and sometimes even the foreground of Bellow's novel. When Sammler lectures on this revolutionary cauldron to Dr. Lal, Margotte, and Shula at the Gruner home near New Rochelle, he draws a perceptive distinction between two modern views of nature. The first is urban man's craving for a return to nature in the form of "a park, a zoo, a botanical garden, a world's fair, an Indian reservation" (227). This, of course, is a civilized, orderly, controlled approach to nature, but in the revolutionary sixties there is an opposite, disruptive force at work:

> there are always human beings who take it upon themselves to represent or interpret the old savagery, tribalism, the primal fierceness of the fierce, lest we forget prehistory, savagery, animal origins. It is even said, here and there, that the real purpose of civilization is to permit us all to live like primitive people and lead a neolithic life in an automated society. (227)

"Prehistory, savagery, animal origins"—this is what Bellow's protagonist is confronted with daily in New York, this modern "Sodom and Gomorrah" (304). It is as if the evolutionary process were reversed and atavism, the revolutionary password. Bellow, like Dos Passos and Wallant, expresses this social criticism through a great many animal images, particularly those depicting apes and monkeys. When, for example, Mr. Sammler tries to give at Columbia University a guest lecture on the Bloomsbury Circle, he is crudely interrupted and insulted by dissidents in the audience. The civilized, Oxonian scholar is astonished by "All this confused sex-excrement-militancy, explosiveness, abusiveness, tooth-showing, Barbary ape howling" (43). These radical students are "like the spider monkeys in the trees, . . . defecating into their hands, and shrieking, pelting the explorers below." Later, when Shula takes Dr. Lal's NASA manuscript a second time, Sammler empathizes with the distraught scientist and wryly defends his motivation for wanting to leave earth and colonize the moon: "humankind kept doing the same stunts over and over. . . . Barking, hissing, ape-chatter, and spitting" (174). But Sammler never loses sight of man's other side, his "civilized, orderly, controlled" approach to nature. Repelled by the simian characteristics, he can still marvel at the regularity of workers, "however rebellious at heart" (146), as they arrive at their jobs and perform their assigned tasks. "For such a volatile and restless animal, such a high-strung curious animal, an ape subject to so many diseases, to anguish, boredom, such discipline, such drill, such strength for regularity, such assumption of responsibility, such regard for order (even in disorder) is a mystery, too" (146–47). An even greater part of this mystery is man's capacity for love. Sammler must continue to believe that "there were times when Love seemed life's great architect. Weren't there?" (174). Though this hope dims at times, he does see it glow in Shula's, Margotte's, and Elya's love for him and his love for them.

Ape-monkey-baboon imagery reappears throughout *Mr. Sammler's Planet* as Bellow describes the gallery of eccentrics that populate his novel and as he satirizes the "ape restiveness" (237) of the times. Walter Bruch, for example, an occasional visitor in his sixties, insists on describing to his reluctant listener, Artur Sammler, his erotic fettishism with women's bare arms. Sammler does not want to hear all the sordid details, but Bruch, using Sammler as his psychiatrist or guru, pleads for his understanding: "His flat nose dilated, his mouth open, he was spurting tears and, apelike, twisting his shoulders, his trunk" (60). At F. A. O. Schwarz, Bruch buys himself toys, "wind-up monkeys who combed their hair in a mirror, who banged cymbals and danced jigs, in little green jackets or red caps" (61), and plays with them in his room alone. When Bruch tells a joke, "he rolled with laughter. Ape-like, he put his hands on his paunch and closed his eyes, letting the tongue hang out of his blind head" (284). Shula Sammler's atrocious wig, which at least one hair dresser has refused to set, is composed of "mixed yak and baboon hair and synthetic fibers" (34). Less farcical, but still contributing to the light tone and comic book fantasy of men in rocketships, is Dr. Lal's defense of space travel as more than mere "show biz" (217). The new technology, he tells Sammler, will impress people more than new personalities. "The astronauts may not seem so very heroic. More like superchimpanzees."

The creatureliness of man can also be seen in several dog images, such as Sammler's observing in the bearded Dr. Lal "The sensitivity of a hairy creature; the animal brown of his eyes; the good breeding of his attentive posture" (211). Bellow introduces Sammler himself on the second page with a similar image: "the good eye was dark-bright, full of observation through the overhanging hairs of the brow as in some breeds of dog" (4). Sammler thinks of his crazy Israeli son-in-law as "poor dog-laughing Eisen" (294), but when Wallace refers to his dying father as "like a dog in the manger" (241), Sammler objects to this demeaning figure of speech and would like to see Wallace show more respect for Elya. Dogs in *Mr. Sammler's Planet* more generally are connected with the pollution and sexuality of the modern urban environment. Reference has already been made to the "dog-fouled . . . grass" in parks and "doggish hind-sniffing charm," but the most erotic animal image to depict the sexual exhibitionism of the sixties is Sammler's description of the students hired by Shula to read to him: "he no longer wanted these readers with the big dirty boots and the helpless vital pathos of young dogs with their first red erections . . ." (37). Dog imagery takes on even darker connotations when Sammler remembers seeing these animals as scavengers during the 1967 Arab-Israeli war. As a correspondent, he saw many dead Arabs lying in the desert: "Swollen gigantic arms, legs, roasted in the sun. The dogs ate human roast" (250). Mr. Sammler's evident dislike of dogs is summed up in his wry observation of the feces in parks: "One would have said that only the Eskimos had nearly so much to do with dogs as this local branch of mankind. The veterinarians must be sailing in yachts, surely. Their fees were high" (116).

Further evidence of Sammler's view of the creatureliness of modern man is found in the Stuyvesant Park scene when he stops to sit for ten minutes to read Dr. Lal's manuscript and get his mind off the dying Elya. "He noted a female bum drunkenly sleeping like a dugong, a sea cow's belly rising, legs swollen purple; a short dress, a mini-rag. At a corner of the fence, a wino was sullenly pissing on newspapers and leaves" (106). He also sees some younger people, barefoot, wearing woolen ponchos, looking Peruvian: "Natives of somewhere. Innocent, devoid of aggression, opting out, much like Fredinand the Bull. No *corrida* for them; only smelling flowers under the lovely cork tree." This couple reminds him of "the Eloi of H. G. Wells' fantasy *The Time Machine*. Lovely young human cattle herded by the cannibalistic Morlocks who lived a subterranean life and feared light and fire." As Bellow moves easily from the amusing image of the dugong to the scatology of the wino, from the lovable Ferdinand to the cannibalistic Morlocks, he reinforces his view of modern man's animal nature.

Other animals are referred to in passing in descriptions of Angela, Shula, Emil, Lionel Feffer, and Sammler himself. Angela, who, like Bruch, loves to describe to Sammler all of her amorous adventures, explains how she told her recent lover Wharton Hornicker, "'We're going to fuck all night!' But first she had to have a bath. Because she had been longing all evening for him. 'Oh, a woman is a skunk. So many odors, Uncle'" (71). Bellow describes her "hair with its dyed streaks like raccoon fur, smelling of Arabian musk" (70). Sammler is well aware of "That effect of the hair called frosting, that color under the lioness's muzzle, that swagger to enhance the natural color of the bust!" (31). Shula, whose hearing is much better than her father's, has "keen senses. Idiot ingenuous animal, she had ears like a fox" (201). When she steals Dr. Lal's manuscript from the top of her father's desk, Sammler is distressed but not surprised; he "knew her ways; knew them as the Eskimo knows the ways of the seal. Its breathing-holes" (173). Elya Gruner's loyal chauffeur Emil "had the wolfish North Italian look" (268), and Feffer, "less student than promoter," has a "brown beaver beard" (38). Sammler, as war correspondent in the Middle East, "thought of himself as a camel among the armored vehicles" (142).

None of the above is meant to suggest that Bellow is an allegorist, a Ben Jonson writing *Volpone*. Sammler repeatedly denies that he is a judge of mankind and claims that he is just a curious observer. He claims he dislikes people who have explanations for everything, but he is always trying to explain things to himself and others. When, for example, toward the end of the novel he considers blaming Churchill and Roosevelt for not bombing Auschwitz, he pulls back, because individuals cannot make such judgments. At best, he sees himself as an

> intermediate judge. But never final. Existence was not accountable to him. Indeed not. Nor would he ever put together the inorganic, organic, natural, bestial, human, and superhuman in any dependable arrangement but, however fascinating and original his genius, only idiosyncratically, a shaky scheme, mainly decorative or ingenious. (277)[4]

Here, perhaps, is a clue to Bellow's artistic intentions. No absolute allegorist, he simply observes modern man's creatureliness, fascinated by his bizarre behavior. No rigid schematization is intended, but Bellow's animal imagery, certainly "idiosyncratic" and "ingenious," is far from being "mainly decorative." Part of the novel's dialectic, it functions as interior structure, interweaving characterization and theme.

The most important (and controversial) animal imagery in *Mr. Sammler's Planet* is found in Bellow's treatment of the black pickpocket who displays his genitals to Mr. Sammler as a form of intimidation, a warning to the vulnerable witness of his crimes. A grotesque inversion of the noble savage, Bellow's Queequeg cannibalizes his unsuspecting victims on the New York City buses from Columbus Circle to Verdi Square. Sammler thinks of him in his "camel's hair coat" and "single gold earring" (14) as "this African prince or great black beast." The man's "face showed the effrontery of a big animal" (5), and later, when he traps Mr. Sammler in his hotel lobby and pushes him from behind, the thief never speaks a word. "He no more spoke than a puma would" (49). The pickpocket's exposed penis is described as "a tube, a snake, . . . the tip curled beyond the supporting, demonstrating hand, suggesting the fleshly mobility of an elephant's trunk, though the skin was somewhat iridescent rather than thick or rough" (49). In chapter 2, Sammler remembers the black's penis as "the lizard-thick curving tube in the hand, dusty stale pinkish chocolate color and strongly suggesting the infant it was there to beget. Ugly, odious; laughable, but nevertheless important" (65).

Artur Sammler easily comprehends the meaning of this erotic symbolism. The pickpocket's exhibitionism is his way of expressing power and authority:

> Oh, the transcending, ultimate, and silencing proof. We hold these things, man, to be self-evident. And yet, such sensitive elongations the anteater had, too, uncomplicated by assertions of power, even over ants. But make Nature your God, elevate creatureliness, and you can count on gross results. Maybe you can count on gross results under any circumstances. (55)

Here is the supreme symbol of the sexual revolution of the sixties, sex as primal force, potentate, be-all and end-all of existence. Unfortunately, in making his thief a black man, Bellow has left himself vulnerable to charges of racism. The black pickpocket is the racist stereotype of the black stud and criminal.[5] Bellow could have made his same point about sexual barbarism with a white exhibitionist, but he chose the more exotic eroticism to titillate white readers. Both Wallace and Feffer are fascinated by the black's genitals and try to pump Sammler for descriptive details. Feffer is worried about the old man's naïveté about such things: "You're wise but not hip, and this cat, Mr. Sammler, sounds like a real tiger" (119–20). The dialogue between Wallace and his uncle on the drive to New Rochelle would be even more delightfully humorous than it is, were it not for the undertones of racism. When Sammler is reluctant to supply the anatomical description Wallace requests, Wallace presses on: "Oh, Uncle, suppose I were a zoologist who had never seen a live leviathan but you knew Moby Dick from the whaleboat? Was is sixteen, eighteen inches?" (185). Wallace asks if it was "uncircumcised" and then wonders "if women really prefer that kind of thing." Sammler answers, "'I assume they have other interests in addition,'" but Wallace disagrees: "That's what they say. But you know you can't trust them. They're animals, aren't they" (185). As the "intermediate judge," Sammler tries to soften Wallace's mysogyny: "Temporarily there is an animal emphasis." Wallace's angry reply is to call his sister Angela "a pig . . . a swine" (186). Later, as Sammler reflects on his traumatic encounter with the black, he reviews its meaning: "unbottoning his puma-colored coat in puma silence to show himself. Was this the sort of fellow called by Goethe *eine Natur*? A primary force?" (282). Accordingly, when a few pages later Bellow describes this man beating Feffer, who has photographed him in action on the bus, he emphasizes the black's "intense animal-pressing power," as Feffer's assailant rises on his toes in his "alligator shoes! In fawn-colored trousers!" (288)[6]

Bellow's animal imagery is unlike that used by Emile Zola and Frank Norris. In their naturalistic novels, Zola and Norris describe characters (for instance, the miners in *Germinal*, the dentist in *McTeague*) in terms of animals to emphasize their victimization by environmental and hereditary forces over which they have no control. These characters are caught up in sexual drives and needs that they cannot understand; they cannot escape from the inherent violence that ultimately destroys them. According to Charles Walcutt, a character like McTeague

> probably thinks and chooses, but the novel concerns itself with the objects and actions that exist outside of his mind; in the crises, the actions of the leading characters are fully treated, while the accompanying cerebration is assumed to be part or function of the action rather than its cause. The causes are physical, instinctive, and dependent upon external circumstance.[7]

The differences between Norris and Bellow are obvious. In *Mr. Sammler's Planet*, there is very little external action. The objects and actions that stimulate Sammler's mind exist for no other purpose. Sammler's cerebration is the raison d'être of the novel. Where Norris's atavism underscores his protagonist's pathetic lack of free will, Bellow endows his protagonist with an intelligence that enables him to transcend his creaturely needs and limitations. Artur Sammler may be dependent on the patronage of Elya Gruner for his survival in America, but the brilliance of Sammler's mind and his self-deprecating sense of humor raise him far above the level of Norris's brontosaurus.

Bellow is above all an intellectual writer. He is fascinated by the challenge of ideas, old and new, and his protagonists forever seek an intellectual synthesis that will make sense of an urban world that is often anarchic and irrational. In his serach for language to express this meaning, to give form and order to the seeming chaos of existence, Bellow frequently draws on nature to clarify the abstract. He is no transcendentalist like Emerson and Thoreau, insisting on a fixed, mystical correspondence between the seen and unseeable. He is, however, the eternal storyteller who draws on the natural and familiar to make understandable the speculative and philosophical. Thus animals, insects, birds, fish, flowers, plants, geological formations, and even planets, become vehicles for ideas; metaphors to carry philosophical observations that might otherwise be dry and uninteresting. In this manner, these images become an integral part of the novel's rich interior structure.

Bellow's novel is filled with examples of nature images used for this purpose. When Sammler thinks how modern intellectuals spend so much time explaining things to others who do not listen anyway, he conceives of man's soul as a bird: "The soul wanted what it wanted. It had its own natural knowledge. It sat unhappily on superstructures of explanation, poor bird, not knowing which way to fly" (3–4). Later, when he is unsuccessfully trying to convince the amoral Shula that she was wrong in stealing Dr. Lal's manuscript, Sammler's harassed soul is conceived of again in terms of bird imagery: "It seemed . . . that inside him . . . was a field in which many hunters at cross-purposes were firing bird-shot at a feather apparition assumed to be a bird. Shula had meant to set him a test. Was he the real thing or wasn't he?" (199). When Dr. Lal, at supper in Elya's New Rochelle home, tries to explain that man cannot comprehend things going on in his head and may thus delude himself, he draws the following analogy: "In very much the same way as a lizard or a rat or a bird cannot comprehend being organisms. But a human being, owing to dawning comprehension, may well feel that he is a rat who lives in a temple" (225). Sammler has his own analogy in contemplating those areas of his brain where he stores private thoughts during "internal consultation." He humbly sees them as "mental dry courses in his head, of no interest to anyone else perhaps — wadis, he believed such things were called, small ravines made by the steady erosion of preoccupations. The taking of life was one of these" (144). One last example of this kind of nature metaphor used to vivify mental activities or philosophical observations is Sammler's pointing out that man is incapable of comprehending his own biological and chemical subtlety: "They say our protoplasm is like sea water. Our blood has a Mediterranean base. But now we live in a social and human sea" (227).[8]

In *Mr. Sammler's Planet*, Dr. Govinda Lal is, at times, a reflector of Artur Sammler as both men wish for a world of order, for rational explanations of enigmatic phenomena. When Lal tells Sammler that "to desire to live without order is to desire to turn from the fundamental biological governing principle" (216), he expresses dryly and scientifically what Sammler explains with a fascinating analogy: "It is sometimes necessary to repeat what all know. All mapmakers should place the Mississippi in the same location, and avoid originality. It may be boring, but one has to know where he is. We cannot have the Mississippi flowing towards the Rockies for a change" (228). But Bellow cannot resist allowing even Dr. Lal an occasional literary flourish.[9] For example, after his just quoted appeal for a life of order, he attacks modern madness and impulsive behavior and makes the sage observation that "the ant was once a hero, but now the grasshopper is the whole show" (216). A little later, in this same dialogue with Sammler, Lal defends the need for interplanetary exploration despite its huge costs when the money is needed so desperately for social services on this planet. Lal uses an analogy that draws heavily on nature imagery. From the moment of birth, Lal says, man is propelled outward. "To see the sidereal archipelagoes is one thing, but to plunge into them, into a dayless, nightless universe, why, that, you see, makes sea-depth petty, the leviathan no more than a polliwog — " (222). These contrasts between ants and grasshoppers, polliwogs and leviathans, with their echoes of ancient parables, add a mythological flavor to a novel that asks its readers to give serious thought to the possibility of man's leaving his familiar habitat and venturing into the immensities of outer space.

Like one of his favorite philosophers, Søren Kierkegaard, Sammler believes that the world of the finite and usual is all that man needs in his pursuit of knowledge of the infinite. Sammler recalls with pleasure ". . . Kierkegaard's comical account of people traveling around the world to see rivers and mountains, new stars, birds of rare plumage, queerly deformed fishes, ridiculous breeds of men — tourists abandoning themsleves to the bestial stupor which gapes at existence and thinks it has seen something" (62). Like Emerson and Thoreau, Kierkegaard makes fun of those travelers always seeking the "extraordinary in the world. . . . They themselves wanted to be the birds of rare plumage, the queerly deformed fishes, the ridiculous breeds of men" (62–63). Artur Sammler sees such ridiculous figures every day, close at home, in the streets and parks of New York. In a Whitmanesque catalogue of the eccentrics he sees on Broadway, he lists "the barbarian, redskin, or Fiji, the dandy, the buffalo hunter, the desperado, the queer, the sexual fantasists, the squaw, bluestocking, princess, poet, painter, prospector, troubador, guerilla, Che Guevera, the new Thomas à Becket" (147). In short, "Madness makes interest" (146).

Madness also makes clutter. Bellow has great fun using plant, flower, and other organic imagery to describe Margotte Arkin, who is a little better housekeeper than Shula, but not by much. Like Shula, Margotte saves junk, breeds it. Her uncle does not enjoy the jungle she surrounds him with in the apartment.

> She planted avacado pits, lemon seeds, peas, potatoes. Was there anything ever so mangy, trashy, as those potted objects? Shrubs and vines dragged on the ground, tried to rise on grocer's string hopefully stapled fanwise to the ceiling. The stems of the avacadoes looked like the sticks of fireworks, falling back after the flash, and produced a few rusty, spiky, anthrax-damaged nitty leaves. (21)

Cautioning the reader against reading too much symbolism into the description of her plants, Bellow facetiously adds, "This botanical ugliness, the product of so much fork-digging, watering, so much breast and arm, heart and hope, told you something, didn't it? First of all, it told you that the individual facts were filled with messages and meanings, but you couldn't be sure what the messages meant" (21). An example of the excessive analysis Sammler objects to is Margotte's drawing on the organic imagery of trees and plants to explain to her uncle her understanding of Hannah Arendt's theory of "the banality of evil." The thousands of German workers — the Lumpenproletariat — the masses who simply did their daily jobs with no monstrous spirit of evil and made the Nazi bureaucracy function smoothly are, she explains, what Arendt had in mind behind her striking phrase: "It's like instead of a forest with enormous trees, you have to think of small plants with shallow roots" (16). Sammler quickly tires of this intellectual discussion, but not before attacking Arendt's theory, explaining that it was part of the German genius to make "the century's greatest crime look dull . . ." (18). German methodology, whether in war industry or "aesthetic fanaticism," that is, "the aesthetic machine, the philosophic machine, the mythomanic machine, the culture machine . . . !" was all part of the effort "to promote the foolish ideas of Weimar intellectuals" (19). To Sammler, "the important consideration was that life should recover its plenitude, its normal contented turgidity. All the old fusty stuff had to be blown away, of course, so we might be nearer to nature. To be nearer to nature was necessary in order to keep in balance the achievements of modern Method."

Sammler, who is getting a headache from all of this analysis, conjectures that Margotte "wanted a bower in her living room, a screen of glossy leaves, flowers, a garden, blessings of freshness and beauty — something to foster as woman the germinatrix, the matriarch of reservoirs and gardens" (21). In short, she represents "Humankind, crazy for symbols, trying to utter what it doesn't know itself." Worst of all, he concludes, "these frazzled plants would not, could not respond. There was not enough light. Too much clutter." Bellow has never had much respect for the literary critic as obsessive symbol hunter, and here he makes his point again, at the same time that he uses all the plant imagery as a delightful part of the characterization of Sammler's niece. It is hard to dislike a person who, "in honor of spring. . . . had set forsythia in Mason jars" (126).

A wonderfully comic example of the kind of pseudo-scientific pretense at intellectuality that Bellow scorns is Sammler's recollection of a public television program that he and Margotte watched one night. A "singular botanist" attached a lie detector "to flowers and recorded the reaction of roses to gentle and violent stimuli. Stridency made them shrink, he said. A dead dog cast before them caused aversion. A soprano singing lullabies had the opposite effect" (258). Sammler concludes "that the investigator himself, his pale leer, his wild stern police nose would distress roses, African violets."

Flower imagery is also used to characterize the eccentric Shula. To seduce Dr. Lal, she makes a dramatic entrance dressed in a kind of sari which covers her head correctly, but not her bust. She is wearing no undergarments. "She was extremely white — citrus-thick skin, cream cheeks — and her lips, looking fuller and softer than ever, were painted a peculiar orange color. Like the Neapolitan cyclamens Sammler admired in the botanical garden" (206). The morning after the flood in Elya's home, Sammler finds his daughter in the garden talking to the flowers. "It was warm. Tulips, daffodils, jonquils, and a paradise of gusts. Evidently she asked the flowers how they were today. No answers required. Brilliant instance sufficed. She herself was a brilliant instance of something organically strange" (258). Sammler the great analyzer concludes that his no longer married daughter with her thinning hair is attracted by "the natural abundance, growth power, exuberance that she admired in flowers" (263). Observing her "among the blond openmouthed daffodils, which were being poured back and forth by the wind, her father believed that she was in love" with Dr. Lal. Wallace, who had earlier observed his cousin Shula "whispering to the flowers in the garden" (177), attributes her strange behavior to "Those talking flowers. The garden of live flowers" in *Alice in Wonderland*, which he used to read to her.

Wallace himself could easily step out of the pages of *Alice in Wonderland*. He is the twentieth-century advantaged intellectual who cannot find himself, a descendant of Bellow's Eugene Henderson, the quintessential "becomer"; Wallace has "nearly" become a physicist, mathematician, lawyer "(he had even passed the bar and opened an office, once)" (88), an engineer, "a Ph. D. in behavioral science," a licensed pilot, an alchololic, and a homosexual. His latest scheme is to go into business with Lionel Feffer taking aerial photographs of the trees and shrubs around country homes. The plan is to show the pictures to the homeowner and offer to "identify the trees and shrubs on the place and band them handsomely in Latin and English," because "People feel ignorant about the plants on their property" (99). The entrepreneurs will have to hire a graduate student in botany. Later, when Feffer describes this business enterprise to Sammler, he admits it is a little "hokey," but insists that it has great potential and they are thinking of going national. "We'll need regional plant specialists. The problem would be different in Portland, Oregon, from Miami Beach or Austin, Texas" (111). Feffer, a fledgling con artist, tries to impress Sammler by quoting the first sentence of Aristotle's *Metaphysics:* "All men by nature desire to know," but quickly confesses, "I never got much farther, but I figured the rest must be out of date anyway. However, if they desire to know, it makes them depressed if they can't name the bushes on their own property. They feel like phonies. The bushes belong. They themselves don't" (111)[10] Feffer compares labeling trees to psychiatrists' tagging patients with names of disorders to give them a psychological boost. If people want things named or renamed," he confidently concludes, "you can make dough by becoming a taxonomist."

Bellow is at his comic best in characterizing Wallace, whose bizarre behavior keeps him in constant trouble. Once he flew to Tangiers to buy a horse to visit Morocco and Tunisia and was robbed in Morocco but still managed to ride into Russia on horseback before being detained in Soviet Armenia. Another time he carelessly parked his father's Rolls and let it slip into the bottom of a reservoir. Wallace attributes his unusual experiences to the fact that he is a Gemini: "Lily of the valley is my birth flower," he tells his uncle. "Did you know the lily of the valley was very poisonous?" (244). This "poisonous" influence continues to plague him, as he floods his dying father's home while looking in the pipes for hidden money and crash lands an airplane after scraping the wheels off on a house. With whimsical understatement, Sammler gently reproves his nephew: "You've done a lot of peculiar things. No one can call you boring" (101). And much later, reflecting on Margotte's potted plants, Wallace's incipient shrub business, and Shula's talking to the flowers, Sammler jokes that "It would be too bad if the first contacts of plants were entirely with the demented. Maybe I'd better have a word with them myself" (259).

Since Sarah Blacher Cohen has written the definitive study of Bellow's humor,[11] it is unnecessary here to elaborate on the author's comic use of language (already evident throughout this chapter), except to point out the frequency of nature imagery as a part of this humor. Once again it is Bellow's instinctive return to the familiar and usual to explain the abstract and unusual. That the result is often humorous simply adds to the novel's transcendence over the dismal reality and pain of existence.

Though man's vaunted intellect raises him above the animals, Bellow never allows him to get too complacent or conceited. Insect and amphibian imagery serves to deflate the filling balloon. Sammler, for example, finds Dr. Lal very likable, but thinks of him "as an Eastern curiosity, a bushy little planet-buzzing Oriental demon, mentally rebounding from limits like a horsefly from a glass" (223). As Sammler observes several small planes in the air above New Rochelle, he is correct in assuming that Wallace is "piloting one of them. Unto himself a roaring center. To us, a sultry beetle, a gnat propelling itself through blue acres" (267). When Sammler is surprised at how much Feffer knows about campus security and the Pinkertons at Columbia, he tells the young man, "I am astonished by the amount of information that sticks to you. You remind me of a frog's tongue. It flips out and comes back covered with gnats" (113).

Sometimes the nature image is less comical and more grotesque. The resulting humor mixes a little involuntary shiver with the laugh. This trait is what Bellow once said was characteristic of Yiddish fiction: "Laughter and trembling are so curiously mingled that it is not easy to determine the relation of the two."[12] In *Mr. Sammler's Planet*, Shula's pet chicken is a case in point. Shula kept an Easter chick in the bathroom of their twelfth-floor apartment when her father lived with her after her return from Israel. "The hen with yellow legs in his room on his documents and books was too much one day" (27).

The claustrophobia of the apartment and the ugly yellow legs trigger off the memory of the few months he had hidden in the mausoleum in Poland to escape death. "And during this period there was a yellow tinge to everything, a yellow light in the sky. In this light, bad news for Sammler, bad news for humankind, bad information about the very essence of being was diffused" (90). Sammler thinks of Elya Gruner's impending death and dreads what remains for him — "that bad literalness, the yellow light of Polish summer heat behind the mausoleum door. It was the light also of that china-cabinet room in the apartment where he suffered confinement with Shula-Slava" (92). And when Sammler recalls life in Cracow before World War II, he remembers "desperate darkness, the dreary liquid yellow mud to a depth of two inches over the cobblestones in the Jewish streets" (31–32). The mud in this last passage contributes to the negative connotations of yellow which Sammler associates with Shula's pet chicken, his migraine headaches, and the strange light in the sky around the Polish mausoleum.

But yellow in *Mr. Sammler's Planet* can also have mixed connotations. The sunset can be so beautiful to a city dweller that the "maladroit" (17) Margotte forgets to lock the window after admiring the view, and her apartment is robbed. This same mixture of the pleasant and unpleasant can be seen when Margotte goes off to inform Dr. Lal of the location of his stolen manuscript, and Bellow describes the white Spry sign beginning to flash across the Hudson, "while in the sunset copper the asphalt belly of the street was softly disfigured, softly rank, with its manhole covers" (134). The most beautiful poetic image to describe the sun is found late in the novel when Sammler reflects on his Polish adventures and flight to Israel. In Athens, he was waiting for an El Al plane to take off when "Just then the sun ran up from the sea like a red fox" (249). The most traditional sun image appears when Sammler returns to the streets of New York after his interrupted lecture at Columbia. His vision seems strangely improved as he sees things more sharply. It is early spring, and he sees "the dogwood white, pink, blooming crabapple," and the tulips near Rockefeller Center. "The sun shone as if there were no death" (44). However, the corrective appears somewhat later as the April sunshine in New York City reminds him of the Polish spring thirty years ago when he, his wife, and other victims had to dig their own grave. Rarely does Sammler have an unadulterated thought about spring. As he contemplates the coming fullness of spring in New York, he thinks of "The Cross County, the Saw Mill River, the Henry Hudson thick with reviving grass and dandelions, the oven of the sun baking green life again" (277). To Sammler, "Spring lost the touch of winter and got the summer rankness" (279). The negative connotations of the sun as an "oven" and "summer rankness" help prepare the reader for Sammler's sober reflection that green growth in modern urban America has lost its pastoral quality: "green in the city had lost its association with peaceful sanctuary. The old-time poetry of parks was banned. Obsolete thickness of shade leading to private meditation. Truth was not slummier and called for litter in the setting—leafy reverie? A thing of the past" (279).

While the sun is a traditional metaphor for truth and fertility, the truth it reveals can be dismaying and oppressive. Feeling sorry for Wallace, who had to land his plane without wheels, and for the black pickpocket bloodied by Eisen, Sammler sees "everything with heightened clarity. . . . To see was delicious. Oh, of course! An extreme pleasure! The sun may shine, and be a blessing, but sometimes shows the fury of the world. Brightness like this, the vividness of everything, also dismayed him" (298). Looking out the window, Sammler notices that "the streaked glass ran with light like honey. A barrage of sweetness and intolerable brightness was laid down" (298). When Angela is angered in the hospital by his criticism of her inappropriate miniskirt, "the sunlight was yellow, sweet. It was horrible" (300). More horrible is Sammler's vivid recollection of the swollen Arab corpses in the Gaza Strip and "the great sun wheel of white desert in which these Egyptian corpses and machines were embedded . . ." (252).

As important as sun imagery is in *Mr. Sammler's Planet*, of even greater significance are those images involving the moon. Their importance lies in their connection with the novel's central theme—the degraded quality of life in urban America in the 1960s and man's option of starting life afresh in the lunar environment. According to Porter, "The moon serves in the novel as the central symbol for both the goal of advanced technology and the future of Man. But, in Sammler's view, the technological advances appear to be occurring in a moral void, and thus the future of Man is uncertain, another major theme" (172). Bellow's views here are a twentieth-century extension of the Adamic theme traced so brilliantly by R. W. B. Lewis in *The American Adam*. According to Lewis, "the American myth saw life and history as just beginning. It described the world as starting up again under fresh initiative, in a divinely granted second chance for the human race, after the first chance had been so disastrously fumbled in the darkening Old World."[13] Bellow explores in *Mr. Sammler's Planet* the possibility that mankind has been given a third chance. Sammler is intrigued by Lal's theories, although he cannot accept them.[14] He likes Lal's philosophical and social thoughtfulness. Lal "seemed aware, for instance, that the discovery of America had raised hopes in the sinful Old World of a new Eden. 'A shared consciousness,' Lal had written, 'may well be the new America. Access to central data mechanisms may foster a new Adam'" (135). Thus it is evident that moon imagery in Bellow's novel is not used merely for romantic or aesthetic embellishment, but is an integral part of the novel's dialectic. Sammler's discussions with Dr. Lal not only give dramatic form to the theory of colonization of the moon, but also enable Bellow to probe moral, social, even philosophical and theological implications of such scientific achievement.

Moon imagery as aesthetic embellishment or affective setting has only minor use in *Mr. Sammler's Planet*. As Sammler arrives with the chauffeur at Elya's suburban home, he can momentarily forget the pollution and decay of the city and relax in the pleasant countryside. He remembers how as a refugee in 1947, he "had been astonished" at the sight of the Gruner family playing badminton on their vast, trim lawn which was now "lighted by the moon. . . . The elms were thick, old — older than the combined ages of all the Gruners. Animal eyes appeared in the headlights, or beveled reflectors set out on the borders of paths shone: mouse, mole, woodchuck, cat, or glass bits peering from grass and bush" (191). Inside, "The moon rinsed the curtains and foamed like peroxide on the nap of the white heavy carpets" (192). Passages from Shakespeare and Milton spring to Sammler's mind, both involving the moon. The line from Shakespeare is quoted when he reflcts on the reasons for Shula's behavior and attributes it to her love for him and the absence of a lover in her life. He thinks of the lovesick Cleopatra's lines when Antony is dying. The world without Antony would be to he like a sty: "There is nothing left remarkable Beneath the visiting moon" (197). Earlier in the novel, when Wallace was doing a crossword puzzle and asked his uncle for a word meaning dance, Sammler supplied "morrice" and remembered a line from Milton's *Comus*: "Now to the Moon in wavering Morrice move" (97), explaining, "It's the fishes, by the billions, I believe, and the seas themselves, performing the dance."[15]

Thoughts of moon colonization help keep Sammler's mind from thoughts of the dying Elya: "He could not cope with the full sum of facts about him. Remote considerations seemed to help — the moon, its lifelessness, its deathlessness. A white corroded pearl" (105). Chapter 2 begins with Dr. Lal's lecture notes, dry, basic, scientific facts about the size and environment of the moon. Later, when Sammler stops in Stuyvesant Park to read some of Lal's manuscript, he is fascinated by the biophysicist's speculation on the kinds of plants that might be able to grow there, speculation on organisms possibly capable of adapting themselves in exposed lunar conditions. Were there no plants which might cover the moon's surface? Water and carbon dioxide would have to be present, extremes of temperature would have to be withstood. Lichens, thought Govinda, possibly could make it. Also certain members of the cactus family. The triumphant plant, a combination of lichen and cactus, certainly would look weird to the eyes of man. But life's capacities are even now inconceivably diverse. What impossibilities has it not faced? Who knows what the depths of the seas may yet yield? Creatures, perhaps even one to a species. A grotesque individual which has found its equilibrium under twenty miles of water. (107)[16]

Artur Sammler is just such a tough hybrid, a combination of cactus and lichen, capable of surviving in a hostile environment. With his one "opaque guppy eye" (255), Sammler might also qualify as "a grotesque individual which has found its equilibrium." Striving for humility, however, he denies his uniqueness. Others have also had painful experiences and somehow endured them. "Surely some Navaho, Apache must have fallen into the Grand Canyon, survived, picked himself up, possibly said nothing to his tribe" (137).

The opening line of Dr. Lal's notebook, *The Future of the Moon*, asks, "How long . . . will this earth remain the only home of Man?" (51). Right after his confrontation with the black pickpocket, Sammler thinks that this might be the time to leave Earth: "A time to gather stones together, a time to cast away stones. Considering the earth itself not as a stone cast but as something to cast oneself from — to be divested of. To blow this great blue, white, green planet or to be blown from it" (51). Feffer urges Sammler to appear on a television talk show, tell about the pickpocket, and "denounce New York. You should speak like a prophet, like from another world" (122).

But Sammler refuses to succumb to despair, although he is constantly tested. He refuses to denounce New York, as Feffer requests. Bellow's Old Testament prophet can see both sides. He realizes that with future colonization of the moon, earth will no longer be the center of the universe. "The earth [is] a memorial park, a merry-go-round cemetery. The seas powdering our bones like quartz, making sand, grinding our peace for us by the aeon" (135). Nevertheless, we also "know from photographs the astronauts took, the beauty of the earth, its white and its blue, its fleeces, the great glitter afloat. A glorious planet."

Artur Sammler remains hopeful. Schopenhauer, he tells Dr. Lal, once called the Jews "vulgar optimists," but Sammler defends his people: "Optimists? Living near the crater of Vesuvius, it is better to be an optimist" (209). Unlike Wallace, who is the 512th person to phone Pan Am for a reservation for a trip to the moon ("Isn't the moon great? They're buzzing away around it" [182]), Sammler tells his nephew that he would rather go to "the ocean bottom. In Dr. Piccard's bathysphere. I seem to be a depth man rather than a height man. I do not personally care for the illimitable. The ocean, however deep, has a top and bottom whereas there is no sky ceiling" (183–84). Ben Siegel's comment on this passage bears quoting. Siegel sees Sammler's "sympathies . . . with the limited, the definite, indeed with the bottom of the sea, which embodies, he feels, a descent into dense tangibility, into cool inward finiteness."[17] To Sammler, according to Siegel, "These elements symbolize . . . man's duties and depth. Yet only a few among the young see that dealing with the near, the commonplace, the responsible is what makes saints and heroes."

Sammler finds it hard to conceive of earth's eventual destruction six billion years from now, when the sun explodes, as some scientists predict.

> Six billion years of human life! It lames the heart to contemplate such a figure. Six billion years! What will become of us? Of the other species, yes, and of us? How will we ever make it? And when we have to abandon the earth, and leave this solar system for another, what a moving day that will be. But by then humankind will have become very different. Evolution continues. (190–91)

Sammler refuses to take such apocalyptic fears too seriously. He has seen too much, lived too long. Most humans somehow learn how to carry on, to cope with the terms of existence. Man's natural instinct to live is too strong to allow apocalypse. As Bellow's elderly protagonist sips coffee in the garden of Elya's home in the country, with his one good eye he observes the natural beauty around him and has a remarkable vision: "Black fluid, white light, green ground, the soil heated and soft, penetrated by new growth. In the grass, a massed shine of particles, a turf-buried whiteness, and from this dew, wherever the sun could reach it, the spectrum flashed: like night cities seen from the jet, or the galactic sperm of worlds" (266). Here is no stale cynicism of Sodom and Gomorrah or whores of Babylon. A man who can conceive of the dew as being "the galactic sperm of worlds" has the imagination of a poet. Such "rhetorical leaps of imagination" (the words are Sarah Cohen's)[18], skewer the reader's attention and are wonderfully appropriate in a novel that pits the erotic against the scientific and cosmic.

Porter is correct when he criticizes the major weakness of *Mr. Sammler's Planet* as "the unsatisfactory relationship between theme and form."[19] True, Artur Sammler's tempered optimism is not supported by the events of the novel (e.g., the death of Elya Gruner and the refusal of the unrepentant Angela to forgive her father), but Porter is misleading in criticizing the novelist for failing "to find adequate 'objective correlatives,' a set of concretions which embody his ideas and emotions in coherent and organic fashion."[20] To Porter, "the use of animal and water imagery seems ultimately too pat in the movements between reflection and action. The ideas are important, frequently expressed with eloquence, and often intensely felt, but the form is thin."[21] This criticism is only partly valid. The connection between abstract ideas and the actions that embody them *is* thin, but Dr. Lal is closer to the mark when he praises Sammler's gift of condensation, his ability to express his philosophical and social views in a clear and vivid manner. Sammler, like his creator, *does* fall short of Sydney Smith's exhortation, "Short views, for God's sake, short views" (114), but the cornucopia of organic images drawn from the world of animals, birds, water, flowers, vegetation, stars, and planets enriches the novel's coherence, embodies its major themes, and provides that "solidity of specification" which Henry James, in "The Art of Fiction," called "the supreme virtue of a novel. . . ."[22]

NOTES

Introduction

1. From Joyce Carol Oates, "Imaginary Cities: America," *Literature and the Urban Experience: Essays on the City and Literature*, ed. Michael C. Jaye and Ann Chalmers Watts (New Brunswick: Rutgers University Press, 1981), 11. Copyright © 1981 by Rutgers, The State University of New Jersey.

2. "Nature," in *The Portable Emerson*, ed. Carl Bode and Malcolm Cowley (New York: Viking Press, 1981), 8.

3. Mary McCarthy, "One Touch of Nature," in *The Handwriting on the Wall and Other Literary Essays* (New York: Harcourt Brace & World, 1970), 194.

4. McCarthy, "One Touch of Nature," 189.

5. James T. Farrell, "In Search of an Image," in *The League of Frightened Philistines* (New York: Vanguard, 1945), 156–57.

6. Farrell, "In Search of an Image," 157.

7. Blanche Housman Gelfant, *The American City Novel* (Norman: University of Oklahoma Press, 1954), 18. Copyright © 1954 by the University of Oklahoma Press.

8. Irving Howe, "The City in Literature," *Commentary*, May, 1971, 65.

9. Leo Marx, *The Machine in the Garden: Technology and the Pastoral Ideal in America* (New York: Oxford University Press, 1969), 228.

10. Quoted by permission of New York University Press from Jonathan Baumbach, *The Landscape of Nightmare: Studies in the Contemporary American Novel* (New York: New York University Press, 1965), 120. Copyright © 1965 by New York University.

11. Edgar Branch, "*Studs Lonigan*, Symbolism and Theme," *College English* 23 (October–May, 1961–62): 192. Copyright © 1961 by the National Council of Teachers of English. Quoted with permission.

Chapter One

1. *National Review*, January 16, 1968, 31.

2. Ibid., 30.

3. Ibid., 31.

4. Blanche Housman Gelfant, *The American City Novel* (Norman: Univer-

sity of Oklahoma Press, 1954), 145. Copyright © 1954 by the University of Oklahoma Press.

5. Joseph Warren Beach, "*Manhattan Transfer*: Collectivism and Abstract Composition," in *Dos Passos, the Critic and the Writer's Intention*, ed. Allen Belkind (Carbondale: Southern Illinois University Press, 1971), 68. This essay is a condensed version of Beach's chapter in his *American Fiction: 1920–1940* (New York: Macmillan, 1941).

6. Gelfant, *American City Novel*, 144.

7. Ibid., 144–45.

8. Quoted in Linda Wagner, *Dos Passos, Artist as American* (Austin: University of Texas Press, 1979), 49. Copyright © 1979 by the University of Texas Press. Wagner is quoting from Dos Passos, "The beginning of the Contemporary Chronicles," University of Virginia collection, 2, 4. For a shortened version, see "Contemporary Chronicles," *Carleton Miscellany* 2, no. 2 (Spring 1961): 25–29.

9. George Knox, "Dos Passos and Painting," in *Dos Passos, the Critic and the Writer's Intention*, ed. Belkind, 248.

10. Ibid., 264.

11. Gelfant, *American City Novel*, 142.

12. E. D. Lowry ("*Manhattan Transfer*: Dos Passos' Wasteland," in *Dos Passos: A Collection of Critical Essays*, ed. Andrew Hook [Englewood Cliffs: Prentice Hall, 1974]), argues that Dos Passos is closer to T. S. Eliot than to Crane, Dreiser, or Farrell, "writers with whom he is frequently bracketed" (53). To Lowry, "the most obvious similarity between *The Waste Land* and *Manhattan Transfer* is their use of the structural principle of dissociation and recombination." E. D. Lowry's *Manhattan Transfer*: Dos Passos' Wasteland" originally, appeared in *The University Review* (30:1, October 1963). Excerpts are reprinted here with the permission of *New Letters/The University Review* and the Curators of the University of Missouri-Kansas City.

13. Gelfant, *American City Novel*, 143.

14. Ibid., 144.

15. R. W. Stallman, Introduction to *The Red Badge of Courage* by Stephen Crane (New York: Random House, 1951), p. xviii. Copyright © 1951 by Random House, Inc.

16. Quoted by Stallman, ibid., xviii.

17. Ibid., xix.

18. Richard Chase, Introduction to *The Red Badge of Courage and Other Writings* by Stephen Crane, ed. Richard Chase (Boston: Houghton Mifflin, 1960), xiv. Copyright © by Houghton Mifflin. Used by permission.

19. Helen Gardner, *Art through the Ages: Renaissance, Modern, and Non-European Art*, 6th ed. rev. by Horst de la Croix and Richard G. Tansey (New York: Harcourt Brace Jovanovich, 1975), 2:692.

20. Ibid., 2:695.

21. John Dos Passos, *Manhattan Transfer* (1925; reprint, Boston: Houghton Mifflin, 1963), 257. Hereafter, all references to *Manhattan Transfer* will be to this Sentry edition.

22. The word *tinfoil*, which does not appear in the epigraph, is a favorite of Dos Passos and a good example of his impressionistic interest in reflections of the sun.

23. Other characters are associated with the sun in various ways. Jimmy Herf sees it as a liberating force that can revitalize his stagnant life. Unhappy with his newspaper job, he wants to run away to South America. "God I like the sun," he cries; "I wish it'd been real Colombia . . ." (174). When Joe Harland, destitute and fighting despair, is kicked out by Mrs. O'Keefe, his friend's mother, "The sultry afternoon sun was like a blow on his back" (24). The day Jimmy and Stan are having Stan's muffler fixed at

a garage, it is very hot: "The dusty afternoon sunlight squirmed in bright worms of heat on his face and hands" (177). Characteristic of Dos Passos, the implications of the sun images are mixed. He is more interested here in the impressionistic moment than in his naturalistic theme.

24. Twenty-seven times, according to David Vanderwerken in "*Manhattan Transfer*: Dos Passos' Babel Story," *American Literature* 49 (May, 1977): 253.

25. In the epigraph that introduces the first section of *Manhattan Transfer*, Dos Passos compares the mass of crushed people exiting the ferryboat to "*apples fed down a chute into a press*" (3).

26. An interesting fog image reinforces this technique of blurred perspective. Toward the end of the last chapter of section 2, "One More River to Jordan," Ellen, bored with all the talk of politics, asks Jimmy to take her home from a restaurant. "Eighth Avenue was full of fog that caught at their throats. Lights bloomed dimly through it, faces loomed, glinted in silhouette and faded like a fish in a muddy aquarium" (264). The image of the muddy aquarium first appears in the epigraph to this same chapter, but without the fog. In the epigraph it is snowing, and the faces of the people in the Cosmopolitan Café, surrounded by "*blue and green opal rifts of smoke . . . blob whitely round the tables like illassorted fishes*" (255). Dos Passos likes the fish image so well, he repeats it again much later in a description of Martin Schiff: "His face with its big eyes and bone glasses swam through the smoke of the restaurant like a fish in a murky aquarium" (360).

27. Murray Baumgarten, *City Scriptures: Modern Jewish Writing* (Cambridge, Mass.: Harvard University Press, 1982), 2. Quoted by permission.

28. In addition to Dos Passos' animal imagery, there are several miscellaneous references to snakes, toads, turtles, and rats. Only the snake images merit attention here. The snake as Satanic image is suggested when the ambulance-chasing lawyer George Baldwin is having an affair with Nellie McNiel while Gus is in the hospital. As they embrace and kiss in the dark apartment, Dos Passos writes melodramatically that "Snakes of light from the streetlamp wound greenly about them" (19). More important is a phallic image that startles the New Yorkers as much as it does the readers of *Manhattan Transfer*; a newspaper article mentions a large snake that suddenly appeared before noon. It "crawled out of a crack in the masonry of the retaining wall of the reservoir at Fifth Avenue and Fortysecond Street . . ." (19). This strange local news probably struck Dos Passos as having symbolic value in a story about insidious corruption in the big city.

29. Wagner quotes some additional lyrics of this nursery rhyme that tell how the monkey got drunk and was crushed by the sneezing elephant. Wagner correctly observes that the "innocuous nursery song used as a chapter title and refrain comes to have sinister connotations . . ." (54), but she mistakenly limits its association to Ellen. It refers to all of the characters. She is also wrong when she identifies Ellen with "Long legged Jack of the Isthmus." The one to escape the flood is Jimmy Herf, as has been pointed out earlier in this chapter.

30. In chapter 3 ("Revolving Doors") of the third section, Jimmy, working nights as a reporter, uses the same metaphor ("squirrel-cage") to complain to Ellen about their cramped apartment (330).

31. The anonymous hobo tells two frightened boys that "There's more wickedness in one block in New York City than there was in a square mile in Nineveh. . . ." (381) and that earthquake insurance will not help when God "smokes out the city like you would a hornet's nest and he picks it up and shakes it like a cat shakes a rat" (370).

32. When one of Ellen's suitors explains that he waited to propose until she was

"free," she answers cynically, "We're none of us that ever . . ." (267). Linda Wagner points out that Dos Passos considered "Tess of 48th Street or The Story of a Pure Woman" as a possible title for his novel and that "most of her scenes in the first half . . . depict her victimization" (50), but the analogy is somewhat strained.

33. In the next chapter, George Baldwin has just had a fight with his wife Cecily and fears that a messy divorce will hurt his political future. He is trapped in a loveless marriage. In a variation of the bird-in-the-cage motif, Dos Passos describes the skyscrapers being built in New York: "Across Park Avenue the flameblue sky was barred with the red girder cage of a new building" (185).

34. The same is true of fruit images. Dos Passos frequently describes people's faces as looking like apples.

35. Ellen has romantic nature fantasies also. When she first meets Jimmy at a café, she tells him to order a gin fizz while she finishes her tea. "I love to see people drink gin fizzes. It makes me feel that I'm in the tropics sitting in a jujube grove waiting for the riverboat to take us up some ridiculous melodramatic river all set about with fever trees" (179).

36. While walking with Ellen in Central Park, Harry Goldweiser proposes and offers her his fortune. He tells her that his success as a Broadway producer was "like planting seed and you're their flower" (203).

37. Toward the end of the novel, when yet another suitor (George Baldwin) proposes to the frigid Ellen, Dos Passos turns away from organic images of sunshine and flowers to those of a patient anesthetized from pain and an inanimate figure captured forever in a photograph: "Through dinner she felt a gradual icy coldness stealing through her like novocaine. . . . It seemed as if she had set the photograph of herself in her own place, forever frozen into a single gesture" (375). These inorganic images culminate in the same paragraph in the image of Ellen as a figurine: "Ellen felt herself sitting with her ankles crossed, rigid as a procelain figure under her clothes, everything about her seemed to be growing hard and enameled, the air bluestreaked with cigarettesmoke, was turning to glass."

38. Dos Passos uses woods and forest images to mythicize the thick dark beauty of Ellen's hair. The men in her life are drawn to it to their peril. In bed with Ellen, Jimmy "knew the deep woods of her hair, he loved her" (330). When Ellen complains that at an audition she was asked to remove her hat, her former husband Jojo Oglethorpe replies, "That was so that I should look upon the forbidden forests of your hair" (340).

39. This is an interesting example of Dos Passos' use of repetition and variation to unify his novel. About forty pages earlier, he described Jimmy lying in bed, sleepless on a hot night. "There came on the air through the window a sourness of garbage, a smell of burnt gasoline and traffic and dusty pavements, a huddled stuffiness of pigeonhole rooms where men and women's bodies writhed alone tortured by the night and the young summer" (194). The addition of the organic image of the twisted "roots of the potbound plants" is an effective extension of Dos Passos' theme and gives the writing an incremental pattern.

40. Here is another effective example of the symmetry of parallel scenes that helps unify the multiplicity of episodes and characters in the novel. In chapter 2 of the first section, Bud Korpenning walks down Broadway on blistered feet, "past empty lots where tin cans glittered among grass and sumach bushes and ragweed, between ranks of billboards and Bill Durham signs, past shanties and abandoned squatters' shacks, past gulches heaped with wheelscarred rubbishpiles where dumpcarts were dumping ashes and clinkers . . ." (23).

41. Vanderwerken, "Manhattan Transfer: Dos Passos' Babel Story," 256.

42. Ibid., 262.

43. Charles C. Walcutt, *American Literary Naturalism: A Divided Stream* (Minneapolis: University of Minnesota Press, 1956), 280.

44. Ibid., 281.

45. Vanderwerken, "*Manhattan Transfer*: Dos Passos' Babel Story," 266.

Chapter Two

1. Frederick Hoffman, "The Scene of Violence: Dostoevsky and Dreiser," *Modern Fiction Studies* 6, no. 2 (Summer 1960): 92–93. Copyright 1960, by Purdue Research Foundation, West Lafayette, Indiana. Quoted with permission.

2. Edgar Branch, "*Studs Lonigan*, Symbolism and Theme," *College English* 23 (December 1961): 192. Copyright © 1961 by the National Council of Teachers of English. Quoted with permission.

3. Donald Pizer, "James T. Farrell: *Studs Lonigan*," in *Twentieth-Century American Literary Naturalism* (Carbondale: Southern Illinois University Press, 1982), 23.

4. Quotations from *Studs Lonigan: A Trilogy* (New York: Random House, 1963) are from the Modern Library edition and will be cited in the text. The abbreviations *YL*, *YMSL*, and *JD* representing *Young Lonigan* (1932), *The Young Manhood of Studs Lonigan* (1934), and *Judgment Day* (1935).

5. Richard Mitchell, "*Studs Lonigan*: Research in Morality," *Centennial Review* 6 (1962): 206.

6. Ibid., 207. Ann Douglas sees the church in *Studs Lonigan* as an ally of mass culture. "At best, Studs' parents and their friends go to church in much the same spirit Studs and his gang go to the movies, to have their prejudices reinforced and their discontent siphoned off in fantasy." "*Studs Lonigan* and the Failure of History in Mass Society: A Study in Claustrophobia," *American Quarterly* 29 (1977): 492.

7. One of Farrell's effective techniques in unifying the episodic structure of the trilogy is his echoing certain motifs used earlier. In *The Young Manhood*, for example, Studs takes Lucy to Fran's school dance. As they walk along the street, she snaps her fingers and sings the words to a song she hears on a Victrola. The lyrics are similar to those in the later scene with Studs and Catherine: "'*Don't mind the rain, / It's bound to come again, / For when the clouds go rolling by . . .*'" (*YMSL*, 277). In this instance, the song is not being used for counterpoint as in *Judgment Day*, but its sentimentality and hopeful optimism reinforce Studs's blissful, romantic mood and help him momentarily forget his syphilis.

8. Farrell was upset by those critics who misinterpreted his novel, especially his characterization of Studs. He angrily denied that Studs was "a slum character." "Alfred Kazin says that I summon the characters before the bar . . . and condemn them all. But I don't pass moral judgments on them. Statements like this show a lack of understanding of the book. Studs is not presented unsympathetically." Dennis Flynn and Jack Salzman, "An Interview with James T. Farrell," *Twentieth Century Literature* 22, no. 1 (February, 1976): 2. Ann Douglas's view is closer to Farrell's. To her, Studs, "For all his vaunted toughness, is what we call a 'nice guy,'" especially when he is contrasted with Weary Reilley, "the least likeable character in the book; by being all the things Studs thinks he wants to be, Weary makes us aware of how much better Studs is than his self-designated ideal." "*Studs Lonigan* and the Failure of History," 500.

9. Branch, "*Studs Lonigan*, Symbolism and Theme," 193.

10. On page 7 of *Young Lonigan* there is a significant passage in which Studs identifies Lucy with the sun. He is reminiscing about a day in the sixth grade when he

walked Lucy home. "It had been a windy day in March, without any sun. The air had seemed black, and the sky blacker, and all the sun that day had been in his thoughts of her. He had had all kinds of goofy, dizzy feelings that he liked." He remembers how he did not want to leave Lucy "because when he did he knew the day would get blacker" (*YL*, 8). On page 56, in her white dress, Lucy looks beautiful to Studs, "like a flame." On page 29 of *The Young Manhood* she is "like a growing flower" and, much later, just before his disillusionment, "she was like something beautiful in a mist" (*YMSL*, 293). The highest praise that Studs bestows on her is in *The Young Manhood* when Studs has been revisiting the old neighborhood and finds Lucy's former house empty: "every block, every store was somehow connected in his mind with her. It was as if she was like God, and her spirit was in everything in the neighborhood, only it wasn't any more" (*YMSL*, 66).

11. Donald Pizer, who reads the *Studs Lonigan* trilogy as "a tragic morality play, . . . a moral allegory in which all that the Everyman protagonist encounters in experience is directly related to his potential damnation or salvation" (20), sees Lucy and Weary as "polar opposites in relation to Studs" (21). To Pizer, "Lucy, because she offers to Studs an opportunity for expression of his deepest nature through communion with others, constitutes his potential for growth." Thus she and Weary "function like the 'good' and 'evil' angels in a medieval morality play. Lucy is spirit, Weary the world; Lucy speaks to Studs' inner ear of love, Weary of pride" (22). But the problem with this reductive interpretation is that Pizer ignores Farrell's irony in characterizing Lucy. Pizer seems to accept Studs's later description of Lucy as "'a saint or a beautiful queen, or a goddess'"; actually, Farrell portrays Lucy as a tease, an imperfect goddess who fails to encourage Studs's gentle, more sensitive side. Only toward the end of his chapter does Pizer acknowledge Farrell's irony. Studs, he says, out of his longing for Lucy, has made "an avatar of spirituality in an average teenager" (35).

12. On page 131 of *Young Lonigan*, Studs himself is identified with the sun.

13. Branch, "*Studs Lonigan*, Symbolism and Theme," 192.

14. University of Iowa, 1950.

15. Branch, "*Studs Lonigan*, Symbolism and Theme," 192–93.

16. Flynn and Salzman, "An Interview with James T. Farrell," 3.

17. Ibid., 4.

18. "The Author as Plaintiff: Testimony in a Censorship Case," in *Reflections at Fifty* (New York: Vanguard Press, 1954), 195.

Chapter Three

1. Bonnie Lyons, "Appendix," in *Henry Roth: The Man and His Work* (New York: Cooper Square, 1976), 169–70. Permission granted by Cooper Square Publishers, Totowa, New Jersey.

2. Ibid., 169.

3. Bonnie Lyons, "The Symbolic Structure of Henry Roth's *Call It Sleep*," *Contemporary Literature* 13 (1972): 186–203, and *Henry Roth: The Man and His Work*; James Ferguson, "Symbolic Patterns in *Call It Sleep*," *Twentieth Century Literature* 14 (January, 1969): 211–20; and Mary Edrich Redding, "Call It Myth: Henry Roth and *The Golden Bough*," *Centennial Review* 18, no. 2 (Spring 1974): 180–95.

4. John S. Friedman, "On Being Blocked & Other Literary Matters: An Interview: Henry Roth," *Commentary*, August 1977, 29.

5. Henry Roth, *Call It Sleep* (1934; reprint, New York: Avon, 1964), 58. Hereafter, page references to Roth's novel will be given in the text.

6. The power of the 550 volts is vividly experienced by both David and the reader, as Roth switches from predatory bird imagery to powerful mountain goats in combat. *"He kicked — once. Terrific rams of dark- / ness collided; out of their shock space / toppled into havoc"* (419).

7. Lyons, *Henry Roth: the Man and His Work*, 60.

8. Redding, "Call It Myth," 185.

9. Gary Epstein, "Auto-Obituary: The Death of the Artist in Henry Roth's *Call It Sleep*," quoted with permission from *Studies in American Jewish Literature*, ed. Daniel Walden (Spring 1979): 40–41.

10. Redding, "Call It Myth," 181. Redding relates David to the myth "of the corn-baby believed to be born on the harvest field as the incarnation of the corn-spirit, and celebrated in Prussia with the mock birth ritual in which the last sheaf, called 'the Bastard,' is 'delivered'" (188).

11. Lyons, *Henry Roth: The Man and His Work*, 58.

12. Redding, "Call It Myth," 182. Redding finds various parallels between David's story and Dionysus myths, especially when the child Dionysus playfully brandishes Zeus the father's lightning bolt. She also finds some interesting parallels between Dionysus' narcissism and David's preoccupation with mirrors, a form of solipsism. Particularly interesting for this study is Redding's discussion of death and resurrection myths that tie ". . . Dionysus (and also Demeter) to the corn-myths; and the persistence with which cattle and bulls appear in the agricultural rituals as a whole parallels the dual identification with vegetation and bulls" (184–85).

13. "Call It Myth," 186.

14. *Henry Roth: The Man and His Work*, 44.

15. In chapter 5 of "The Rail," the boys describing the pursuit of Sadie Salmonowitz's escaped canary reveal how they saw "annuder kinerry" (293), as they spied on a bathing woman (Genya) through the skylight and saw her private parts.

16. Mircea Eliade, *Rites and Symbols of Initiation: The Mysteries of Birth and Rebirth*, trans. Willard R. Trask (New York: Harper & Row, 1965), 70. A good example of such ascension imagery in *Call It Sleep* is found in the scene where Rabbi Pankower has David read Hebrew to impress the elderly visitor, Reb Schulim. As David recognizes the Isaiah passage, he becomes very excited and puts much feeling into his recitation. His voice becomes "a chant, a hymn, as though a soaring presence behind the words pulsed and stressed a meaning. A cadence like a flock of pigeons, vast, heaven-filling, swept and wheeled, glittered, darkened, kindled again, like wind over prairies" (367).

17. In the opening paragraph of chapter 19 of "The Rail," Roth reverses the roles and identifies David with a cat. After playing pimp for Leo, David delays as long as possible his return to his parents' apartment. Looking out of a third floor window, he sees a cat: "in the greying yard below, a lean grey cat leaped at the fence, missed the top and clawed its way up with intent and silent power. And he upward also, wearily" (385).

18. Redding, "Call It Myth," 193.

19. Lyons, *Henry Roth: The Man and His Work*, 108.

20. Ibid., 53–54.

21. Redding, "Call It Myth," 189.

22. Murray Baumgarten, in *City Scriptures: Modern Jewish Writing* (Cambridge, Mass.: Harvard University Press, 1982), 5–6, also finds transcendence in Roth's novel: "No longer limited by his mother's experience of the city in terms of her village past, aware now that his home is not the boundary of his identity, David has embarked upon the development and articulation of his person in psychic and geographic terms. As

he begins to project a possible identity in terms of his father's role as worker and citydweller, David moves from psychological processes through geographic space into the religious encounter that will determine the possibilities of his life" (5–6). Quoted by permission.

23. Lyons, *Henry Roth: The Man and His Work*, 42. Roth's words are from page 59.

24. Bonnie Lyons uses the coal as one of her examples: "The symbol of the coal . . . combines opposing or conflicting meanings. Because it is black and dirty, coal has inevitable connections with uncleanness for David. When he is told the story of Isaiah's purification by God's coal, he is unable to reconcile the blackness of the coal he knows with purity: 'But coal makes smoke and ashes. So how clean?' (Roth, 230). He cannot accept the purifying aspects of coal, for he connects coal with the cellar . . ." (46).

25. In chapter 5 of "The Rail," Roth combines an erotic image with a weather simile to convey David's sense of violation when the boys in the street describe the naked woman (Genya) stepping out of her washtub: "Like flying hail against his nakedness their sharp cries stunned and flayed him" (294).

26. The beginning of chapter 4 of "The Coal" has a more important example, but it has been quoted frequently by the critics: "Two months had passed since David entered the cheder. Spring had come and with the milder weather, a sense of weary contentment, a curious pause in himself as though he were waiting for some sign, some seal that would forever relieve him of watchfulness and forever insure his well-being" (221).

27. Theresa R. Mooney, "The Explicable 'It' of Henry Roth's *Call It Sleep*," quoted with permission form *Studies in American Jewish Literature*, ed. Daniel Walden (Spring 1979): 12.

28. Mooney, "The Explicable 'It,'" 13.

29. Ibid., 12.

30. *Henry Roth: The Man and His Work*, 107.

31. Bonnie Lyons, "An Interview with Henry Roth," *Shenandoah* 25 (1973): 63. Copyright © 1973 by Washington and Lee University, quoted from *Shenandoah: The Washington and Lee University Review* with the permission of the editor. The rest of Roth's answer bears repeating: "The only thing I think he feels triumphant about . . . was that for one brief second he was able to summon something up that unified the world. But at the same time, in the process of doing that, he couldn't do it scot-free. He paid a price. And maybe the unification attained that way is again a storming of the heavens. It is not the way a true unification is attained. By a slow laborious development one gets there, but not all at once in mortal splendor."

32. Carol A. Binkert, "The Complexities of Light and Dark Imagery in Henry Roth's *Call It Sleep*" (Seminar paper, Wayne State University, 1984).

33. "At the time I thought this was a beautiful symbol of power destroying— what? The child was symbolically destroyed although he lived on. Something was destroyed in him, I don't know exactly what—perhaps it was his childhood." "An Interview with Henry Roth," 63.

34. Binkert, "The Complexities of Light and Dark Imagery," 22.

35. Baumgarten, *City Scriptures*, 7.

36. Epstein, "Auto-Obituary," 39.

37. "Semioticists might note that the electricity David encounters is the fundamental binary opposition of the code of this city. It is its power for good as well as for evil, the energy that defines it as a city, just as Isaiah's God is the condition and force that makes him human" (Baumgarten, *City Scriptures*, 8).

38. Lyons, "Interview with Henry Roth, March 1977," quoted with permission from *Studies in American Jewish Literature*, ed. Daniel Walden (Spring 1979): 57.

39. Binkert, "The Complexities of Light and Dark Imagery," 3.

40. Lyons, *Henry Roth: The Man and His Work*, 48. Baumgarten arrives at a similar conclusion: "When David puts the dipper into the crack in the street leading to the third rail, he makes contact with the ultimate power of his world and his city. He contacts the electricity that powers the trolleys, the transportation system that makes it one city and gives it shape as an urban landscape." *City Scriptures*, 8.

41. Lyons, *Henry Roth: The Man and His Work*, 49.

42. Irving Howe, "Life Never Let Up," review of *Call It Sleep*, by Henry Roth, *New York Times Book Review*, October 25, 1964, 1, 60, 61.

Chapter Four

1. Harriette Arnow, *The Dollmaker* (1954; reprint, New York: Macmillan, 1967), 129. Hereafter, all references in the text are to this Collier edition.

2. "The Ax Helve," *The Poetry of Robert Frost: The Collected Poems*, ed. Edward Connery Lathem (New York: Henry Holt, 1975), 186.

3. Walter Havighurst, in his review of *The Dollmaker* in the *Saturday Review* (April 24, 1954, 12) wishes that Arnow's novel had "been more selective, and more readable; as it is, it moves like a steamroller, ponderous and ineluctable." Glenda Hobbs agrees. After speaking of "minor confusions" involving the novel's religious symbolism, she criticizes Arnow's excessive documentation of Gertie's daily life, arguing that "the reader may crave a more structured, foreshortened vision of Gertie's world rather than a recreation of it." ("A Portrait of the Artist as Mother: Harriette Arnow and *The Dollmaker*," *Georgia Review* 33, no. 4 [Winter 1979]: 851–66, © 1979 by Glenda Hobbs. Reprinted by permission of *The Georgia Review*.) Hobbs's criticism has some validity, but these flaws are minor in view of Arnow's memorable accomplishment.

4. Hobbs, "A Portrait of the Artist as Mother," 862.

5. Leo Marx, *The Machine in the Garden: Technology and the Pastoral Ideal in America* (1964; reprint, New York: Oxford University Press, 1969), 32.

6. Ibid., 16.

7. Ibid., 17.

8. Gertie shows the same compassion for trees when Cassie asks her to whittle a doll. Gertie "searched until she found a smooth-barked little hickory sprout, so crooked it could never grow into a proper tree and from it cut a piece not much longer than her middle finger but with a little branch on either side" (52). At the end of chapter 3, Gertie observes her twelve-year-old, Reuben, who shares her love of nature, "take his pocket knife and cut a little crooked cedar away from a straight one so that the straight one could grow" (56).

9. Arnow's metaphorical description of the wind as a cat many chapters later is more threatening and dynamic than Sandburg's and Eliot's metaphors of the fog as a cat in "Chicago" and "Prufrock." In *The Dollmaker*, a weary and lonesome Gertie has been confined indoors for three weeks by bad weather. "Far away across the vacant land past the railroad tracks, the wind's whine mingled with the trains and the steel mill's roar. Then, there was the shriek of it as it leaped against her unit, poking and prying like a white cat determined to claw its way through the cardboard walls. Defeated, it would cry in the chimney, sob with a long woo-wooing by the walls, then be gone with a higher, shriller shrieking as it leaped through the telephone wires" (312). Gertie cannot get away from the white cat even indoors. "No matter how cold it was outside,

the kitchen, unlike the rest of the house, was always hot, and the white cat [the Icy Heart refrigerator] purred."

10. Wilton Eckley, *Harriette Arnow* (Boston: Twayne, 1974), 38. Copyright © 1974 and quoted with permission of Twayne Publishers, a division of G. K. Hall & Co., Boston.

11. Hobbs, "A Portrait of the Artist as Mother," 858.

12. *Saturday Review*, 12.

13. "Joyce Carol Oates on Harriette Arnow's *The Dollmaker*," in *Rediscoveries*, ed. David Madden (New York: Crown, 1971), 61.

14. Dorothy Lee, "Harriette Arnow's *The Dollmaker*: A Journey to Awareness," *Critique: Studies in Modern Fiction* 20, no. 2 (1978): 97.

15. Ibid., 97–98.

16. Ibid., 98.

17. Hobbs, "A Portrait of the Artist as Mother," 865.

18. Eckley, *Harriette Arnow*, 126.

Chapter Five

1. Bernard Malamud, "Pleasures of the Fast Payoff," *New York Times Book Review*, August 28, 1983, 3. Copyright © 1983 by the New York Times Company. Reprinted by permission.

2. Bernard Malamud, *Idiots First* (New York: Dell, 1963), 177.

3. Carl Jung, *Contributions to Analytical Psychology* (New York: Harcourt Brace, 1928), 248.

4. Jonathan Baumbach, "All Men Are Jews: *The Assistant* by Bernard Malamud," in *The Landscape of Nightmare* (New York: New York University Press, 1965), 120.

5. James M. Mellard, "Malamud's *The Assistant:* The City Novel as Pastoral," *Studies in Short Fiction*, 5 (1967): 2.

6. Sandy Cohen, "*The Assistant*: Ceremony of Innocence," in *Bernard Malamud and the Trial by Love* (Amsterdam: Rodopi N.V., 1974), 40.

7. Ibid., 41.

8. Mellard, "Malamud's *The Assistant*: The City Novel as Pastoral," 14. See also Max Schulz, "Bernard Malamud's Mythic Proletarians," in *Radical Sophistication: Studies in Contemporary Jewish-American Novelists* (Athens, Ohio: Ohio University Press, 1969). Schulz sees Malamud's novels as combining "the proletarian impulse of the Jewish intellectual of the 1930's" with "a mythic pattern of vegetation ritual and Grail quest" (56), thus combining realism and symbolism, social commentary and myth. "The historical determinism of socialism merges with the cyclical inevitability of mythos; the proletarian hero winning justice for society with the mythic hero renewing life for the community" (57). Sidney Richman concludes that "What lies at the heart of *The Assistant* is a ritual composed of fragments of myth, Catholicism, and Judaic thought — all pressed into the services of the author's 'mystical' humanism" (*Bernard Malamud* [Boston: Twayne, 1966], 71. Copyright © 1966 and quoted with the permission of Twyane Publishers, a division of G. K. Hall & Co., Boston.)

9. Sandy Cohen points out that myth serves "merely in the background" of *The Assistant* and does not dominate characterization and plot as it did in *The Natural*. However, though the seasonal cycle "never obtrudes into the thoughts and motivations of the characters" (37), it *is* part of their subconsciousness and characterization.

10. Letter from Bernard Malamud to Mrs. Maryann D. Greenstone, June 24, 1969.

11. Richman, *Bernard Malamud*, 65.

12. Ibid., 42.

13. Ibid., 51.

14. Bernard Malamud, *The Assistant* (New York: Farrar Straus and Cudahy, 1957), 206. Hereafter, page numbers will be cited in the text.

15. Iska Alter, "The Natural, The Assistant, and American Materialism," in *The Good Man's Dilemma: Social Criticism in the Fiction of Bernard Malamud* (New York: AMS Press, 1981), 20. Quoted by permission of AMS Press, Inc.

16. Ward Minogue's surname suggests *minnow*. For such a vicious criminal, the minnow seems inappropriate, but Malamud, if he chose the name for reasons other than its Irishness, is perhaps suggesting the smallness of this petty hood, this blackmailer, the smallest fish in the water.

17. Mellard overlooks the fish symbolism in the names of some of the characters in *The Assistant*, and, in his pursuit of vegetation rituals, mistakenly argues that "fish in the novels [of Malamud] are associated with principles of fertility and life . . ." ("Malamud's Novels: Four Versions of Pastoral," *Crtique* 9 [1967]: 12). This statement may be valid for *The Natural, A New Life*, and *The Fixer*, but not *The Assistant*.

18. Baumbach, "All Men Are Jews," 119.

19. In "Malamud's Novels: Four Versions of Pastoral," Mellard claims that "The most satisfying sexual relationships are almost invariably at least begun in natural settings . . ." (11). When, however, he offers Frank's rape of Helen as an example, his argument sounds bizarre. Cohen is also misleading when he says that "The Parkway, like all wooded areas, represents pastoral innocence and freedom in Malamud's theogony" (*Trial by Love*, 43). Such generalizations overlook Malamud's irony.

20. Alfred Kazin, "Fantasist of the Ordinary," review of *The Assistant* by Bernard Malamud, *Commentary* 24 (July, 1957): 90.

21. Joan Zlotnick points out that moon imagery helps associate Frank with St. Francis, who in his canticle "Laudis Creaturarum" invoked, among other of God's creations, "Sister Moon" ("Malamud's *The Assistant*: Of Morris, Frank, and St. Francis," *Studies in American Jewish Literature* 1 (Winter 1975): 23.

22. Malamud uses a simple but effective nature image to describe the duality of Frank at the beginning of chapter 6. The perspective is Helen's, as she realizes that she is falling in love with her father's mysterious assistant: "One day he seemed unknown, lurking at the far end of an unlit cellar; the next he was standing in sunlight, a smile on his face, as if all she knew of him and all she didn't, had fused into a healed and easily remembered whole" (130). The thrust of the entire novel is an attempt to fuse the two halves of his split personality.

23. Zlotnick points out that Malamud uses images of birds and snow as well as of the moon to link Frank with St. Francis. Such "Images associated with the saint are prevalent, but more importantly, St. Francis is an ideal pursued by Frank, the embodiment of an ethic embraced by the old Jewish grocer, and a vehicle for expressing the Malamudian idea that at its core Judaism is a moral code, one which is shared by all men — St. Francis included — who love and suffer for their fellow man" ("Of Morris, Frank, and St. Francis," 21).

24. On page 198, when Frank finally confesses to Morris his part in the robbery of the store, he feels tremendous relief described in terms of singing birds: "Having said this [the confession], the clerk experienced a moment of extraordinary relief — a treeful of birds broke into song; but the song was silenced . . . ," when Morris reveals that he had already figured out Frank's complicity.

25. Nikos Kazantzakis, "Francis and Clare," in *Saint Francis of Assisi* (New York: Simon and Schuster, 1962), 245–54, © 1962 by Simon and Schuster, Inc., rpt. in Lawrence Cunningham, ed., *Brother Francis: An Anthology of Writings by and about St. Francis*

of Assisi (New York: Harper and Row, 1972), 128–38. Page numbers in the text are from the Cunningham anthology.

26. This same mixture can be seen in the imagery of bananas, associated once with Frank and once with Morris. In chapter 2, Frank tells Morris, "I always have this dream where I want to tell somebody something on the telephone so bad it hurts, but then when I am in the booth, instead of a phone being there, a bunch of bananas is hanging on a hook" (37). The other example appears in chapter 6, when Karp thinks of Morris as a "shlimozel." It wasn't Karp's fault that Morris "was inept, unfortunate." But "because he was, his troubles grew like bananas in bunches" (149).

27. Mellard, "Malamud's Novels: Four Versions of Pastoral," 13.

28. Mellard, "Malamud's *The Assistant*: The City Novel as Pastoral," 11.

29. As quoted in *Contemporary Authors: A Bio-Bibliographical Guide to Current Authors and Their Works*, ed. Barbara Harte and Carolyn Riley (Detroit: Gale Research, 1969), 5–8:725. Copyright © 1963, 1969 by Gale Research Company. Reprinted by permission of the publishers.

Chapter Six

1. Edward Lewis Wallant, *The Pawnbroker* (New York: Harcourt, Brace and World, 1961), 3. Hereafter page numbers will be cited in the text.

2. Occasionally, though, Wallant does indulge in the pathetic fallacy. For example, awakening one night from a horrible nightmare of his wife's violation in the Nazi prison camp, Sol "turned his violet-starred vision on the rest of the room, on the window from which a *tender* breeze came, filtered through the heavy foliage, and then, finally, on the length of his own body, shining with sweat" (169–70; my italics). Another example occurs in chapter 22, where Wallant alternates the horrors of Sol's nightmares with the soothing beauty of nature. When Sol remembers discovering his wife's naked body in the pile of victims ready for the crematorium, "His eyes ripped themselves open to stare at the moonlight on his bedroom wall. The trees *whispered* outside" (224; my italics). Minutes later, "Some birds twittered bewilderedly *as though they thought it a black morning*" (my italics). But when Wallant's writing is at its best, he drops such sentimentality as in the following: "it was morning with none of the quality of newness mornings can have. He sat on the edge of the bed and stared at the light through the trees, wincing every so often, as though his skin had been removed during the night. The bright, pink light of the sun looked like the reflection of some monstrous fire burning a hideous fuel" (225).

3. Wallant, says Max F. Schulz, "portrays man's nature as inextricably linked to the fact of being an animal (pervasive bestial imagery underscores this assumption). He sees the mire in which man breathes and moves as the necessary condition of his spiritual illumination." "Edward Lewis Wallant and Bruce Jay Friedman: The Glory and the Agony of Life," in Max F. Schulz, *Radical Sophistication: Studies in Contemporary Jewish/American Novelists* (Athens, Ohio: Ohio University Press, 1969), 183. Quoted with the permission of Ohio University Press.

4. August is Sol's "bad month, the period of his own mistral, a time when he felt healed scars as a veteran might recall his wounds in damp weather" (91).

5. Leo Gurko argues that although Wallant, "an urban landscapist," sees the city as an inferno, he still finds hope "in this urban hell." "The city is a nightmare but contains at some inscrutable source within itself the seeds of its own resurrection." Wallant "believes uncannily in the regenerative powers of the city, and his novels bear intimate witness to the rebirth of his wounded characters inside the urban framework." "Edward

Lewis Wallant as Urban Novelist," *Twentieth Century Literature* 20, no. 4 (October, 1974): 254. Sol's aiming the feeble light of the flashlight at the burning sun seems to validate Gurko's view of that "inscrutable" resistance in man which ultimately leads to his transcendence.

6. On page 211, as Marilyn dozes on the deck chair of the Hudson River excursion boat, Sol observes that "A tiny pulse in her strong neck throbbed faintly, as though an invisible moth fluttered its wings against her flesh. A tendril of her shiny, dark blond hair swung gently against her cheek."

7. The identification of Marilyn with "A cool refreshing breeze" echoes a passage a few pages earlier when Sol, sickened by the vulturism of his sister, thinks he might take "a little holiday in October, walk in some New England wood and just breathe without regret or poignance the pleasant cold air so free of unnatural smells" (95).

8. In the opening chapter of the novel, as Sol plods along the bank of the Harlem River, he "watched the quiet flow of the water. Ironically, he noted the river's deceptive beauty. Despite its oil-green opacity and the indecipherable things floating on its filthy surface, somehow its insistent direction made it impressive" (4). However, there is "No fear that *he* could be taken in by it; he had the battered memento of his body and his brain to protect him from illusion" (6).

9. David Galloway cites this pastoral dream, along with Sol's outing on the Hudson with Marilyn Birchfield and his memory of a childhood ride on the Vistula, as signaling "the character's rebirth, an event ceremonially blessed by the rain that falls outside as the pawnbroker dreams of this sunny summer day." *Edward Lewis Wallant* (Boston: Twayne, 1979), 78. Copyright © 1979 and quoted with the permission of Twayne Publishers, a division of G. K. Hall & Co., Boston.

10. Wallant reminds the reader of Sol's dream of this European picnic with its butterflies when on the following morning of the anniversary of his horrible loss, a spastic butterfly collector enters the shop and cannot untie a parcel, which Sol opens by cutting the cord with a razor, revealing "a framed glass of brilliantly colored butterflies" (251).

11. In the preface to his book on Wallant, Galloway lists "the loss of the sustaining contact with nature" as one of the "familiar contemporary themes" in Wallant's fiction. *Edward Lewis Wallant*, 10. In the passage just quoted from the novel, Sol's choice of language effectively reveals his relaxed posture and mellowed feelings. In no other passage in the book does he use such vapid colloquialisms as "quite" and "very." Heretofore his command of language has been clipped and precise.

12. Rather appropriately, Sol and Marilyn discover their mutual enjoyment of Chekhov's *A Day in the Country*. Galloway points out the theme of "the regenerative aspects of nature" in the Russian work, adding that Chekhov "pays a moving tribute to the simple people who have learned 'not from books, but in the fields, in the woods, on the riverbank,' and while their knowledge cannot erase the injustices of the world, it can help to ease the painful loneliness of two orphaned children." *Edward Lewis Wallant*, 82.

13. Eliot's description of the polluted Thames, the drifting barges, "dry sterile thunder without rain," the sound of "the cicada / And dry grass singing," and "the dry stone no sound of water" ("The Waste Land" in *The Collected Poems 1909–1962* by T. S. Eliot [New York: Harcourt, 1963]) — all have their counterparts in *The Pawnbroker*. Sol also quotes "The Love Song of J. Alfred Prufrock" one evening after work ("I grow old . . . I grow old . . . / I shall wear the bottoms of my trousers rolled" [55]) and then decides to visit Tessie. Although Sol is capable of having intercourse with Tessie, he is as mechanical and unromantic as Eliot's "carbuncular" clerk in "The Waste Land,"

who visits the "tired" typist and engages "her in caresses / Which still are unreproved, if undesired."

14. John G. Parks, "The Grace of Suffering: The Fiction of E. L. Wallant," *Studies in American Jewish Literature*, no. 5; *The Varieties of Jewish Experience*, ed. Daniel Walden (Albany: State University of New York Press, 1986), 113. Baumbach suggests that Sol's bitter cynicism "betrays for all the blackness of its vision an underlying moral (and human) commitment. Sol assumes responsibility, as human being, for the worst atrocities of behavior of his species — behavior which appears to him, by any stretch of possibility, unredeemable. The numbness which protects him from the horrors of the world serves also as a defense against himself — against the risk of trust." *The Landscape of Nightmare* (New York: New York University Press, 1965), 142.

15. A natural image that Wallant uses in *The Pawnbroker* to describe Sol's death wish is the sea. The most important passage in which this archetypal symbol appears is in chapter 18, when Sol walks to the river in the evening after having seen Jesus and the three other conspirators huddled in a restaurant. As he breathes the slightly cooler air by the river, "A dark barge moved at a funeral pace, and he stood watching it pass under one bridge after another, heading for the invisible sea. A sudden yearning raked him, and he imagined himself lying flat on his back on a barge as somber and silent as that one, moving toward the sea, seeing one bridge after another obscure the sky briefly, feeling the water grow bigger beneath him, spread to the endlessness of open ocean, with stars over him so distant that there was no way to judge movement by them, and all quiet except for the murmurous, tending sea and him lying there with folded hands, floating in eternal peace . . ." (187–88).

16. Schulz, "Edward Lewis Wallant and Bruce Jay Friedman," *Radical Sophistication*, 179. Parks puts it more simply: Wallant's "fiction shows that it is only through suffering that we can discover our full humanity" ("The Grace of Suffering," 111).

Chapter 7

1. Saul Bellow, *Mr. Sammler's Planet* (New York: Viking Press, 1970), 224. Hereafter, all references in the text are to this edition.

2. An early anecdote about an Israeli gaucho who raises nutrias ("greedy Beasts") for fur hats and coats offers an example of Mr. Sammler's earlier state of cold indifference. When Sammler saw these little animals in Galilee, "they were heavy, their coats shone, opulent and dense" (25). The Israeli "cowpuncher from the pampas" told Sammler that he butchered the animals himself by hitting them on the head with a stick, feeling no tenderness toward any favorite; he explained his impassivity by observing "that nutrias were very stupid."

3. In *Whence the Power? The Artistry and Humanity of Saul Bellow* (Columbia: University of Missouri Press, 1974), M. Gilbert Porter points out that ". . . Sammler does some hind-sniffing of his own: '[Wallace] often transmitted to Sammler in warm weather (perhaps Sammler's nose was hypersensitive) a slightly unclean odor from the rear. The merest hint of fecal carelessness'" (*Sammler*, 87; Porter, 171n).

4. Ben Siegel sees "The holocaust and his own escape from the grave [as] . . . the experiences by which Sammler measures all events. . . . Clearly intellect and knowledge, Sammler has learned, are not enough: without a conscience man is merely an intellectual animal. Wanting to understand this planet's creatures, he tries to look and listen without judging." "Saul Bellow and Mr. Sammler: Absurd Seekers of High Qualities," in *Saul Bellow: A Collection of Critical Essays*, ed. Earl Rovit (Englewood Cliffs: Prentice Hall, 1975), 128.

5. Sammler scoffs at the popular idea "of the healing power of black. The dreams of nineteenth-century poets polluted the psychic atmosphere of the great boroughs and suburbs of New York" (33). America's new erotic freedom reminds him of Gauguin and "the hibiscus-covered exotic ease of Samoa."

6. According to Porter, "The animal imagery which Sammler uses to describe the pickpocket reveals the primitive nature of his predatory activities, the counterpart to his primitive sexual force" (*Whence the Power?*, 167). In general, Bellow employs animal imagery in this novel, "though perhaps heavy-handedly, to depict human beastialty, savagery, and grotesqueness" 178).

7. Charles C. Walcutt, *American Literary Naturalism: A Divided Stream* (Minneapolis: University of Minnesota Press, 1956), 128–29.

8. Porter makes a very interesting comment on Bellow's use of water imagery in *Mr. Sammler's Planet*. It "is used skillfully to suggest overpopulation, immensity, turbulence, mystery, death, and the influence of the moon on the earth" (*Whence the Power?*, 178). In the long philosophical scene between Sammler and Dr. Lal, "Water imagery is appropriate . . . for several reasons. First, because water occupies two-thirds of the earth's surface, it is a suitable metaphor for the overcrowded conditions which both Sammler and Lal describe. The turbulence of the water matches the turbulence of the teeming multitudes, frantically seeking gratification or release, even in the form of escape to another planet; and the mystery of the sea is equivalent to the mystery of human death, which Sammler ponders. The moon exerts influence on the tides just as human behavior and direction are affected by the prospects of advanced technology leading to inhabitation of the moon, the subject matter of this section. The scene ends appropriately with Wallace flooding the house, a microcosmic counterpart, however comical, to The Flood, which according to biblical account God sent to destroy sinful man. Sammler fears, of course, that we are nearing that point again" (174–75).

9. Dr. Lal tells Sammler that since his earliest work in biophysics he has been convinced "that nature, more than an engineer, is an artist. Behavior is poetry, is metaphorical order, is metaphysics. . . . the body of an individual is electronically denser than the tropical rain forest is dense with organisms. And all of these existences are, it often suggests itself, poems" (222).

10. Ironically, much later in the novel, Wallace admits to his uncle that he has no feelings for his family's New Rochelle house, "no desire for roots." Sammler's sarcastic reply is: "No, of course not. Roots? Roots are not modern. That's a peasant conception, soil and roots. Peasantry is going to disappear" (245).

11. Sarah Blacher Cohen, *Saul Bellow's Enigmatic Laughter* (Urbana: University of Illinois Press, 1974).

12. Saul Bellow, Introduction to *Great Jewish Short Stories*, ed. Saul Bellow (New York: Dell, 1963), 12.

13. R. W. B. Lewis, *The American Adam: Innocence, Tragedy, and Tradition in the Nineteenth Century* (Chicago: University of Chicago Press, 1955), 5. Copyright © The University of Chicago, 1955.

14. According to Siegel, "Every Bellow wanderer is caught up in this 'urban clutter' of noise, dirt, and smell, and each is forced to recognize that all dreams of escape — geographic or spatial — are sentimental nonsense" ("Saul Bellow and Mr. Sammler," 125).

15. Cohen has a very interesting gloss on this Milton reference: "To suggest how much we are under the moon's sway, Bellow has Sammler recall a line from Milton's *Comus*: 'Now to the Moon in wavering Morrice move' (97). Milton was referring to the fishes and seas 'performing the dance' (97), but Bellow is implying that in this age we, the higher orders of creation, are equally influenced by the moon and do our

equivalent aerospace dances. To Sammler, such cosmic gyrations also resemble the bizarre feats depicted in science fiction" (*Bellow's Enigmatic Laughter*, 206).

16. Margotte's plants and those recommended by Dr. Lal for planting on the moon are both "tough members of the plant kingdom" (53), but the practical Lal has "hops and sugar beets in mind."

17. Siegel, "Saul Bellow and Mr. Sammler," 129.

18. Cohen, *Bellow's Enigmatic Laughter*, 203.

19. Porter, *Whence the Power?*, 179.

20. Ibid., 179–80.

21. Ibid., 180.

22. In *The Portable Henry James*, ed. Morton Dauwen Zabel (New York: Viking Press, 1951), 403.

Selected Bibliography

General

Baumbach, Jonathan. *The Landscape of Nightmare: Studies in the Contemporary American Novel*. New York: New York University Press, 1965.

Baumgarten, Murray. *City Scriptures: Modern Jewish Writing*. Cambridge, Mass.: Harvard University Press, 1982.

Clough, Wilson O. *The Necessary Earth: Nature and Solitude in American Literature*. Austin: University of Texas Press, 1964.

Farrell, James T. "In Search of an Image." In *The League of Frightened Philistines and Other Papers*, 154–60. New York: Vanguard, 1945.

Festa-McCormick, Diana. *The City as Catalyst*. Cranbury, N.Y.: Associated University Presses, 1979.

Fine, David M. *The City, the Immigrant and American Fiction, 1880–1920*. Metuchen, N.J.: Scarecrow Press, 1977.

Gates, Robert A. *The New York Vision: Interpretations of New York City in the American Novel*. Lanham, Md.: University Press of America, 1987.

Gelfant, Blanche. *The American City Novel*. Rev. ed. Norman: University of Oklahoma Press, 1970.

Howe, Irving. "The City in Literature." *Commentary* 51 (May, 1971): 61–68.

Jaye, Michael C., and Chalmers Watts, eds. *Literature and the Urban Experience: Essays on the City and Literature*. New Brunswick: Rutgers University Press, 1981.

McCarthy, Mary. "One Touch of Nature." In *The Handwriting on the Wall and Other Literary Essays*, 189–213. New York: Harcourt Brace & World, 1970.

Machor, James Lawrence. *Pastoral Cities: Urban Ideals and the Symbolic Landscape of America*. Madison: University of Wisconsin Press, 1987.

Marx, Leo. *The Machine in the Garden: Technology and the Pastoral Ideal in America*. New York: Oxford University Press, 1969.

Pike, Burton. *The Image of the City in Modern Literature*. Princeton: Princeton University Press, 1981.

Schmitt, Peter J. *Back to Nature: The Arcadian Myth in Urban America*. New York: Oxford University Press, 1969.

Squier, Susan M., ed. *Women Writers and the City: Essays in Feminist Literary Criticism.* Knoxville: University of Tennessee Press, 1986–87.

Tanner, Tony. *Scenes of Nature, Signs of Man: Essays in 19th and 20th Century American Literature.* Cambridge: Cambridge University Press, 1988.

Walcutt, Charles C. *American Literary Naturalism: A Divided Stream.* Minneapolis: University of Minnesota Press, 1956.

John Dos Passos, *Manhattan Transfer*

Beach, Joseph Warren. "*Manhattan Transfer*: Collectivism and Abstract Composition." In *Dos Passos, the Critic and the Writer's Intention*, ed. Allen Belkind, 54–69. Carbondale: Southern Illinois University Press, 1971. Longer version originally published in Joseph Warren Beach, *American Fiction: 1920–1940.* New York: Macmillan, 1941.

Brantley, John D. *The Fiction of John Dos Passos.* Paris: Mouton, 1968.

Clark, Michael. *Dos Passos's Early Fiction, 1912–1938.* Cranbury, N.J.: Susquehanna University Press, 1987.

Dos Passos, John. "What Makes a Novelist." *National Review*, January 16, 1968, 29–32.

Gates, Robert A. "The Dynamic City: John Dos Passos' *Manhattan Transfer.*" In *The New York Vision: Interpretations of New York City in the American Novel*, 63–89. Lanham, Md.: University Press of America, 1987.

Gelfant, Blanche. "John Dos Passos: The Synoptic Novel." In *The American City Novel*, 133–74. Rev. ed. Norman: University of Oklahoma Press, 1970.

John Dos Passos special issue. *Modern Fiction Studies* 26 (Autumn 1980).

Knox, George. "Dos Passos and Painting." In *Dos Passos, the Critic and the Writer's Intention*, ed. Allen Belkind, 242–64. Carbondale: Southern Illinois University Press, 1971.

Lowry, E. D. "*Manhattan Transfer*: Dos Passos' Wasteland." In *Dos Passos: A Collection of Critical Essays*, ed. Andrew Hook, 53–60. Englewood Cliffs: Prentice Hall, 1974.

Ludington, Townsend. *John Dos Passos: A Twentieth Century Odyssey.* New York: E. P. Dutton, 1980.

Vanderwerken, David. "*Manhattan Transfer*: Dos Passos' Babel Story," *American Literature* 49 (May, 1977): 253–67.

Wagner, Linda. *Dos Passos, Artist as American.* Austin: University of Texas Press, 1979.

Wrenn, John H. *John Dos Passos.* New York: Twayne, 1961.

James T. Farrell, *Studs Lonigan: A Trilogy*

Branch, Edgar. *James T. Farrell.* Boston: Twayne, 1971.

Butler, Robert James. "Parks, Parties, and Pragmatism: Time and Setting in James T. Farrell's Major Novels." *Essays in Literature* 10 (Fall 1983): 241–54.

Douglas, Ann. "*Studs Lonigan* and the Failure of History in Mass Society: A Study in Claustrophobia." *American Quarterly* 29 (1977): 487–505.

Farrell, James T. "The Author as Plaintiff: Testimony in a Censorship Case." In *Reflections at Fifty*, 188–223. New York: Vanguard Press, 1954.

Flynn, Dennis, and Jack Salzman. "An Interview with James T. Farrell." *Twentieth Century Literature* 22, no. 1 (February, 1976): 1–10.

Gelfant, Blanche. "James T. Farrell: The Ecological Novel." In *The American City Novel*, 175–227. Norman, Oklahoma: University of Oklahoma Press, 1954.

Mitchell, Richard. "*Studs Lonigan*: Research in Morality." *Centennial Review* 6 (1962): 202–14.

Pizer, Donald. "James T. Farrell: *Studs Lonigan*." In *Twentieth-Century American Literary Naturalism: An Interpretation*, 17–38. Carbondale: Southern Illinois University Press, 1982.

Henry Roth, *Call It Sleep*

Epstein, Gary. "Auto-Obituary: The Death of the Artist in Henry Roth's *Call It Sleep*." *Studies in American Jewish Literature* 5, no. 1 (Spring 1979): 37–45.

Ferguson, James. "Symbolic Patterns in *Call It Sleep*." *Twentieth Century Literature* 14 (January, 1969): 211–20.

Friedman, John S. "On Being Blocked & Other Literary Matters: An Interview: Henry Roth." *Commentary*, August, 1977, 27–38.

Lyons, Bonnie. *Henry Roth: The Man and His Work*. New York: Cooper Square, 1976.

———. "An Interview with Henry Roth." *Shenandoah* 25 (Fall 1973): 48–71.

———. "Interview with Henry Roth, March 1977." *Studies in American Jewish Literature* 5, no. 1 (Spring 1979): 50–58.

———. "The Symbolic Structure of Henry Roth's *Call It Sleep*." *Contemporary Literature* 13 (1972): 186–203.

Mooney, Theresa. "The Explicable 'It' of Henry Roth's *Call It Sleep*." *Studies in American Jewish Literature* 5, no. 1 (Spring 1979): 11–18.

Redding, Mary Edrich. "Call It Myth: Henry Roth and *The Golden Bough*." *Centennial Review* 18, no. 2 (Spring 1974): 180–95.

Harriette Arnow, *The Dollmaker*

Eckley, Wilton. *Harriette Arnow*. Boston: Twayne, 1974.

Hobbs, Glenda. "A Portrait of the Artist as Mother: Harriette Arnow and *The Dollmaker*." *Georgia Review* 33, no. 4 (Winter 1979): 851–66.

Lee, Dorothy. "Harriette Arnow's *The Dollmaker*: A Journey to Awareness." *Critique: Studies in Modern Fiction* 20, no. 2 (1978): 92–98.

Oates, Joyce Carol. "An American Tragedy." *New York Times Book Reveiw*, January 24, 1971, 12–16.

Bernard Malamud, *The Assistant*

Alter, Iska. "*The Natural, The Assistant*, and American Materialism." In *The Good Man's Dilemma: Social Criticism in the Fiction of Bernard Malamud*, 1–26. New York: AMS Press, 1981.

Astro, Richard, and Jackson Benson, eds. *The Fiction of Bernard Malamud*. Corvallis, Ore.: Oregon State University Press, 1977.

Baumbach, Jonathan. "All Men Are Jews: *The Assistant*, by Bernard Malamud." In *The Landscape of Nightmare: Studies in the Contemporary Novel*, 101–22. New York: New York University Press, 1965.

Cohen, Sandy. "*The Assistant*: Ceremony of Innocence." In *Bernard Malamud and the Trial by Love*, 37–55. Amsterdam: Rodopi N.V., 1974.

Hays, Peter L. "The Complex Pattern of Redemption in *The Assistant*." *Centennial Review*, no. 2 (Spring 1969): 200–214.

Kazin, Alfred. "Fantasist of the Ordinary." Review of *The Assistant*, by Bernard Malamud. *Commentary* 24 (July, 1957): 89–92.

Mellard, James M. "Malamud's *The Assistant*: The City Novel as Pastoral." *Studies in Short Fiction* 5 (1967): 1–11.

———. "Malamud's Novels: Four Versions of Pastoral." *Critique: Studies in Modern Fiction* 9 (1967): 5–19.

Richman, Sidney. *Bernard Malamud*. Boston: Twayne, 1966.

Salzberg, Jack, ed. *Critical Essays on Bernard Malamud*. Boston: G. K. Hall, 1987.

Schulz, Max. "Bernard Malamud's Mythic Proletarians." In *Radical Sophistication: Studies in Contemporary Jewish/American Novelists*, 56–68. Athens, Ohio: Ohio University Press, 1969.

Zlotnick, Joan. "Malamud's *The Assistant*: Of Morris, Frank, and St. Francis." *Studies in American Jewish Literature* 1 (Winter 1975): 20–23.

Edward Lewis Wallant, *The Pawnbroker*

Ayo, Nicholas. "The Secular Heart: The Achievement of Edward Lewis Wallant." *Critique: Studies in Modern Fiction* 12 (1970): 86–94.

Davis, W. V. "Fathers and Sons in the Fiction of Edward Wallant." *Research Studies at Washington State University* 40 (1972): 53–55.

———. "The Renewal of Dialogical Immediacy in Edward Lewis Wallant." *Renascence* 24 (Winter 1972): 59–69.

Galloway, David. *Edward Lewis Wallant*. Boston: Twayne, 1979.

Gurko, Leo. "Edward Lewis Wallant as Urban Novelist." *Twentieth Century Literature* 20, no. 4 (October, 1974): 252–61.

Lewis, R. W. "The Hung-Up Heroes of Edward Lewis Wallant." *Renascence* 24 (Winter 1972): 70–84.

Lorch, Thomas. "The Novels of Edward Lewis Wallant." *Chicago Review* 19 (1967): 78–91.

Parks, John G. "The Grace of Suffering: The Fiction of E. L. Wallant." *Studies in American Jewish Literature*, no. 5 (1986): 111–18.

Schulz, Max. "Edward Lewis Wallant and Bruce Jay Friedman: The Glory and Agony of Life." In *Radical Sophistication: Studies in Contemporary Jewish/American Novelists*, 173–97. Athens, Ohio: Ohio University Press, 1969.

Stanford, Raney. "The Novels of Edward Wallant." *Colorado Quarterly* 17 (September, 1969): 393–405.

Saul Bellow, *Mr. Sammler's Planet*

Clayton, John. *Saul Bellow: In Defense of Man*. Rev. ed. Bloomington: Indiana University Press, 1979.

Cohen, Sarah Blacher. "This Droll Mortality." In *Saul Bellow's Enigmatic Laughter*, 176–210. Urbana: University of Illinois Press, 1974.

Dutton, Robert R. *Saul Bellow*. Rev. ed. Boston: Twayne, 1982.

Fuchs, Daniel. *Saul Bellow: Vision and Revision*. Durham: Duke University Press, 1984.

Galloway, David. "*Mr. Sammler's Planet*: Bellow's Failure of Nerve." *Modern Fiction Studies* 19, no. 1 (Spring 1973): 17–28.

Harris, James Neil. "One Critical Approach to *Mr. Sammler's Planet*. *Twentieth Century Literature* 18 (October, 1972): 235–50.

Kremer, S. Lillian. "The Holocaust in *Mr. Sammler's Planet*." *Saul Bellow Journal* 4, no. 1 (1985): 19–32.

Opdahl, Keith M. *The Novels of Saul Bellow: An Introduction*. University Park: Pennsylvania State University Press, 1967.

Pifer, Ellen. "'Two Different Speeches': Mystery and Knowledge in *Mr. Sammler's Planet*." *Mosaic* 18, no. 2 (1985): 17–32.

Porter, M. Gilbert. *Whence the Power? The Artistry and Humanity of Saul Bellow*. Columbia: University of Missouri Press, 1974.

Rodrigues, Eusebio L. *Quest for the Human: An Exploration of Saul Bellow's Fiction*. Lewisburg, Pa.: Bucknell University Press, 1981.

Schulz, Max. "Mr. Bellow's Perigee, or, The Lowered Horizon of *Mr. Sammler's Planet*." In *Contemporary American-Jewish Literature*, ed. Irving Malin, 117–33. Bloomington: Indiana University Press, 1973.

Seventieth Birthday Issue. *Saul Bellow Journal* 4, no. 2 (1985).

Siegel, Ben. "Saul Bellow and Mr. Sammler: Absurd Seekers of High Qualities." In *Saul Bellow: A Collection of Critical Essays*, ed. Earl Rovit, 122–34. Englewood Cliffs: Prentice Hall, 1975.

Wilson, Jonathan. *On Bellow's Planet: Readings from the Dark Side*. Rutherford, N.J.: Dickenson University Press, 1985.

Index